THE EAGLE
OF THE
NINTH

MAR CVS

ROSEMARY SUTCLIFF

THE EAGLE
OF THE
NINTH

Illustrated by

C. WALTER HODGES

LONDON
OXFORD UNIVERSITY PRESS

Oxford University Press Ely House, London W. 1

GLASGOW NEW YORK TORONTO MELBOURNE WELLINGTON
CAPE TOWN SALISBURY IBADAN NAIROBI LUSAKA ADDIS ABABA
BOMBAY CALCUTTA MADRAS KARACHI LAHORE DACCA
KUALA LUMPUR SINGAPORE HONG KONG TOKYO

First published 1954
Reprinted 1955, 1957, 1959, 1961, 1963, 1967, 1969

Printed in Great Britain by Richard Clay (The Chaucer Press), Ltd.,
Bungay, Suffolk

Foreword

Sometime about the year 117 A.D., the Ninth Legion, which was stationed at Eburacum where York now stands, marched north to deal with a rising among the Caledonian tribes, and was never heard of again.

During the excavations at Silchester nearly eighteen hundred years later, there was dug up under the green fields which now cover the pavements of Calleva Atrebatum, a wingless Roman Eagle, a cast of which can be seen to this day in Reading Museum. Different people have had different ideas as to how it came to be there, but no one knows, just as no one knows what happened to the Ninth Legion after it marched into the northern mists.

It is from these two mysteries, brought together, that I have made the story of ' The Eagle of the Ninth '.

R. S.

RETURN JOURNEY

ESCA'S DOUBLE BACK

NORTHERN
AND HADRIAN'S WALLS

MILES

0   50   100

CALEDONIA

CRUACHAN

L.LOMOND
Are Cluta (Dumbarton)
DUMNONII

HIBERNIA

EPIDII

Trinomontium
(Melrose)

VALENTIA

SELGOVAE

NOVANTAE

Borcovicus
Chilurnium

Segedunum
(Wallsend)

Luguvallium
(Carlisle)

Eburacum
(York)

Deva (Chester)

Isca Silurium
(Caerleon)

Glevum (Gloucester)

Aquae
Sulis
(Bath)

Calleva Atrebatum
(Silchester)

FOREST OF SPINAII

Regnum (Chichester)

Dubris
(Dover)

Isca Dumnoniorum
(Exeter)

Anderida
(Pevensey)

Durinum
(Dorchester)

—MANN—

Contents

CONTENTS

I

FRONTIER FORT

F ROM the Fosseway westward to Isca Dumnoniorum the
road was simply a British trackway, broadened and
roughly metalled, strengthened by corduroys of logs in
the softest places, but otherwise unchanged from its old estate,
as it wound among the hills, thrusting farther and farther into
the wilderness.

It was a busy road and saw many travellers: traders with
bronze weapons and raw yellow amber in their ponies' packs;
country folk driving shaggy cattle or lean pigs from village to
village; sometimes a band of tawny-haired tribesmen from
farther west; strolling harpers and quack-oculists, too, or a
light-stepping hunter with huge wolf-hounds at his heel; and
from time to time a commissariat wagon going up and down to
supply the Roman frontier post. The road saw them all, and
the cohorts of the Eagles for whom all other travellers must
make way.

There was a cohort of leather-clad auxiliaries on the road

today, swinging along at the steady Legion's pace that had brought them down from Isca Silurium at twenty miles a day; the new garrison coming to relieve the old one at Isca Dumnoniorum. On they went, following the road that now ran out on a causeway between sodden marsh and empty sky, now plunged into deep boar-hunted forest, or lifted over bleak uplands where nothing grew save furze and thorn-scrub. On with never a halt nor a change of rhythm, marching century by century, the sun bright on the Standard at their head, and the rolling dust-cloud kicked up over the pack-train behind.

At the head of the column marched the Pilus Prior Centurion, the cohort Commander, the pride that shone from him showing clearly that this was his first command. They were, he had long since decided, a command worthy of anyone's pride; six hundred yellow-haired giants recruited from the tribes of Upper Gaul, with the natural fighting power of mountain cats, drilled and hammered into what he firmly believed to be the finest auxiliary cohort ever to serve with the Second Legion. They were a newly joined cohort; many of the men had not yet proved themselves in action, and the spear-shaft of their Standard had no honours on it, no gilded laurel wreath nor victor's crown. The honours were all to win—perhaps during his command.

The Commander was a complete contrast to his men: Roman to his arrogant finger-tips, wiry and dark as they were raw-boned and fair. The olive-skinned face under the curve of his crested helmet had not a soft line in it anywhere—a harsh face it would have been, but that it was winged with laughter lines, and between his level black brows showed a small raised scar that marked him for one who had passed the Raven Degree of Mithras.

Centurion Marcus Flavius Aquila had seen little of the Eagles until a year ago. His first ten years had been lived quietly with his mother on the family farm near Clusium, while his father soldiered in Judaea, in Egypt, and here in Britain. They had been going to join his father in Britain, but before the time came for them to do so, rebellion had flared up among the northern tribes, and the Ninth Hispana, his father's Legion, had marched north to deal with it, and never came marching back.

His mother had died soon afterwards, leaving him to be brought up in Rome by a rather foolish aunt and the plump and purse-proud official who was her husband. Marcus had loathed the official, and the official had loathed Marcus. They saw everything with different eyes. Marcus came of a line of soldiers—one of those Equestrian families who, when the rest of their kind had turned from soldiering to trade and finance, had kept to the old way of life, and remained poor but held their noses high in consequence. The official came of a line of officials, and his code of life was quite other than Marcus's. Neither of them had a shred of understanding for each other's ideas, and they had both been thankful when Marcus was eighteen and could apply for a centurion's commission.

Marcus, his eyes narrowed into the sun as he marched, smiled to himself a little wryly, as he remembered how almost pathetically thankful that plump official had been. (Tramp, tramp, tramp, said the cohort's feet behind him.)

He had asked to be sent to Britain, though it meant starting in an auxiliary cohort instead of a line-of-battle one, partly because his father's elder brother had settled there when his own years of soldiering were done, but mostly because of his father. If ever anything became known of the lost Legion, it would be known first in Britain, and it might even be that here in Britain he would find out something for himself.

Marching down the Isca Dumnoniorum road in the run-honey evening light, he found himself thinking about his father. He had very vivid memories of a slight, dark man with laughter lines at the corners of his eyes, who had come home from time to time, and taught him to fish, to play 'Flash the Fingers', and throw a javelin. He remembered vividly that last leave of all. His father had just been appointed to command the First Cohort of the Hispana, which meant having charge of the Eagle and being something very like second-in-command of the Legion beside; and he had been like a jubilant boy about it. But his mother had been faintly anxious, almost as if she knew. . . .

'If it was any *other* Legion!' she had said. 'You have told me yourself that the Hispana has a bad name.'

And his father had replied: 'But I would not have it any other Legion if I could. I held my first command in the Hispana, and a man's first Legion is apt to hold chief place in his heart ever after, be its name good or bad; and now that I go back to it as First Cohort, we will see whether there is nothing can be done to better its name.' He had turned to his small son, laughing. 'Presently it will be your turn. It has fallen on evil days, but we will make a Legion of the Hispana yet, you and I.'

Looking back across the years, Marcus remembered that his father's eyes had been very bright, like the eyes of a man going into action; and the light had caught suddenly in the great flawed emerald of the signet-ring he always wore, striking from it a spark of clear green fire. Odd how one remembered things like that: little things that somehow mattered.

(Tramp, tramp, tramp, came the sound of the cohort's feet behind him.)

It would be pleasant, he thought, if Uncle Aquila was like his father. He had not met his uncle yet; after learning his foot-drill he had arrived in Britain in the sleety days of late autumn, and been sent straight up to Isca; but he had a rather vague invitation to spend his leave with him at Calleva, when he had any leave to spend. It would be very pleasant if Uncle Aquila was like his father.

Not of course that he and his uncle were likely to have much to do with each other. In a few years' time he would probably be serving in quite a different part of the Empire, since a cohort centurion seldom moved up all the way in the same Legion.

All the way . . . from his present rank right up to his father's rank of First Cohort; and after that? For most of the men who got so far there was nothing after that, but for the out-standing few who went farther—as Marcus intended to go farther—the ways divided there. One could become a camp commandant, as Uncle Aquila had done, or one could go on, by way of the Praetorian Guard, to try for command of a Legion. Legion Commanders were almost always men of Senator's rank, with no experience of soldiering save a year's service as Military Tribune in their youth; but by long custom the two Egyptian Legions were exceptions to the rule. They were commanded by professional soldiers; and an Egyptian Legion had been Marcus's shining goal for as long as he could remember.

But one day, when he had finished with the Eagles, when he had made an honourable name and become Prefect of his Egyptian Legion, he would go home to the Etruscan hills, and perhaps even buy back the old farm, which the plump official had ruthlessly sold to defray expenses. For a moment he remembered almost painfully the sunlit courtyard flickered over with the shadow of pigeons' wings, and the wild olive-tree in the loop of the stream, on a twisted root of which he had once found a kind of gall growing, that was shaped something like a little bird. He had cut it from the root with the new knife his father had given him, and spent much loving care, all one absorbed summer evening, trimming and carving feathers on it. He had that little bird still.

The road topped a gentle rise, and suddenly Isca Dumnoniorum lay before them, with the fortress-crowned Red Mount dark with shadows against the evening sky; and Marcus came back to the present with a jerk. The farm in the Etruscan hills could wait until he was old and tired and famous; in the present was the glory of his first command.

The British town was spread below the southern scarp of the Mount; a sprawling huddle of reed-thatched roofs, every colour from the gold of honey to the black of dried peat, according to the age of the thatch; with the squared, clean lines of the Roman forum and basilica looking oddly rootless in their midst; and the faint haze of wood-smoke lying over all.

The road led straight through the town and up to the cleared slope beyond, to the Praetorian gate of the fort; here and there, crimson or saffron-cloaked men turned to look at the cohort as it swung by, a look that was reserved rather than hostile. Dogs sat scratching in odd corners, lean pigs rooted among the garbage piles, and women with bracelets of gold or copper on very white arms sat in hut doorways, spinning or grinding corn. The blue smoke of many cooking-fires curled up into the quiet air, and the savoury smell of many evening meals mingled with the blue reek of wood-smoke and the sharper tang of horse-droppings, which Marcus had by now come to associate with all British towns. Little that was Roman was here as yet, despite the stone-built forum. One day there would be straight streets, he supposed, and temples and bath-houses and a Roman way of life. But as yet it was a place where two worlds met without mingling: a British town huddled under the dominion of the turf ramparts where once the tribe had had its stronghold and now the Roman sentries paced up and down. He looked about him under the curve of his helmet as he marched, knowing that this place would be part of his life for the next year; then looked up to the turf ramparts, and saw a Roman banner drooping in the still air, and the tall crest of a sentry burning in the sunset, and heard a trumpet-call ring out, as it seemed, from the fiery sky.

·   ·   ·   ·   ·

'You have brought clear skies with you,' said Centurion Quintus Hilarion, lounging in the window of the Commander's quarters, and peering into the night. 'But Hercle! you need not expect it to last.'

'As bad as that?' said Centurion Marcus Aquila, who was seated on the table.

'Quite as bad as that! It rains always, here in the west, save when Typhon, the father of all ills, brews up a mist to come between a man and his own feet. By the time you have served your year here you will have toadstools sprouting out of your ears, the same as me, *and* not from the damp alone!'

'From what beside?' inquired Marcus with interest.

'Oh, lack of company, for one thing. I am a sociable soul

myself; I like my friends around me.' He turned from the window, and folded up on to a low cushioned bench, hugging his knees. 'Ah well, I am off to rub away the blue mould as soon as I have marched the troops back to Isca.'

'Going on leave?'

The other nodded. 'Long leave, lovely leave, among the fleshpots of Durinum.'

'Durinum—that is your home?' asked Marcus.

'Yes. My father retired and settled there a few years ago. There is a surprisingly good circus, and plenty of people— pretty girls too. A pleasant enough place to get back to, out of the wilds.' An idea seemed to strike him. 'What shall you do when *your* leave falls due? I suppose, coming out from home, you have no one here to go to?'

'I have an uncle at Calleva, though I have not yet met him,' Marcus said, 'and certainly there is no one at home I should want to spend my leave with.'

' Father and mother both dead? ' inquired Hilarion with friendly interest.

' Yes. My father went with the Ninth Legion.'

' Pericol! You mean when they—— '

' Disappeared. Yes.'

' So. That is bad! ' said Hilarion, wagging his head. ' A deal of ugly stories, there were—still are, for that matter; and of course, they did lose the Eagle.'

Instantly Marcus was up in arms to defend his father and his father's Legion. ' Since not a man of the Legion came back, it is scarcely a matter for wonder that neither did the Eagle,' he flashed.

' Surely not,' agreed Hilarion amicably. ' I was not blowing on your father's honour, so you can keep your feathers on, my Marcus.' He looked up at the other with a wide, friendly grin, and suddenly Marcus, who had been ready to quarrel with him the instant before, found himself grinning back.

It was several hours since Marcus had marched his cohort across the hollow-ringing bridge, answering the sentry's challenge, ' Fourth Gaulish Auxiliaries of the Second Legion, come to relieve this garrison.' Dinner was over, in the officers' mess, with the Quartermaster, the Surgeon, and the double complement of ranker centurions. Marcus had taken charge of the pay-chest keys—in a garrison as small as this there was no paymaster; and for the past hour, here in the Commander's quarters in the Praetorium, he and Hilarion had been going through the office work of the frontier fort. Now, crested helmets and embossed breastplates laid aside, the two of them were taking their ease.

Through the doorless opening Marcus could see almost the whole of the sleeping-cell, the narrow cot piled with gay native rugs, the polished oaken chest, the lamp-bracket high on the bare wall, and nothing more. The outer room held the battered writing-table on which Marcus was sitting, a cross-legged camp-stool, the cushioned bench to represent comfort, another chest for the record rolls, and a bronze pedestal lamp of peculiarly hideous design.

In the little silence that had fallen between them, Marcus looked round him at the austere room in the yellow flood of lamplight, and to him it seemed beautiful. But though it would be his tomorrow, for this one night he was a guest here, and he looked back to his host with a quick smile of apology for having looked too soon at his surroundings with the eye of mastery.

Hilarion grinned. ' You will not be feeling like that this day next year.'

' I wonder,' said Marcus, swinging one sandalled foot and idly watching the swing of it. ' What does one do here, beside growing toadstools? Is there good hunting? '

' Good enough; it is the one thing to be said for this particular corner of the Empire. Boar and wolf in the winter, and the forest swarms with deer. There are several hunters below in the town, who will take you out for the price of the day's work. Unwise to go alone, of course.'

Marcus nodded. ' Have you any advice for me? I am new to this country.'

The other considered. ' No, I think not.' Then he sat up with a jerk. ' Yes, I have, if no one has warned you already. But it has nothing to do with the hunting. It is the priest-kind—the wandering Druids. If one of them appears in the district, or you get the least idea that there is one about, look to your weapons. Good advice, that is.'

' The Druids? ' Marcus was surprised and puzzled. ' But surely Suetonius Paulinus dealt with them once and for all, sixty years ago? '

' As an organized priesthood, maybe; but as easily hold off these heathen mists with a palm-leaf umbrella as end the Druids by destroying their stronghold. They spring up still, from time to time, and wherever they do spring up, there is likely to be trouble for the Eagles. They were the heart and soul of British resistance in the early days, and even now, when there is any sign of unrest among the tribes, you can wager your sandals there is a holy man at the bottom of it.'

' Go on,' Marcus prodded, as the other seemed to have finished. ' This becomes interesting.'

ɴ

'Well, the thing is this. They can preach holy war, and that is ever the most deadly kind, for it recks nothing of consequences.' Hilarion spoke slowly, as though he was thinking the thing out as he went along. ' The frontier tribes are not like those of the south coast, who were half Romanized before ever we landed; they are a wild lot, and superbly brave; but even they have mostly come to think that we are not fiends of darkness, and they have enough sense to see that destroying the local garrison will only mean a punitive expedition and their homes and standing crops burned, and a stronger garrison with a heavier hand thereafter. But let one of their holy men lay hold of them, and all that goes whistling down the wind. They cease to think whether there can be any good come of their rising, cease to think at all. They are keeping faith with their gods by smoking out a nest of the unbelievers, and what happens after is no concern of theirs, for they are going West of the Sunset by the warriors' road. And when you get men into that state there is apt to be trouble coming.'

Outside in the quiet darkness the trumpets sounded for the second watch of the night. Hilarion uncurled himself and stood up. ' We had best do Late Rounds together tonight,' he said, and reached for his sword, slipping the baldrick over his head. ' I am native born,' he added as though in explanation. ' That is how I come to have some understanding of these matters.'

' I imagined that you must be.' Marcus tested a buckle of his own equipment. ' You have had no holy man round here, I suppose? '

' No, but my predecessor had a certain amount of trouble just before I took over, and the trouble-maker slipped through his fingers and disappeared. We lived a month or two on Vesuvius —all the more so as the harvest was bad for the second year running—but it never erupted.'

Footsteps sounded outside, and a red light glimmered at the window; and they went out together to the Duty Centurion, who stood outside with a flaring torch. The clashing Roman salute was exchanged, and they set out on their tour of the

darkened fort, from sentry-post to sentry-post along the rampart
walk, from guard-point to guard-point, with the low exchange
of the password; lastly to the small lighted room in the Praetorium where the pay-chest was kept and the Standard stood
against the wall, and between rounds the Duty Centurion sat
with his drawn sword on the table before him, through the
night.

Marcus thought: 'After tonight it will be for me alone to
follow the centurion's torch from guard-post to guard-post,
from barrack block to horse-lines, seeing that all is well with the
frontier of the Empire.'

Next morning, after the formal take-over ceremony in the
forum, the old garrison marched out. Marcus watched them
go, out across the ditch and downhill between the crowding
hovels of the native town whose reed-thatched roofs were gold-
dusted by the morning sun. Century after Century, marching
away up the long road that led to Isca; and at their head the
glint of gold and crimson that was the cohort Standard. He
narrowed his eyes into the piercing light, and watched that
coloured glint till it disappeared into the brightness of the
morning. The last driver of the baggage-train dropped out of
sight beyond the lift of the road, the rhythmic tramp-tramp-
tramp of heavily sandalled feet ceased to pulse through the
sunlit air, and Marcus was alone with his first command.

II

FEATHERS IN THE WIND

BEFORE many days had passed, Marcus had slipped so completely into the life of the frontier fort that it seemed as though he had never known any other. The plan of all Roman forts was much the same, and the pattern of life lived in them, so that knowing one meant knowing them all, whether it was the stone-built camp of the Praetorian Guard itself, or a baked mud fort on the Upper Nile, or this one at Isca Dumnoniorum, where the ramparts were of rammed turf, and the cohort Standard and the officers were all housed together in one small square of wattle-and-daub buildings round a colonnaded courtyard. But after a few days Marcus began to know the individualities that made every camp different, after all, from every other; and it was these differences, rather than the samenesses, that made him feel at home in Isca. An artist of some long-departed garrison had scratched with his dagger a beautiful leaping wild cat on the bath-house wall, and someone less gifted had scratched a very rude picture of a centurion he had not liked; you could tell that it was a centurion, by the vine staff and the centurion's mark > scored beneath it. There was a martin's nest under the eaves of the shrine where the Standard was housed, and an odd and untraceable smell behind Number Two storehouse. And in one corner of the officers' courtyard, some past commander, homesick for the warmth and colour of the South, had planted a rose-bush in a great stone wine-jar, and already the buds were showing crimson among the dark leaves. That rose-bush gave Marcus a sense of continuance; it was a link between him and those who had been before him, here on the frontier, and the others who would come after. It must have been there a long time, and it was becoming pot-bound; he thought that in the

autumn he would see about having a proper bed made
for it.

It took him a little while to settle down with his officers.
The Surgeon, who appeared, like the Quartermaster, to be a
fixture, was a gentle soul, content enough in his backwater so
long as it contained sufficient of the fiery native spirit; but the
Quartermaster himself was something of a trial, a little red
angry man who had missed promotion and grown overfull of his
own importance in consequence. Lutorius, who commanded
the fort's one squadron of Dacian Horse, spent all his friendliness on his horses and was reserved to the point of sullenness
with all men, even his own. Marcus's five ranker centurions
were all so much older and more experienced than he was that
at first he was uncertain how to deal with them. It was not
easy, with less than a year with the Eagles behind him, to tell
Centurion Paulus that he was overfond of using his vine-staff
on his men's backs; or make Centurion Galba understand that,
whatever might be the custom in other cohorts, the centurions
of the Fourth Gaulish were not going to take bribes from their
men for letting them off fatigues, while he was in command.
But he managed it somehow, and the odd thing was that though
both Galba and Paulus raged inwardly at the time, and even
talked to each other about puppies, there was a better understanding between them and the Cohort Commander afterwards.
And between Marcus and his second-in-command there was a
good working understanding from the first, which grew to
a warm liking as time went by. Centurion Drusillus, like
most of his kind, was promoted from the ranks; he was a
veteran of many campaigns, full of odd wisdom and hard
counsel; and Marcus had need of such, that summer. Day
started with the trumpets sounding Cockcrow from the ramparts, and ended with Late Rounds; and between came all the
complicated pattern of parades and fatigues, patrols out and in,
stables, arms drill. He had to be his own magistrate too; he
had to deal with the situation when one of his men claimed that
a tribesman had sold him a worthless dog; or a tribesman com-
plained that someone from the fort had stolen his poultry; or

when the Dacians and the Gauls fell out over some obscure question of a tribal god whom he had never heard of before.

It was hard work, especially in the earliest days, and he was thankful for Centurion Drusillus; but the work was in his blood, just as farming was, and it was work that he loved. And it was not all work: there was the occasional day's hunting too—good hunting, even as Hilarion had said.

His usual guide and companion on the trail was a Briton not many years older than himself, a hunter and horse-dealer, Cradoc by name. And on a morning of late summer he went down from the fort, carrying his hunting-spears, to pick up Cradoc according to custom. It was very early, the sun not yet up, and the mist lying like a white sea between the hills. Scent would lie low and heavy on such a morning, and he sniffed the dawn chill like a hound. And yet he could not find his usual pleasure in the fine hunting morning, for he was worried. Not very worried, but enough to take the keen edge off the blade of his enjoyment; turning over in his mind the rumour that had been drifting through the fort for the past day or two—the rumour of a wandering Druid having been seen in the district. Oh, no one had actually seen him themselves; it was much more vague than that. None the less, remembering Hilarion's warning, he had checked up as best he could, without of course the least result. But even if there *were* something in the wind, there would be no result—nothing to be got even from the few men who held official positions from Rome; if their first loyalty was to Rome they would know nothing; if it was to their Tribe they would tell nothing. Probably there was not a scrap of truth in the story; it was just one of those floating rumours that blew up from time to time, like a wind out of nowhere. But he would keep his eyes and ears open, all the same, especially as once again, for the third year running, the harvest was going to be a poor one. You could tell that from the faces of the men and women, as well as you could from their little fields, where the corn stood thin and shrivelled in the ear. A bad harvest was always the time to look for trouble.

As he threaded his way among the crowding huts beyond the forum, it struck Marcus again how untouched this place was by Rome. The tribe found the forum and basilica useful to hold their markets in. One or two men had laid aside their hunting-spears to become Roman officials, occasionally one even saw a Roman tunic. There were wine-shops everywhere, the craftsmen of the town made things to please the garrison, and everybody else sold them dogs, skins, vegetables, and fighting-cocks, while the children scrambled after the auxiliaries for denarii. But all the same, here in Isca Dumnoniorum, Rome was a new slip grafted on to an old stock—and the graft had not yet taken.

He reached the cluster of huts that were Cradoc's, and turned aside at the house-place door, whistling a few bars of the latest tune running in the Legions, with which he was used to announce his arrival. The leather apron over the doorway was drawn aside at once, but instead of the hunter, there appeared a girl with a solemn sunburned baby on her hip. She was tall, as were most British women, and carried herself like a queen; but the thing that Marcus noticed about her was the look on her face: a queer, guarded look, as though she had drawn a veil behind her eyes so that he should not see in.

'My man is out behind with his chariot team. If the Commander goes to look, he will find him,' she said, and stepped back, letting the leather apron fall between them.

Marcus went to look. The sound of the hunter's voice and a horse's soft whinny gave him his direction, and making his way between the wood-pile and a tethered cock whose feathers shone with metallic colours among the duller hens, he reached the doorway of a stable hut, and looked in. Cradoc turned to the doorway as he appeared, and gave him a courteous greeting.

Marcus returned it—by this time he spoke the Celtic tongue fluently, though with an appalling accent—but he was staring into the shadows behind the other man. ' I did not know you drove the Royal Fours in these parts,' he said.

'We are not above learning some lessons from Rome. Have you never chanced to see my team before?'

Marcus shook his head. 'I did not even know you for a charioteer, though I suppose I might have guessed. The British are all charioteers.'

'The Commander is mistaken,' Cradoc said, drawing his hand down a glossy neck. 'The British can all drive after a fashion; not everyone is a charioteer.'

'You, I take it, are a charioteer?'

'I am accounted among the best of my tribe,' Cradoc said with quiet dignity.

Marcus had moved in from the doorway. 'May I see your team?' he asked, and the other stood aside for him without a word.

The four were loose in their stable, and they came to him almost like dogs to sniff inquiringly at his breast and outstretched hands; four superbly matched black chariot ponies. He thought of the Arab team he had sometimes driven in Rome. These were smaller—under fourteen hands, he judged —thicker coated, and for their size a little more heavily built, but in their way they seemed to him without match; the heads that turned to him gentle and intelligent, the ears pricked and delicate as flower petals, the quivering nostrils lined with vivid red, the breasts and haunches deep and powerful. He turned from one to another, moving among them, fondling them, running a practised hand over their lithe bodies from proud crest to sweeping tail.

Before he left Rome, Marcus had been in a fair way to becoming a charioteer, in Cradoc's sense of the word, and now desire woke in him, not to possess this team, for he was not one of those who must be able to say ' Mine ' before they can truly enjoy a thing, but to have them out and harnessed; to feel the vibrating chariot floor under him, and the spread reins quick with life in his hands, and these lovely, fiery little creatures in the traces, his will and theirs at one.

Turning, with a soft muzzle against his shoulder, he said, ' Will you let me try your team? '

' They are not for sale.'

' If they were, I could not afford to buy them. I asked that I might try them.'

' The Commander also is a charioteer? ' Cradoc said.

At the Saturnalia Games last year, Marcus had been put up to race a borrowed team against a staff officer, reputed to be the finest driver in the Legion; and he had won. ' I am accounted the best in my Legion,' he said.

Cradoc did not seem to think his question answered. ' I doubt if you could handle these black jewels of mine.'

' Will you take a wager on it? ' Marcus asked, his eyes suddenly cool and bright, and his mouth smiling.

' A wager? '

' That I will handle your team to your satisfaction, over ground of your own choosing.' Marcus slipped a brooch from the shoulder of his rough cloak, and held it out, the red cornelian with which it was set gleaming faintly in the shadows. ' This fibula against—against one of your hunting-spears. Or if that does not suit you, name your own stakes.'

Cradoc did not look at the fibula. He was looking at Marcus, rather as though the young Roman was a horse whose mettle he wished to gauge, and Marcus, facing the cool stocktaking, felt himself flushing. The hunter noticed the angry colour, and the arrogantly raised head, and a queer little twisted smile lifted one side of his mouth. Then, as though satisfied by his scrutiny, he said : ' I will take the wager.'

' When do we put the matter to the test? ' asked Marcus, returning the brooch to the shoulder of his cloak.

' I am taking a draft of horses up to Durinum tomorrow; but in eight days I shall be back. We will hold the trial on my return. And now, it is time that we were away.'

' So be it,' said Marcus; and with a final pat to a glossy neck, he turned and followed Cradoc from the stable. They whistled the waiting hounds to heel, collected hunting-spears from the house-place wall where they had been propped, and disappeared into the wilderness.

.   .   .   .   .

Cradoc was away longer than he expected, and the harvest, such as it was (there would be many hungry in Isca Dumnoniorum that winter), was gathered in by the time the trial took place. Marcus was turning over in his mind the question of getting in extra grain supplies when he arrived at the appointed meeting ground, a wide stretch of level land in the curve of the river, to find the other waiting for him. Cradoc flung up an arm in greeting as he appeared from the woodshore, and springing into the chariot, turned the team and came thundering towards him through the swaying fern at a gallop. The sun flashed back in spars of light from the bronze ornaments on the breasts and foreheads of the team, and the long hair of the charioteer was flying like his ponies' manes. Marcus stood his ground, though with an uncomfortable tightening of his stomach, until at the last moment the ponies were brought to a rearing halt almost on top of him and the charioteer ran out along the yoke-pole and stood poised against the sky.

' A pretty trick,' said Marcus, grinning up at him. ' I have heard of it before, but never seen it until today.'

The other laughed and stepped back into the chariot, and as he brought the team round, Marcus side-stepped and sprang in beside him. The reins and the many-folded lash changed hands, and Cradoc drew back into the spearman's place, with a hand on the wickerwork side of the chariot. 'Take them across to the dead ash-tree yonder, for a start.'

'All in good time,' said Marcus. 'I am not yet ready.'

The ponies were harnessed Roman fashion, the two inner to the yoke-pole, the two outer by traces to the axles. So far, so good; but the chariot was another matter. Until now his driving had all been done in a Roman racing chariot, a mere cockle-shell with room for no one but the driver; this thing was twice as big, though fairly light, and the open front gave one a sense of being on top of the team which was new to him. To get the best out of chariot and team, certain allowances must be made. Holding the carefully separated reins high, in the approved Colosseum manner, his feet wide planted on the interlaced straps of the chariot bed, he set the fidgeting team in motion; easily at first, getting the feel of them, then steadying them from a trot into a canter, as he headed for the silvery target of the dead ash-tree. Just before it, he wheeled them, obedient to Cradoc's direction, and sent them weaving delicately down the curved row of javelins that the other had stuck upright in the turf before his arrival, in the same way that he had woven the white Arabs between the practice posts on Mars Field, his speed quickening to a gallop, but with never a grazed wheel-hub to disgrace him. He took the team through every trick and test that their master ordered, until the moment came for a final burst of speed, and they were sweeping at full gallop round the mile-wide curve of the wood-shore.

To Marcus that moment was always like being born from one kind of life into another. So must an arrow feel when it leaves the bow! It had been hot and sultry in the old life, but in this one the cool wind flowed against him like water, pressing his thin scarlet tunic into his body, singing past his ears above the soft thunder of the ponies' flying hooves. He crouched lower, feeling the chariot floor buoyant and vibrating under his wide-set feet, feeling the reins quick with life in his hands, his will flowing out along them to the flying team, and their response flowing back to him, so that they were one. He called to them in the Celtic tongue, urging them on.

'On, brave hearts! On, bold and beautiful! Thy mares shall be proud of thee, the tribe shall sing thy praises to their children's children! Sweff! Sweff, my brothers!'

For the first time he loosed the lash, letting it fly out and flicker like dark lightning above their ears without ever touching them. The forest verge spun by, the fern streaked away beneath flying hooves and whirling wheels. He and his team were a comet shooting down the bright ways of the sky; a falcon stooping against the sun. . . .

Then, on a word from Cradoc, he was backed on the reins, harder, bringing the team to a rearing halt, drawn back in full gallop on to their haunches. The wind of his going died, and the heavy heat closed round him again. It was very still, and the shimmering, sunlit scene seemed to pulse on his sight. Before the wheels had ceased to turn, Cradoc had sprung down and gone to the ponies' heads. After the first plunging moment, they stood quite quiet, their flanks heaving a little, but not over-much.

'Well?' demanded Marcus, rubbing the back of his hand across his wet forehead.

Cradoc looked up at him, unsmiling. 'The Commander begins to be a charioteer,' he said.

Marcus laid by reins and lash, and stepped down to join him. 'I have not driven a team to better these,' he said, and curved his arm over an arched neck. 'Do I win my spear?'

'Come and choose it for yourself, before you go back to the fort,' said the other. He had brought sweet crusts with him in the breast of his tunic, and he held them out on his open palms to the soft questing lips of the ponies. 'These four are the jewels of my heart. They are descended out of the Royal Stables of the Iceni, and there are few could handle them better than the Commander.' And there was a queer note of regret in his voice, for which there seemed no reason; but Marcus was to remember it afterwards.

They drove back slowly, walking the ponies through the summer evening.

'It will not harm them to stand for a little, now that they have cooled off,' Cradoc said, as, after threading their way through the confused huddle of the town, he pulled up before his own house-place. He drew the reins over the ponies' heads and turned to the dark doorway, calling, 'Guinhumara, bring out to me my spears.'

The leather apron had been drawn back to let in what air there was, and the red fire glowed in the centre of the house-place. Marcus saw the tall girl rise without a word—she had been turning wheat cakes among the hot ash for her man's supper—and melt into the darkness of some inner place. Several dogs which had been lying in the piled fern, with the small brown baby sleeping in their midst, came out with waving tails to fawn around their master, but the baby slept on, sucking its thumb. In a few moments the girl came back and joined them in the doorway, carrying a sheaf of spears whose polished blades caught the evening light like so many tongues of flame.

'The Commander and I have laid a wager,' said Cradoc.
'His brooch against one of my hunting-spears. He has won,
and now he is come to choose his spear.' As he spoke, he took
one from the sheaf and stood leaning on it with a gesture that
said quite plainly, ' But not this one.'

Those that were left were fine weapons, beautiful as were all
the weapons of the Celts, perfectly balanced and deadly; some
light for throwing, some broad-bladed for close work, some for
war, some for hunting. The girl handed them to Marcus one
by one, and he tested and examined them, finally picking one
with a slender, barbed blade and a cross-piece just below the
neck. 'This one,' he said. 'It shall be this one, for when I
hunt boar with your husband this winter.' He smiled at her,
but she did not smile back; her face had the same veiled look
that he remembered on it before. She stepped back without a
word, and carried the remaining spears with her into the house-
place. But Marcus had already turned to the hunter, for that
other spear had caught his interest, and been in his mind even
while he made his choice. It was to the rest of the sheaf what a
king is to his bodyguard; the shaft darkened with much
handling, the iron blade perfect in shape as a laurel leaf, engraved with a strange and potent design that swirled like the
eddies in running water. The weight of the head was counter-
balanced by a ball of enamelled bronze on the butt, and about
its neck was a collar of blue-grey heron's feathers.

'I have not seen the like of this before,' Marcus said. 'It is a
war spear, is it not? '

Cradoc's hand caressed the smooth shaft. 'It was my
father's war spear,' he said. 'It was in his hand when he
died—up yonder under our old ramparts where the fortress
walls stand now. See, the mark is still upon it . . . his own
blood, and the blood of his enemy.' He parted the heron's
feathers to show the neck of the shaft blackened by an old stain.

A little while afterwards, carrying his newly-won boar spear,
Marcus made his way back towards the Praetorian gate.
Children and hounds were playing together in the low sunshine,
and here and there a woman in a hut doorway called the even-

ing greeting to him as he passed. It all seemed very peaceful, and yet he was filled with an uneasy feeling that the peace was only a film—a veil like that which the girl Guinhumara had drawn behind her eyes—and that underneath, something very different was stirring. Again he remembered Hilarion's warning.

For the collar of the old war spear had been lately renewed, and the heron's feathers were still bright with the lustre of a living bird.

In all likelihood that spear had been refurbished many times, kept bright by a son in memory of his father; and yet, he wondered suddenly, in how many of these thatched homesteads had an old spear been put in fighting trim? Then he shook his shoulders impatiently, and strode on at a quickened pace up the steep way to the gate. He was simply growing toadstools, even as Hilarion had prophesied. All this because of a few feathers. Yet even a feather might show which way the wind blew.

If only they could have had a good harvest!

III

ATTACK!

IN the dark hour before the dawn, two nights later, Marcus was roused out of his sleep by the Duty Centurion. A pilot lamp always burned in his sleeping-cell against just such an emergency, and he was fully awake on the instant.

'What is it, Centurion?'

'The sentries on the south rampart report sounds of movement between us and the town, sir.'

Marcus was out of bed and had swung his heavy military cloak over his sleeping-tunic. 'You have been up yourself?'

The centurion stood aside for him to pass out into the darkness. 'I have, sir,' he said with grim patience.

'Anything to be seen?'

'No, sir, but there is something stirring down there, for all that.'

Quickly they crossed the main street of the fort, and turned down beside a row of silent workshops. Then they were mounting the steps to the rampart walk. The shape of a sentry's helmet rose dark against the lesser darkness above the breastwork, and there was a rustle and thud as he grounded his pilum in salute.

Marcus went to the breast-high parapet. The sky had clouded over so that not a star was to be seen, and all below was a formless blackness with nothing visible save the faint pallor of the river looping through it. Not a breath of air stirred in the stillness, and Marcus, listening, heard no sound in all the world save the whisper of the blood in his own ears, far fainter than the sea in a conch-shell.

He waited, breath in check; then from somewhere below came the kee-wick, kee-wick, wick-wick, of a hunting owl, and a moment later a faint and formless sound of movement that was gone almost before he could be sure that he had not imagined it. He felt the Duty Centurion grow tense as a strung bow beside him. The moments crawled by, the silence became a physical pressure on his eardrums. Then the sounds came again, and with the sounds, blurred forms moved suddenly on the darkness of the open turf below the ramparts.

Marcus could almost hear the twang of breaking tension. The sentry swore softly under his breath, and the centurion laughed.

'Somebody will be spending a busy day looking for his strayed cattle!'

Strayed cattle; that was all. And yet for Marcus the tension had not snapped into relief. Perhaps if he had never seen the new heron's feathers on an old war spear it might have done, but he had seen them, and somewhere deep beneath his thinking mind the instinct for danger had remained with him ever since. Abruptly he drew back from the breastwork, speaking quickly to his officer. 'All the same, a break-out of cattle might make good cover for something else. Centurion, this is my first command: if I am being a fool, that must excuse me. I am going back to get some more clothes on. Turn out the cohort to action stations as quietly as may be.'

And not waiting for a reply, he turned, and dropping from the rampart walk, strode off towards his own quarters.

In a short while he was back, complete from studded sandals to crested helmet, and knotting the crimson scarf about the waist of his breastplate as he came. From the faintly lit

c

doorways of the barrack rows, men were tumbling out, buckling sword-belts or helmet-straps as they ran, and heading away into the darkness. 'Am I being every kind of fool?' Marcus wondered. 'Am I going to be laughed at so long as my name is remembered in the Legion, as the man who doubled the guard for two days because of a bunch of feathers, and then turned out his cohort to repel a herd of milch-cows?' But it was too late to worry about that now. He went back to the ramparts, finding them already lined with men, the reserves massing below. Centurion Drusillus was waiting for him, and he spoke to the older man in a quick, miserable undertone. 'I think I must have gone mad, Centurion; I shall never live this down.'

'Better to be a laughing-stock than lose the fort for fear of being one,' returned the centurion. 'It does not pay to take chances on the Frontier—and there was a new moon last night.'

Marcus had no need to ask his meaning. In his world the gods showed themselves in new moons, in seed-time and harvest, summer and winter solstice; and if an attack were to come, the new moon would be the time for it. Holy War. Hilarion had understood all about that. He turned aside to give an order. The waiting moments lengthened; the palms of his hands were sticky, and his mouth uncomfortably dry.

The attack came with a silent uprush of shadows that swarmed in from every side, flowing up to the turf ramparts with a speed, an impetus that, ditch or no ditch, must have carried them over into the camp if there had been only the sentries to bar the way. They were flinging brushwood bundles into the ditch to form causeways; swarming over, they had poles to scale the ramparts, but in the dark nothing of that could be seen, only a flowing up and over, like a wave of ghosts. For a few moments the utter silence gave sheer goose-flesh horror to the attack; then the auxiliaries rose as one man to meet the attackers, and the silence splintered, not into uproar, but into a light smother of sound that rippled along the ramparts: the sound of men fiercely engaged, but without giving

tongue. For a moment it endured; and then from the darkness came the strident braying of a British war-horn. From the
ramparts a Roman trumpet answered the challenge, as fresh
waves of shadows came pouring in to the attack; and then
it seemed as if all Tartarus had broken loose. The time for
silence was past, and men fought yelling now; red flame
sprang up into the night above the Praetorian gate, and was
instantly quenched. Every yard of the ramparts was a reeling,
roaring battle-line as the tribesmen swarmed across the breastwork to be met by the grim defenders within.

How long it lasted Marcus never knew, but when the attack
drew off, the first cobweb light of a grey and drizzling dawn
was creeping over the fort. Marcus and his second-in-command
looked at each other, and Marcus asked very softly, ' How long
can we hold out? '

' For several days, with luck,' muttered Drusillus, pretending
to adjust the strap of his shield.

' Reinforcements could get to us in three—maybe two—
from Durinum,' Marcus said. ' But there was no reply to our
signal.'

' Little to wonder in that, sir. To destroy the nearest signal
station is an obvious precaution; and no cresset could carry the
double distance in this murk.'

' Mithras grant it clears enough to give the smoke column a
chance to rise.'

But there was no sign of anxiety in the face of either of
them when they turned from each other an instant later, the
older man to go clanging off along the stained and littered
rampart walk, Marcus to spring down the steps into the
crowded space below. He was a gay figure, his scarlet cloak
swirling behind him; he laughed, and made the ' thumbs up '
to his troops, calling ' Well done, lads! We will have breakfast
before they come on again! '

The ' thumbs up ' was returned to him. Men grinned, and
here and there a voice called cheerfully in reply, as he disappeared with Centurion Paulus in the direction of the
Praetorium.

No one knew how long the breathing space might last; but at the least it meant time to get the wounded under cover, and an issue of raisins and hard bread to the troops. Marcus himself had no breakfast, he had too many other things to do, too many to think about; amongst them the fate of a half Century under Centurion Galba, now out on patrol, and due back before noon. Of course the tribesmen might have dealt with them already, in which case they were beyond help or the need of it, but it was quite as likely that they would merely be left to walk into the trap on their return, and cut to pieces under the very walls of the fort.

Marcus gave orders that the cresset was to be kept alight on the signal roof; that at least would warn them that something was wrong as soon as they sighted it. He ordered a watch to be kept for them, and sent for Lutorius of the Cavalry and put the situation to him. ' If they win back here, we shall of course make a sortie and bring them in. Muster the squadron and hold them in readiness from now on. That is all.'

' Sir,' said Lutorius. His sulks were forgotten, and he looked almost gay as he went off to carry out the order.

There was nothing more that Marcus could do about his threatened patrol, and he turned to the score of other things that must be seen to.

It was full daylight before the next attack came. Somewhere, a war-horn brayed, and before the wild note died, the tribesmen broke from cover, yelling like fiends out of Tartarus as they swarmed up through the bracken; heading for the gates this time, with tree-trunks to serve as rams, with firebrands that gilded the falling mizzle and flashed on the blade of sword and heron-tufted war spear. On they stormed, heedless of the Roman arrows that thinned their ranks as they came. Marcus, standing in the shooting turret beside the Praetorian gate, saw a figure in their van, a wild figure in streaming robes that marked him out from the half-naked warriors who charged behind him. Sparks flew from the firebrand that he whirled aloft, and in its light the horns of the young moon, rising from his forehead, seemed to shine with a fitful radiance of its own. Marcus said quietly to the archer beside him, 'Shoot me that maniac.'

The man nocked another arrow to his bow, bent and loosed in one swift movement. The Gaulish Auxiliaries were fine bowmen, as fine as the British; but the arrow sped out only to pass through the wild hair of the leaping fanatic. There was no time to loose again. The attack was thundering on the gates, pouring in over the dead in the ditch with a mad courage that took no heed of losses. In the gate towers the archers stood loosing steadily into the heart of the press below them. The acrid reek of smoke and smitch drifted across the fort from the Dexter Gate, which the tribesmen had attempted to fire. There was a constant two-way traffic of reserves and armament going up to the ramparts and wounded coming back from them. No time to carry away the dead; one toppled them from the rampart walk that they might not hamper the feet of the living, and left them, though they had been one's best friend, to be dealt with at a fitter season.

The second attack drew off at last, leaving their dead lying twisted among the trampled fern. Once more there was breathing space for the desperate garrison. The morning dragged on; the British archers crouched behind the dark masses of uprooted blackthorn that they had set up under cover of the first assault, and loosed an arrow at any movement on the ramparts; the next rush might come at any moment. The garrison had lost upward of fourscore men, killed or wounded: two days would bring them reinforcements from Durinum, if only the mizzle which obscured the visibility would clear, just for a little while, long enough for them to send up the smoke signal, and for it to be received.

But the mizzle showed no signs of lifting, when Marcus went up to the flat signal-roof of the Praetorium. It blew in his face, soft and chill-smelling, and faintly salt on his lips. Faint grey swathes of it drifted across the nearer hills, and those beyond were no more than a spreading stain that blurred into nothingness.

'It is no use, sir,' said the auxiliary who squatted against the parapet, keeping the great charcoal brazier glowing.

Marcus shook his head. Had it been like this when the Ninth Legion ceased to be? he wondered. Had his father and all those others watched, as he was watching now, for the far hills to clear so that a signal might go through? Suddenly he found that he was praying, praying as he had never prayed before, flinging his appeal for help up through the grey to the clear skies that were beyond. 'Great God Mithras, Slayer of the Bull, Lord of the Ages, let the mists part and thy glory shine through! Draw back the mists and grant us clear air for a space, that we go not down into the darkness. O God of the Legions, hear the cry of thy sons. Send down thy light upon us, even upon us, thy sons of the Fourth Gaulish Cohort of the Second Legion.'

He turned to the auxiliary, who knew only that the Commander had stood beside him in silence for a few moments, with his head tipped back as though he was looking for something in the soft and weeping sky. 'All we can do is wait,' he said. 'Be ready to start your smother at any moment.' And swinging on his heel, he rounded the great pile of fresh grass and fern that lay ready near the brazier, and went clattering down the narrow stairway.

Centurion Fulvius was waiting for him at the foot with some urgent question that must be settled, and it was some while before he snatched another glance over the ramparts; but when he did, it seemed to him that he could see a little farther than before. He touched Drusillus, who was beside him, on the shoulder. 'Is it my imagining, or are the hills growing clearer?'

Drusillus was silent a moment, his grim face turned towards the east. Then he nodded. 'If it is your imagining, it is also mine.' Their eyes met quickly, with hope that they dared not put into any more words; then they went each about their separate affairs.

But soon others of the garrison were pointing, straining their eyes eastward in painful hope. Little by little the light grew:

the mizzle was lifting, lifting . . . and ridge behind wild ridge of hills coming into sight.

High on the Praetorium roof a column of black smoke sprang upward, billowed sideways and spread into a drooping veil that trailed across the northern rampart, making the men there cough and splutter; then rose again, straight and dark and urgent, into the upper air. In the pause that followed, eyes and hearts were strained with a sickening intensity toward those distant hills. A long, long pause it seemed; and then a shout went up from the watchers, as, a day's march to the east, a faint dark thread of smoke rose into the air.

The call for help had gone through. In two days, three at the most, relief would be here; and the uprush of confidence touched every man of the garrison.

Barely an hour later, word came back to Marcus from the northern rampart that the missing patrol had been sighted on the track that led to the Sinister Gate. He was in the Praetorium when the word reached him, and he covered the distance to the gate as if his heels were winged; he waved up the Cavalry waiting beside their saddled horses, and found Centurion Drusillus once again by his side.

' The tribesmen have broken cover, sir,' said the centurion.

Marcus nodded. 'I must have half a Century of the reserves. We can spare no more   A trumpeter with them and every available man on the gate, in case they try a rush when it opens.'

The centurion gave the order, and turned back to him. ' Better let me take them, sir.'

Marcus had already unclasped the fibula at the shoulder of his cloak, and flung off the heavy folds that might hamper him. 'We went into that before. You can lend me your shield, though.'

The other slipped it from his shoulder without a word, and Marcus took it and swung round on the half Century who were already falling in abreast of the gate. ' Get ready to form testudo,' he ordered. ' And you can leave room for me. This tortoise is not going into action with its head stuck out! '

It was a poor joke, but a laugh ran through the desperate
little band, and as he stepped into his place in the column head,
Marcus knew that they were with him in every sense of the
word; he could take those lads through the fires of Tophet if
need be.

The great bars were drawn, and men stood ready to swing
wide the heavy valves; and behind and on every side he had a
confused impression of grim ranks massed to hold the gate,
and draw them in again if ever they won back to it.

' Open up! ' he ordered; and as the valves began to swing
outward on their iron-shod posts, ' Form testudo.' His arm
went up as he spoke, and through the whole column behind
him he felt the movement echoed, heard the light kiss and click
of metal on metal, as every man linked shield with his neigh-
bour, to form the shield-roof which gave the formation its
name. ' Now! '

The gates were wide; and like a strange many-legged beast,
a gigantic woodlouse rather than a tortoise, the testudo was out
across the causeway and heading straight downhill, its small,
valiant cavalry wings spread on either side. The gates closed
behind it, and from rampart and gate-tower anxious eyes
watched it go. It had all been done so quickly that at the foot
of the slope battle had only just joined, as the tribesmen hurled
themselves yelling on the swiftly formed Roman square.

The testudo was not a fighting formation; but for rushing a
position, for a break through, it had no equal. Also it had a
strange and terrifying aspect that could be very useful. Its
sudden appearance now, swinging down upon them with the
whole weight of the hill behind it, struck a brief confusion into
the swarming tribesmen. Only for a moment their wild ranks
wavered and lost purpose; but in that moment the hard-
pressed patrol saw it too, and with a hoarse shout came charging
to join their comrades.

Down swept Marcus and his half Century, down and forward
into the raging battle-mass of the enemy. They were slowed
almost to a standstill, but never quite halted; once they were
broken, but re-formed. A mailed wedge cleaving into the wild

ranks of the tribesmen, until the moment came when the tortoise could serve them no longer; and above the turmoil Marcus shouted to the trumpeter beside him: ' Sound me " Break testudo ".'

The clear notes of the trumpet rang through the uproar. The men lowered their shields, springing sideways to gain fighting space; and a flight of pilums hurtled into the swaying horde of tribesmen, spreading death and confusion wherever the iron heads struck. Then it was ' Out swords ', and the charge driven home with a shout of ' Caesar! Caesar! ' Behind them the valiant handful of cavalry were struggling to keep clear the line of retreat; in front, the patrol came grimly battling up to join them. But between them was still a living rampart of yelling, battle-frenzied warriors, amongst whom Marcus glimpsed again that figure with the horned moon on its forehead. He laughed, and sprang against them, his men storming behind him.

Patrol and relief force joined, and became one.

Instantly they began to fall back, forming as they did so a roughly diamond formation that faced outward on all sides and was as difficult to hold as a wet pebble pressed between the fingers. The tribesmen thrust in on them from every side, but slowly, steadily, their short blades like a hedge of living, leaping steel, the cavalry breaking the way for them in wild rushes, they were drawing back towards the fortress gate—those that were left of them.

Back, and back. And suddenly the press was thinning, and Marcus, on the flank, snatched one glance over his shoulder, and saw the gate-towers very near, the swarming ranks of the defenders ready to draw them in. And in that instant there came a warning yelp of trumpets and a swelling thunder of hooves and wheels, as round the curve of the hill towards them, out of cover of the woodshore, swept a curved column of chariots.

Small wonder that the press had thinned.

The great battle-wains had long been forbidden to the tribes, and these were light chariots such as the one Marcus had driven two days ago, each carrying only a spearman beside the driver; but one horrified glance, as they hurtled nearer behind their thundering teams, was enough to show the wicked, whirling scythe-blades on the war-hubs of the wheels.

Close formation—now that their pilums were spent—was useless in the face of such a charge; again the trumpets yelped an order, and the ranks broke and scattered, running for the gateway, not in any hope of reaching it before the chariots were upon them, but straining heart and soul to gain the advantage of the high ground.

To Marcus, running with the rest, it seemed suddenly that there was no weight in his body, none at all. He was filled through and through with a piercing awareness of life and the sweetness of life held in his hollowed hand, to be tossed away like the shining balls that the children played with in the gardens of Rome. At the last instant, when the charge was almost upon them, he swerved aside from his men, out and back on his tracks, and flinging aside his sword, stood tensed to spring, full in the path of the oncoming chariots. In the breath of time that remained, his brain felt very cold and clear, and he seemed to have space to do quite a lot of thinking. If he sprang for the heads of the leading team, the odds were that he would merely be flung down and driven over without any check to the wild gallop. His best chance was to go for the charioteer. If he could bring him down, the whole team would be flung into confusion, and on that steep scarp the chariots coming behind would have difficulty in clearing the wreck. It was a slim chance, but if it came off it would gain for his men those few extra moments that might mean life or death. For himself, it was death. He was quite clear about that.

They were right upon him, a thunder of hooves that seemed to fill the universe; black manes streaming against the sky; the team that he had called his brothers, only two days ago. He hurled his shield clanging among them, and side-stepped, looking up into the grey face of Cradoc, the charioteer. For one splinter of time their eyes met in something that was almost a salute, a parting salute between two who might have been

friends; then Marcus leapt in under the spearman's descending thrust, upward and sideways across the chariot bow. His weight crashed on to the reins, whose ends, after the British fashion, were wrapped about the charioteer's waist, throwing the team into instant chaos; his arms were round Cradoc, and they went half down together. His ears were full of the sound of rending timber and the hideous scream of a horse. Then sky and earth changed places, and with his hold still unbroken, he was flung down under the trampling hooves, under the scythe-bladed wheels and the collapsing welter of the overset chariot; and the jagged darkness closed over him.

IV

THE LAST ROSE FALLS

O N the other side of the darkness was pain. For a long
time that was the only thing Marcus knew. At first it
was white, and quite blinding; but presently it dulled
to red, and he began to be dimly aware of the other things
through the redness of it. People moving near him, lamplight,
daylight, hands that touched him; a bitter taste in his mouth
which always brought back the darkness. But it was all
muddled and unreal, like a dissolving dream.

And then one morning he heard the trumpets sounding
Cockcrow. And the familiar trumpet-call, piercing through
the unreality like a sword-blade through tangled wool, brought
with it other real and familiar things: the dawn chill on his
face and an uncovered shoulder, the far-off crowing of a real
cock, the smell of lamp-smitch. He opened his eyes, and
found that he was lying flat on his back on the narrow cot in his
own sleeping-cell. Close above him the window was a square
of palest aquamarine in the dusky gold of the lamplit wall, and
on the dark roof-ridge of the officers' mess opposite was a
sleeping pigeon, so clearly and exquisitely outlined against the
morning sky that it seemed to Marcus as though he could make
out the tip of every fluffed-out feather. But of course that was
natural, because he had carved them himself, sitting between
the roots of the wild olive-tree in the bend of the stream. And
then he remembered that that had been a different bird; and
the last shreds of his confusion fell away from him.

So he was not dead, after all. He was faintly surprised, but
not very interested. He was not dead, but he was hurt. The
pain, which had been first white and then red, was still there,
no longer filling the whole universe, but reaching all up and
down his right leg: a dull, grinding throb with little sparks of

37

sharper pain that came and went in the dullness of it. It was
the worst pain that he had ever known, save for the few blinding
moments when the brand of Mithras pressed down between his
brows; but he was not much more interested in it than in the
fact that he was still alive. He remembered exactly what had
happened; but it had all happened so long ago, at the other
side of the blackness; and he was not even anxious, because
Roman trumpets sounding from the ramparts could only mean
that the fort was still safely in Roman hands.

Somebody moved in the outer room and, a moment later,
loomed into the doorway. Marcus turned his head slowly—it
seemed very heavy—and saw the garrison Surgeon, clad in a
filthy tunic, and with red-rimmed eyes and several days'
growth of beard.

' Ah, Aulus,' Marcus said, and found that even his tongue felt
heavy. ' You look—as if you had not been to bed for a month.'

' Not quite so long as that,' said the Surgeon, who had come
forward quickly at the sound of Marcus's voice, and was bending
over him. ' Good! Very good! ' he added, nodding his vague
encouragement.

' How long? ' began Marcus, stumblingly.

' Six days; yes, yes—or it might be seven.'

' It seems—like years.'

Aulus had turned back the striped native rugs, and laid a
fumbling hand over Marcus's heart. He seemed to be counting, and answered only with a nod.

But suddenly everything grew near and urgent again to
Marcus. ' The relief force?—They got through to us, then? '

Aulus finished his counting with maddening deliberateness,
and drew the rugs up again. ' Yes, yes. The best part of a
cohort of the Legion, from Durinum.'

' I must see Centurion Drusillus—and the—the relief force
Commander.'

' Maybe presently, if you lie still,' said Aulus, turning to deal
with the smoking lamp.

' No, not presently. Now! Aulus, it is an order: I am still
in command of this—— '

He tried to crane up on his elbow, and his rush of words ended in a choking gasp. For a few moments he lay very still, staring at the other man, and there were little beads of sweat on his forehead.

' Tch! Now you have made it worse! ' scolded Aulus in a slight fluster. ' That is because you did not lie still, as I bade you.' He picked up a red Samian bowl from the chest top, and slipped an arm under Marcus's head to raise him. ' Best drink this. Tch! tch! It will do you good.'

Too weak to argue, and with the rim of the bowl jolting against his teeth, Marcus drank. It was milk, but with the bitter taste in it which always brought back the darkness.

' There,' said Aulus, when the bowl was empty. ' Now go to sleep. Good boy; now go to sleep.' And he laid Marcus's head back on the folded rug.

Centurion Drusillus came next day, and sitting with his hands on his knees and the shadow of his crested helmet blue on the sunlit wall behind him, gave his Commander a broad outline of all that had happened since he was wounded. Marcus listened very carefully; he found that he had to listen very carefully indeed, because if he did not, his attention wandered: to the crack in a roof-beam, to the flight of a bird across the window, to the pain of his wounds or the black hairs growing out of the centurion's nostrils. But when the centurion had finished, there were still things that Marcus needed to know.

' Drusillus, what became of the holy man? '

' Gone to meet his own gods, sir. Caught between the relief force and ourselves. There was a-many of the tribe went with him.'

' And the charioteer?—my charioteer? '

Centurion Drusillus made the ' thumbs down '. ' Dead as we thought you were when we pulled you from the wreck.'

After a moment's silence, Marcus asked, ' Who brought me in? '

' Why, now, that is hard to say, sir. Most of us had our hand in it.'

'I had hoped to gain time for the rest.' Marcus rubbed the back of one hand across his forehead. 'What happened?'

'Nay now, sir, it was all so quick. . . . Galba doubled back to you, and the rest with him, and it was a time for desperate measures; so we took down the reserves—'twas not much more than a javelin throw—and brought you off.'

'And got cut to pieces by the chariots in doing it?' Marcus asked quickly.

'Not so badly as we might have been. Your wreck broke the weight of the charge.'

'I want to see Galba.'

'Galba is in the sick-block, with his sword arm laid open,' Drusillus said.

'How bad is the damage?'

'A clean wound. It is healing.'

Marcus nodded. 'You will be seeing him, I suppose? Salute him for me, Centurion. Tell him I shall come and compare scars with him if I am on my feet before he is. And tell the troops I always *have* said the Fourth Gaulish was the finest cohort with the Eagles.'

'I will, sir,' said Drusillus. 'Very anxiously inquiring, the troops have been.' He got up, raised an arm heavy with silver good-conduct bracelets in salute, and tramped off back to duty.

Marcus lay for a long time with his forearm across his eyes, seeing against the blackness of his closed lids picture after picture that Drusillus had left behind him. He saw the relief force coming up the road, tramp-tramp-tramp, and the dust rising behind them. He saw the last stand of the tribesmen crumble and the moon-crested fanatic go down. The British town a smoking ruin and the little fields salted by order of the relief force Commander. (Wattle-and-daub huts were easily rebuilt, and salted fields would bear again in three years, but not all the years in eternity would bring back the young men of the tribe, he thought, and was surprised to find that he cared.) He saw dead men, Lutorius among them; he hoped that there would be horses for Lutorius in the Elysian Fields. Most clearly of all, again and again, he saw Cradoc, lying broken among the trampled bracken of the hillside. He had felt very bitter towards Cradoc; he had liked the hunter and thought that his liking was returned; and yet Cradoc had betrayed him. But that was all over. It was not that Cradoc had broken faith; simply that there had been another and stronger faith that he must keep. Marcus understood that now.

Later, the Commander of the relief force came to see him, but the interview was not a happy one. Centurion Clodius Maximus was a fine soldier, but a chilly mannered, bleak-faced man. He stood aloofly in the doorway, and announced that since everything was under control, he intended to continue his interrupted northward march tomorrow. He had been taking troops up to Isca when the Frontier fort's distress signal had reached Durinum and he had been deflected to answer it. He would leave two Centuries to bring the garrison temporarily up to strength, and Centurion Herpinius, who would take command of the fort until Marcus's relief could be sent from Isca, when no doubt fresh drafts of auxiliaries would be sent with him.

Marcus realized that it was all perfectly reasonable. The Relief Force were Legionaries, line-of-battle troops, and in the nature of things a Legionary Centurion ranked above an auxiliary one; and if he, Marcus, was going to be laid by for a while, a relief would of course have to be sent down to take his place until he was once more fit for duty. But all the same, he was annoyed by the man's high-handed manner, annoyed on Drusillus's account, and on his own. Also, quite suddenly, he began to be afraid. So he became very stiff, and very proud, and for the rest of the short and formal interview treated the stranger with an icy politeness that was almost insulting.

Day followed day, each marked off in its passing by lamplight and daylight, food that he did not want, and the changing shadows that moved across the courtyard outside his window. These, and the visits of Aulus and a medical orderly to dress the spear-gash in his shoulder (he had never felt the blade bite, as he sprang in under the spearman's thrust), and the ugly mass of wounds that seared his right thigh.

D

There was some delay about the arrival of his relief from
Isca, for several cohort centurions were down with marsh fever;
and the moon, which had been new when the tribe rose, waxed
and waned into the dark, and the pale feather of another new
moon hung in the evening sky; and all save the deepest and
most ragged of Marcus's wounds were healed. That was when
they told him that his service with the Eagles was over.

Let him only be patient, and the leg would carry him well
enough, one day, Aulus assured him, but not for a long time;
no, he could not say how long. Marcus must understand, he
pointed out with plaintive reasonableness, that one could not
smash a thigh-bone and tear the muscles to shreds and then
expect all to be as it had been before.

It was the thing that Marcus had been afraid of ever since
his interview with Centurion Maximus. No need to be afraid
now, not any more. He took it very quietly; but it meant the
loss of almost everything he cared about. Life with the Eagles
was the only kind of life he had ever thought of, the only kind
that he had any training for; and now it was over. He would
never be Prefect of an Egyptian Legion, he would never be able
to buy back the farm in the Etruscan hills, or gather to himself
another like it. The Legion was lost to him and, with the
Legion, it seemed that his own land was lost to him too; and
the future, with a lame leg and no money and no prospects,
seemed at first sight rather bleak and terrifying.

Maybe Centurion Drusillus guessed something of all this,
though Marcus never told him. At all events he seemed to find
the Commander's quarters a good place to spend every off-duty
moment, just then; and though Marcus, longing to be alone
like a sick animal, often wished him at the other side of the
Empire, afterwards he remembered and was grateful for his
centurion's fellowship in a bad time.

.   .   .   .   .

A few days later, Marcus lay listening to the distant sounds
of the new Commander's arrival. He was still in his old
quarters, for when he had suggested that he should go across to

the sick-block, and leave the two rooms in the Praetorium free for their rightful owner, he was told that other quarters had been made ready for the new Commander, and he was to stay where he was until he was fit to travel—until he could go to Uncle Aquila. He was lucky, he supposed rather drearily, to have Uncle Aquila to go to. At all events he would know quite soon now whether the unknown uncle was like his father.

Now that he could sit up, he could look out into the court-yard, and see the rose-bush in its wine-jar, just outside his window. There was still one crimson rose among the dark leaves, but even as he watched, a petal fell from it like a great slow drop of blood. Soon the rest would follow. He had held his first and only command for just as long as the rose-bush had been in flower. . . . It was certainly pot-bound, he thought; maybe his successor would do something about it.

His successor: whoever that might be. He could not see the entrance to the courtyard, but quick footsteps sounded along the colonnade and then in the outer room, and a moment later the new Commander stood in the doorway; an elegant and very dusty young man with his crested helmet under one arm. It was the owner of the chariot team which Marcus had driven in the Saturnalia Games.

' Cassius! ' Marcus greeted him. ' I wondered if it would be anyone I knew.'

Cassius crossed to his side. ' My dear Marcus; how does the leg? '

' It mends, in its fashion.'

' So. I am glad of that, at all events.'

' What have you done with your bays? ' Marcus asked quickly. ' You are not having them brought down here, are you? '

Cassius collapsed on to the clothes-chest and wilted elegantly. ' Jupiter! No! I have lent them to Dexion, with my groom to keep an eye on them, and him.'

' They will do well enough with Dexion. What troops have you brought down with you? '

'Two Centuries of the Third: Gauls, like the rest. They are good lads, seasoned troops; been up on the wall laying stone courses and exchanging the odd arrow now and then with the Painted People.' He cocked a languid eyebrow. 'But if they can give as good an account of themselves in action as your raw Fourth have done, they will have no need to feel themselves disgraced.'

'I think there will be no more trouble in these parts,' Marcus said. 'Centurion Maximus took good care of that.'

'Ah, you mean the burned villages and salted fields? A punitive expedition is never pretty. But I gather from your embittered tone that you did not take warmly to Centurion Maximus?'

'I did not.'

'A most efficient officer,' pronounced Cassius, with the air of a grey-headed Legate.

'To say nothing of officious,' snapped Marcus.

'Maybe if you saw the report he sent in when he got back to Headquarters, you might find yourself feeling more friendlily disposed towards him.'

'It was good?' asked Marcus, surprised. Centurion Maximus had not struck him as the type who sent in enthusiastic reports.

Cassius nodded. 'Rather more than good. Indeed, before I marched south there was beginning to be talk of some trifle— say a gilded laurel wreath—to make the standard of the Gaulish Fourth look pretty when it goes on parade.'

There was a short silence, and then Marcus said, 'It is no more than we—than they deserve! Look, Cassius, if anything more than talking comes of it, send me word. I will give you the direction to write to. I should like to know that the cohort won its first honours under my command.'

'Possibly the cohort would like to know it too,' said Cassius gruffly, and lounged to his feet. 'I am for the bath-house. I am gritty from head to foot!' He paused a moment, looking down at Marcus, with his air of weary elegance quite forgotten. 'Do not worry. I shall not let your cohort go to ruin.'

Marcus laughed, with a sudden aching in his throat. 'See that you do not, or I swear I shall find means to poison your wine! They are a fine cohort, the best with the Legion: and—good luck to you with them.'

Outside in the courtyard, the last crimson petals fell in a little bright flurry from the rose-bush in the old wine-jar.

V

SATURNALIA GAMES

UNCLE AQUILA lived on the extreme edge of Calleva.
One reached his house down a narrow side street that
turned off not far from the East Gate, leaving behind
the forum and the temples, and coming to a quiet angle of the
old British earthworks—for Calleva had been a British Dun
before it was a Roman city—where hawthorn and hazel still
grew and the shyer woodland birds sometimes came. It was
much like the other houses of Calleva, timbered and red-roofed
and comfortable, built round three sides of a tiny courtyard
that was smoothly turfed and set about with imported roses and
gum-cistus growing in tall stone jars. But it had one pecu-
liarity: a squat, square, flat-roofed tower rising from one
corner; for Uncle Aquila, having lived most of his life in the
shadow of watch-towers from Memphis to Segedunum, could
not be comfortable without one.

Here, in the shadow of his own watch-tower, which he used
as a study, he was very comfortable indeed, with his elderly
wolf-hound Procyon, and the History of Siege Warfare which
he had been writing for ten years, for company.

By the dark end of October, Marcus had been added to the

household. He was given a sleeping-cell opening on to the courtyard colonnade; a lime-washed cell with a narrow cot piled with striped native blankets, a polished citron-wood chest, a lamp on a bracket high against the wall. Save that the door was differently placed, it might have been his old quarters in the Frontier fort, seven days' march away. But most of his days were spent in the long atrium, the central room of the house, occasionally with Uncle Aquila, but for the most part alone, save when Stephanos or Sassticca looked in on him. He did not mind Stephanos, his uncle's old Greek body-slave, who now looked after him as well as his master, but Sassticca the cook was another matter. She was a tall and gaunt old woman who could hit like a man, and frequently did when either of her fellow slaves annoyed her; but she treated Marcus as though he were a small sick child. She brought him little hot cakes when she had been baking, and warm milk because she said he was too thin, and fussed and tyrannized over him, until—for he was very afraid of kindness just then—he came near to hating her.

That autumn was a bad time for Marcus, feeling wretchedly ill for the first time in his life, almost always in pain, and face to face with the wreckage of everything he knew and cared about. He would wake in the dark mornings to hear the distant notes of Cockcrow sounding from the transit camp just outside the city walls, and that did not make it any easier. He was homesick for the Legions; he was desperately homesick for his own land; for now that they seemed lost to him, his own hills grew achingly dear, every detail of sight and scent and sound jewel-vivid on his memory. The shivering silver of the olive-woods when the mistral blew, the summer scent of thyme and rosemary and little white cyclamen among the sun-warmed grass, the songs that the girls sang at vintage.

And here in Britain the wind moaned through the desolate woods, the skies wept, and wet gale-blown leaves pattered against the windows and stuck there, making little pathetic shadows against the steamy glass. There had been wild weather often enough in his own country, but that had been the wild weather of home: here was the wind and rain and wet leaves of exile.

It would have gone less hardly with him if he had had a companion of his own age; but he was the only young thing in the house, for even Procyon had grey hairs in his muzzle, and so he was shut in on himself, and though he did not know it, he was bitterly lonely.

There was just one gleam of light for him in the darkness of that autumn. Not long after he came to Calleva, he had word from Cassius that henceforth the Standard of the Gaulish Fourth would have its gilded laurel wreath to carry on parade; and a little later there came to Marcus himself the award of a military bracelet, which was a thing that he had never for an instant expected. This was not, as the various crowns were, purely a gallantry award; rather it was given for the same qualities which had earned for the Second Legion its titles ' Pia Fidelis '; those titles which were cut deep upon the heavy gold bracelet under the Capricorn badge of the Legion. From the day that it came to him, it was never off Marcus's wrist; and yet it meant rather less to him than the knowledge that his old cohort had won its first laurels.

The days grew shorter and the nights longer, and presently it was the night of the winter solstice. A fitting night for the dark turn of the year, Marcus thought. The inevitable wind was roaring up through the forest of Spinaii below the old British ramparts, driving with it squalls of sleet that spattered against the windows. In the atrium it was warm, for whatever the peculiarities of Uncle Aquila's house, the hypercaust worked perfectly, and for the pleasant look of it rather than for need, a fire of wild-cherry logs on charcoal burned in the brazier hearth, filling the long room with faint, aromatic scent. The light from the single bronze lamp, falling in a golden pool over the group before the hearth, scarcely touched the lime-washed walls, and left the far end of the room in crowding shadows, save for the glim of light that always burned before the shrine of the household gods. Marcus lay propped on one elbow on his usual couch, Uncle Aquila sat opposite to him in his great cross-legged chair; and beside them, outstretched on the warm tessellated floor, Procyon the wolf-hound.

Uncle Aquila was huge; that had been the first thing Marcus noticed about him, and he noticed it still. His joints appeared to be loosely strung together as if with wet leather; his head with its bald freckled top and his bony beautiful hands were big even in proportion to the rest of him, and Authority seemed to hang on him in easy and accustomed folds, like his toga. Even allowing for their twenty years of difference in age, he was not in the least like Marcus's father; but Marcus had long ago ceased to think of him as like, or unlike, anyone. He was simply Uncle Aquila.

The evening meal was over, and old Stephanos had set out a draughts-board on the table between Marcus and his uncle, and gone his way. In the lamplight the ivory and ebony squares shone vividly white and black; Uncle Aquila's men were already in place, but Marcus had been slower, because he was thinking of something else. He set down his last ivory man with a little click, and said: ' Ulpius was here this morning.'

' Ah, our fat physician,' said Uncle Aquila, his hand, which had been poised for an opening move, returning to the arm of his chair. ' Had he anything to say worth the listening to?'

' Only the usual things. That I must wait and wait.' Suddenly Marcus exploded between misery and laughter. ' He said I must have a little patience and called me his dear young man and wagged a scented fat finger under my nose. Fach! He is like the white pulpy things one finds under stones!'

' So,' agreed Uncle Aquila. ' None the less, you *must* wait—there being no help for it.'

Marcus looked up from the board. ' There's the rub. How long can I wait?'

' Hmph?' said Uncle Aquila.

' I have been here two months now, and we have never spoken of the future. I have put it off from one visit of that pot-bellied leech to the next because—I suppose because I have never thought of any life but following the Eagles, and I do not

quite know how to begin.' He smiled at his uncle apolo-
getically. ' But we must discuss it sometime.'

' Sometime, yes : but not now. No need to trouble about the
future until that leg will carry you.'

' But Mithras knows how long that will be. Do you not see,
sir, I cannot go on foisting myself on you indefinitely.'

' Oh, my good lad, do try not to be such a fool ! ' snapped
Uncle Aquila; but his eyes under their jut of brow were
unexpectedly kindly. ' I am not a rich man, but neither am I
so poor that I cannot afford to add a kinsman to my household. You do not get in my way; to be perfectly honest, I
forget your existence rather more than half the time; you play
a reasonably good game of draughts. Naturally you will stay
here, unless of course '—he leaned forward abruptly—' is it that
you would rather go home? '

' Home? ' Marcus echoed.

' Yes. I suppose you still have a home with that peculiarly
foolish sister of mine? '

' And with Uncle-by-Marriage Tullus Lepidus? ' Marcus's
head went up, his black brows twitched almost to meeting point
above a nose which looked suddenly as though there was a very
bad smell under it. ' I'd sooner sit on Tiber-side and beg my
bread from the slum women when they come to fill their water-
pots ! '

' So? ' Uncle Aquila nodded his huge head. ' And now,
that being settled, shall we play? '

He made the opening move, and Marcus answered it. For a
while they played in silence. The lamplit room was a shell of
quiet amid the wild sea-roaring of the wind; the small saffron
flames whispered in the brazier, and a burned cherry log collapsed with a tinselly rustle into the red hollow of the charcoal.
Every few moments there would be a little clear click as Marcus
or his uncle moved a piece on the board. But Marcus did not
really hear the small peaceful sounds, nor see the man opposite,
for he was thinking of things that he had been trying not to
think of all day.

It was the twenty-fourth evening of December, the eve of the winter solstice—the eve of the birth of Mithras; and quite soon now, in camps and forts wherever the Eagles flew, men would be gathering to his worship. In the outposts and the little frontier forts the gatherings would be mere handfuls, but in the great Legionary Stations there would be full caves of a hundred men. Last year, at Isca, he had been one of them, newly initiated at the Bull-slaying, the brand of the Raven Degree still raw between his brows. He ached with longing for last year to be given back to him, for the old life and the comradeship to be given back to him. He moved an ivory man a little blindly, seeing, not the black-and-white dazzle of the board before his eyes, but that gathering of a year ago, filing out by the Praetorian gate and downhill to the cave. He could see the crest of the centurion in front of him up-reared blackly against the pulsing fires of Orion. He remembered the waiting darkness of the cave; then, as the trumpets sounded from the distant ramparts for the third watch of the night, the sudden glory of candles, that sank and turned blue, and sprang up again; the reborn light of Mithras in the dark of the year. . . .

A great gust of wind swooped against the house like a wild thing striving to batter its way in; the lamplight jumped and fluttered, sending shadows racing across the chequered board— and the ghosts of last year were once more a year away. Marcus looked up, and said, as much for the sake of shutting out his own thoughts as for anything else, ' I wonder what possessed you to settle here in Britain, Uncle Aquila, when you could have gone home? '

Uncle Aquila moved his piece with meticulous care before he answered with another question. ' It seems very odd to you, that anyone free to go home should choose to strike his roots in this barbarous country? '

' On a night like this,' said Marcus, ' it seems odd almost past believing.'

' I had nothing to take me back,' said the other, simply. ' Most of my service years were spent here, though it was in Judaea that my time fell due for parting with the Eagles. What have I to do with the South? A few memories, very few.

I was a young man when first I saw the white cliffs of Dubris above the transport galley's prow. Far more memories in the North. Your move. . . .'

Marcus moved an ivory man to the next square, and his uncle shifted his own piece. ' If I settled in the South, I should miss the skies. Ever noticed how changeful British skies are? I have made friends here—a few. The only woman I ever cared a denarius for lies buried at Glevum.'

Marcus looked up quickly. ' I never knew——'

'Why should you? But I was not always old Uncle Aquila with a bald head.'

' No, of course not. What was—she like? '

'Very pretty. She was the daughter of my old Camp Commandant, who had a face like a camel, but she was very pretty, with a lot of soft brown hair. Eighteen when she died. I was twenty-two.'

Marcus said nothing. There seemed nothing to say. But Uncle Aquila, seeing the look on his face, gave a deep chuckle. ' No, you have it all quite wrong. I am a very selfish old man, perfectly well content with things as they are.' And then, after a pause, he harked back to an earlier point in their discussion. ' I killed my first boar in Silurian territory; I have sworn the blood brotherhood with a painted tribesman up beyond where Hadrian's Wall stands now; I've a dog buried at Lugu- vallium—her name was Margarita; I have loved a girl at Glevum; I have marched the Eagles from end to end of Britain in worse weather than this. Those are the things apt to strike a man's roots for him.'

Marcus said after a moment, ' I think I begin to understand.'

' Good. Your move.'

But after they had played a few more moves in silence, Uncle Aquila looked up again, the fine wrinkles deepening at the corners of his eyes. ' What an autumnal mood we have wandered into! We need livening up, you and I.'

'What do you suggest? ' Marcus returned the smile.

' I suggest the Saturnalia Games tomorrow. We may not be able to compete quite on equal terms with the Colosseum, here at Calleva; but a wild-beast show, a sham fight with perhaps a little blood-letting—we will certainly go.'

And they went, Marcus travelling in a litter, for all the world, as he remarked disgustedly, like a Magistrate or a fine lady. They arrived early, but by the time they were settled on one of the cushioned benches reserved for the Magistrates and their families (Uncle Aquila was a Magistrate, though he had not come in a litter), the amphitheatre just outside the East Gate was already filling up with eager spectators. The wind had died down, but the air struck cold, with a clear, chill tang to it that Marcus sniffed eagerly while he pulled the folds of his old military cloak more closely round him. After being so long within four walls, the sanded space of the arena seemed very wide; a great emptiness within the encircling banks up which the crowded benches rose tier on tier.

Whatever else of Rome the British had not taken to, they seemed to have taken to the Games with a vengeance, Marcus thought, looking about him at the crowded benches where townsfolk and tribesmen with their womenfolk and children jostled and shoved and shouted after the best places. There was a fair sprinkling of Legionaries from the transit camp, and Marcus's quick glance picked out a bored young tribune sitting with several British lads all pretending to be equally Roman and equally bored. He remembered Colosseum crowds, chattering, shouting, quarrelling, laying bets and eating sticky sweets. The British took their pleasures a little less loudly, to be sure, but on almost every face was the same eager, almost greedy look that the faces of the Colosseum crowds had worn.

A small disturbance near him drew Marcus's attention to the arrival of a family who were just entering their places on the Magistrates' benches a little to his right. A British family of the ultra-Roman kind, a large, good-natured-looking man, running to fat as men do who have been bred to a hard life and take to living soft instead; a woman with a fair and rather foolish face, prinked out in what had been the height of fashion in Rome two years ago—and very cold she must be, Marcus thought, in that thin mantle; and a girl of perhaps twelve or thirteen, with a sharply pointed face that seemed all golden eyes in the shadow of her dark hood. The stout man and Uncle Aquila saluted each other across the heads between, and the woman bowed. All Rome was in that bow; but the girl's eyes were fixed on the arena with a kind of horrified expectancy.

When the new-comers were settled in their places, Marcus touched his uncle's wrist, and cocked an inquiring eyebrow.

'A fellow Magistrate of mine, Kaeso by name, and his wife Valaria,' Uncle Aquila said. 'Incidentally, they are our next-door neighbours.'

'Are they so? But the little maiden; she is no bud of their branch, surely?'

But he got no answer to his question then, for at that moment a great crashing of cymbals and a fanfare of trumpets announced that the Games were about to begin. All round the crowded circus there was a sudden quietness and a craning forward. Again the trumpets sounded. The double doors at the far side were flung open, and out from their underground lodgements a double file of gladiators came marching into the arena, each carrying the weapons he would use later in the show. Shout on shout greeted their appearance. For a small colonial circus they seemed rather a good lot, Marcus thought, watching them as they paraded round the arena; too good, maybe, though probably they were all slaves. Marcus was something of a heretic where the Games were concerned; he liked well enough to see a wild-beast show, or a sham fight if it were well done, but to put up men—even slaves—to fight to the death for a crowd's amusement, seemed to him a waste.

The men had halted now, before the Magistrates' benches; and in the few moments that they stood there, Marcus's whole attention was caught by one of them: a sword-and-buckler man of about his own age. He was rather short for a Briton, but powerful. His russet-brown hair, flung back by the savage pride with which he carried his head, showed the clipped ear that branded him for a slave. Seemingly he had been taken in war, for his breast and shoulders—he was stripped to the waist—were tattooed with blue warrior patterns. But it was none of these things that Marcus saw, only the look in the wide-set grey eyes that strained back at him out of the gladiator's young sullen face.

'This man is afraid,' said something deep in Marcus. 'Afraid—afraid,' and his own stomach cringed within him.

A score of weapons flashed in the wintry light as they were tossed up with a shout and caught again, and the gladiators wheeled and strode on down the wide curve that led back to their starting point. But the look that he had seen in the young swordsman's eyes remained with Marcus.

The first item on the programme was a fight between wolves and a brown bear. The bear did not want to fight, and was driven into battle by the long curling whip-lashes of the attendants. Presently, amid a great shouting from the on-lookers, it was killed. Its body was dragged away, and with it the bodies of two wolves it had slain; the others were decoyed back into their wheeled cage for another time, and attendants spread fresh sand over the blood in the arena. Marcus glanced, without quite knowing why, at the girl in the dark hood, and saw her sitting as though frozen, her eyes wide and blank with horror in an ashy face. Still oddly shaken by that queer moment of contact with the young gladiator who was so very much afraid, he was filled with a sudden unreasoning anger against Kaeso and his wife for bringing the little maiden to see a thing like this, against all Games and all mobs who came to watch them with their tongues hanging out for horrors, even against the bear for being killed.

The next item was a sham fight, with little damage done save a few flesh wounds. (In the back of beyond, circus masters could not afford to be wasteful with their gladiators.) Then a boxing match in which the heavy cestus round the fighters' hands drew considerably more blood than the swords had done. A pause came, in which the arena was once again cleaned up and freshly sanded; and then a long gasp of expectancy ran through the crowd, and even the bored young tribune sat up and began to take some notice, as, with another blare of trumpets, the double doors swung wide once more, and two

figures stepped out side by side into the huge emptiness of the
arena. Here was the real thing: a fight to the death.

At first sight the two would seem to be unequally armed, for
while one carried sword and buckler, the other, a slight dark
man with something of the Greek in his face and build, carried
only a three-pronged spear, and had over his shoulder a many-
folded net, weighted with small discs of lead. But in truth, as
Marcus knew only too well, the odds were all in favour of the
man with the net, the Fisher, as he was called, and he saw with
an odd sinking of the heart that the other was the young swordsman who was afraid.

'Never did like the net,' Uncle Aquila was grumbling.
'Not a clean fight, no!' A few moments earlier, Marcus had
known that his damaged leg was beginning to cramp horribly;
he had been shifting, and shifting again, trying to ease the
pain without catching his uncle's notice, but now, as the two
men crossed to the centre of the arena, he had forgotten
about it.

The roar which greeted the pair of fighters had fallen to a
breathless hush. In the centre of the arena the two men were
being placed by the captain of the gladiators; placed with
exquisite care, ten paces apart, with no advantage of light or
wind allowed to either. The thing was quickly and com-
petently done, and the captain stepped back to the barriers.
For what seemed a long time, neither of the two moved.
Moment followed moment, and still they remained motionless,
the centre of all that great circle of staring faces. Then, very
slowly, the swordsman began to move. Never taking his eyes
from his adversary, he slipped one foot in front of the other;
crouching a little, covering his body with the round buckler,
inch by inch he crept forward, every muscle tensed to spring
when the time came.

The Fisher stood as still as ever, poised on the balls of his
feet, the trident in his left hand, his right lost in the folds of the
net. Just beyond reach of the net, the swordsman checked
for a long, agonizing moment, and then sprang in. His attack
was so swift that the flung net flew harmlessly over his head,

and the Fisher leapt back and sideways to avoid his thrust, then whirled about and ran for his life, gathering his net for another cast as he ran, with the young swordsman hard behind him. Half round the arena they sped, running low; the swordsman had not the other's length and lightness of build, but he ran as a hunter runs—perhaps he had run down deer on the hunting trail, before ever his ear was clipped—and he was gaining on his quarry now. The two came flying round the curve of the barrier towards the Magistrates' benches, and just abreast of them the Fisher whirled about and flung once more. The net whipped out like a dark flame; it licked round the running swordsman, so intent on his chase that he had forgotten to guard for it; the weight carried the deadly folds across and across again, and a howl burst from the crowd as he crashed headlong and rolled over, helplessly meshed as a fly in a spider's web.

Marcus wrenched forward, his breath caught in his throat. The swordsman was lying just below him, so near that they could have spoken to each other in an undertone. The Fisher was standing over his fallen antagonist, with the trident poised to strike, a little smile on his face, though his breath whistled through widened nostrils, as he looked about him for the bidding of the crowd. The fallen man made as though to raise his hampered arm in the signal by which a vanquished gladiator might appeal to the crowd for mercy; then let it drop back, proudly, to his side. Through the fold of the net across his face, he looked up straight into Marcus's eyes, a look as direct and intimate as though they had been the only two people in all that great amphitheatre.

Marcus was up and standing with one hand on the barrier rail to steady himself, while with the other he made the sign for mercy. Again and again he made it, with a blazing vehemence, with every atom of will-power that was in him, his glance thrusting like a challenge along the crowded tiers of benches where already the thumbs were beginning to turn down. This mob, this unutterably stupid, blood-greedy mob that must somehow be swung over into forgoing the blood it wanted! His gorge

E

rose against them, and there was an extraordinary sense of battle in him that could not have been more vivid had he been standing over the fallen gladiator, sword in hand. Thumbs up! *Thumbs up!* you fools! . . . He had been aware from the first of Uncle Aquila's great thumb pointing skyward beside him; suddenly he was aware of a few others echoing the gesture, and then a few more. For a long, long moment the swordsman's fate still hung in the balance, and then as thumb after thumb went up, the Fisher slowly lowered his trident and with a little mocking bow, stepped back.

Marcus drew a shuddering breath, and relaxed into a flood of pain from his cramped leg, as an attendant came forward to disentangle the swordsman and aid him to his feet. He did not look at the young gladiator again. This moment was shame for him, and Marcus felt that he had no right to witness it.

.   .   .   .   .

That evening, over the usual game of draughts, Marcus asked his uncle: ' What will become of that lad now? '

Uncle Aquila moved an ebony piece after due consideration. ' The young fool of a swordsman? He will be sold in all likelihood. The crowd do not pay to see a man fight, when once he has been down and at their mercy.'

' That is what I have been thinking,' Marcus said. He looked up from making his own move. ' How do prices run in these parts? Would fifteen hundred sesterces buy him? '

' Very probably. Why? '

' Because I have that much left of my pay and a parting thank-offering that I had from Tullus Lepidus. There was not much to spend it on in Isca Dumnoniorum.'

Uncle Aquila's brows cocked inquiringly. ' Are you suggesting buying him yourself? '

' Would you give him house-room? '

' I expect so,' said Uncle Aquila. ' Though I am somewhat at a loss to understand why you should wish to keep a tame gladiator. Why not try a wolf instead? '

Marcus laughed. ' It is not so much a tame gladiator as a

body-slave that I need. I cannot go on overworking poor old Stephanos for ever.'

Uncle Aquila leaned across the chequered board. 'And what makes you think that an ex-gladiator would make you a suitable body-slave?'

'To speak the truth, I had not thought about it,' Marcus said. 'How do you advise me to set about buying him?'

'Send down to the circus slave-master, and offer half of what you expect to pay. And sleep with a knife under your pillow thereafter,' said Uncle Aquila.

VI

ESCA

THE purchase was arranged next day, without much difficulty, for although the price that Marcus could afford was not large, Beppo, the master of the circus slaves, knew well enough that he was not likely to get a better one for a beaten gladiator. So, after a little haggling, the bargain was struck, and that evening after dinner Stephanos went to fetch home the new slave.

Marcus waited for their return alone in the atrium, for Uncle Aquila had retired to his watch-tower study to work out a particularly absorbing problem in siege warfare. He had been trying to read his uncle's copy of the Georgics, but his thoughts kept wandering from Virgil on bee-keeping to the encounter before him. He was wondering for the first time —he had not thought to wonder before—why the fate of a slave gladiator he had never before set eyes on should matter to him so nearly. But it did matter. Maybe it was like calling to like; and yet it was hard to see quite what he had in common with a barbarian slave.

Presently his listening ear caught the sound of an arrival in the slaves' quarters, and he laid down the papyrus roll and turned towards the doorway. Steps came along the colonnade, and two figures appeared on the threshold. ' Centurion Marcus, I have brought the new slave,' said Stephanos, and stepped discreetly back into the night; and the new slave walked forward to the foot of Marcus's couch, and stood there.

For a long moment the two young men looked at each other, alone in the empty lamplit atrium as yesterday they had been alone in the crowded amphitheatre, while the scuff-scuffling of Stephanos's sandals died away down the colonnade.

' So it is you,' the slave said at last.

' Yes, it is I.'

The silence began again, and again the slave broke it. ' Why did you turn the purpose of the crowd yesterday? I did not ask for mercy.'

' Possibly that was why.'

The slave hesitated, and then said defiantly, ' I was afraid yesterday; I, who have been a warrior. I am afraid to choke out my life in the Fisher's net.'

' I know,' Marcus said. ' But still, you did not ask for mercy.'

The other's eyes were fixed on his face, a little puzzled. ' Why have you bought me? '

' I have need of a body-slave.'

' Surely the arena is an unusual place to pick one.'

' But then, I wished for an unusual body-slave.' Marcus looked up with the merest quirk of a smile into the sullen grey eyes fixed so unswervingly on his own. ' Not one like Stephanos, that has been a slave all his life, and is therefore—nothing more.'

It was an odd conversation between master and slave, but neither of them was thinking of that.

' I have been but two years a slave,' said the other quietly.

' And before that you were a warrior—and your name? '

' I am Esca, son of Cunoval, of the tribe of Brigantes, the bearers of the blue war-shield.'

' And I am—I was, a centurion of auxiliaries with the Second Legion,' Marcus said, not knowing quite why he made the reply, knowing only that it had to be made. Roman and Briton faced each other in the lamplight, while the two statements seemed to hang like a challenge in the air between them.

Then Esca put out a hand unconsciously and touched the edge of the couch. ' That I know, for the goaty one, Stephanos, told me; and also that my Master has been wounded. I am sorry for that.'

' Thank you,' Marcus said.

Esca looked down at his own hand on the edge of the couch,

and then up again. 'It would have been easy to escape on my way here,' he said slowly. 'The old goaty one could not have held me back if I had chosen to break for freedom. But I chose to go with him because it was in my heart that it might be you that we went to.'

'And if it had been another, after all?'

'Then I should have escaped later, to the wilds where my clipped ear would not betray me. There are still free tribes beyond the Frontiers.' As he spoke, he drew from the breast of his rough tunic, where it had lain against his skin, a slender knife, which he handled as tenderly as if it had been a thing living and beloved. 'I had this, to my release.'

'And now?' Marcus said, not giving a glance to the narrow, deadly thing.

For a moment the sullenness lifted from Esca's face. He leaned forward and let the dagger fall with a little clatter on to the inlaid table at Marcus's side. 'I am the Centurion's hound, to lie at the Centurion's feet,' he said.

. . . . .

So Esca joined the household and, carrying the spear that marked him for a personal slave and superior to mere household slaves, stood behind Marcus's couch at meals to pour wine for him, fetched and carried and saw to his belongings, and slept on a mattress across his door at night. He made a very good body-slave, so good that Marcus guessed him to have been somebody's armour-bearer in the days before his ear was clipped; a father's, or an elder brother's, perhaps, after the custom of the tribes. He never asked about those days, nor how Esca had come into the Calleva arena, because something about his slave, some inner reserve, warned him that to ask would be an intrusion, a walking in without leave. One day, perhaps, Esca would tell him freely, but not yet.

The weeks went by, and suddenly the rose-bushes in the courtyard were gemmed with swelling leaf-buds, and the air had a sense of quickening that was the first distant promise of spring. Slowly, very slowly, Marcus's leg was mending. It no longer woke him with a stab of pain every time he turned in the night, and he could hobble round the house more and more easily.

As time passed, he got into the way of leaving his stick behind him and walking with a hand on Esca's shoulder instead. It seemed natural to do that, for without quite realizing it, he was slipping more and more often from the master to the friend in his dealings with Esca; though, after that first night, Esca never for an instant forgot the slave in his dealings with Marcus.

That winter there was a lot of trouble with wolves in the district. Driven out from their fastnesses by hunger, they hunted under the very walls of Calleva; and often Marcus would hear their long-drawn cry in the night, setting every dog in the town baying in that frenzy that was half hate and half longing, half enemy hurling defiance at enemy, half kin calling to kin. In the outlying farms of the forest clearings, lambing pens were attacked, and anxious men kept the wolf-guard every night. At a village a few miles away a pony was killed, at another a baby was taken.

Then one day, Esca, going into the town on an errand for Marcus, returned with news of a country-wide wolf hunt planned for next day. It had started simply among the outlying farms, desperate to save their lambing ewes, then gathered to itself professional hunters, and a couple of young officers from the transit camp out for a day's sport; and now it seemed that half the countryside was out to end the menace. He poured it all out to Marcus. The hunters were to meet at such a place, two hours before sunrise; at such another place they were going to drive the thickets with dogs and torches; and Marcus laid aside the belt he was mending, and listened to him as eager to hear as his slave was to tell.

Listening, he longed to be off on that wolf hunt and run the spring fret out of his bones; and he knew that the same longing was hot in his slave. For him, it did not seem likely that there would be any more hunting, but that was no reason why there should be none for Esca. ' Esca,' he said abruptly, when the other had told all that there was to tell. ' It would surely be a good thing if you joined this wolf hunt.'

Esca's whole face lit with eagerness, but after a moment he said, ' It would mean maybe a night and a day that the Centurion must do without his slave.'

' I shall do well enough,' Marcus told him. ' I shall borrow half of Stephanos from my uncle. But what will you do for spears? I left my own for the man who came after me at Isca, else you could have had those.'

' If my Master is sure, really sure, I know where I can borrow spears.'

' Good. Do you go and borrow them now.'

So Esca borrowed the spears he needed, and in the pitch dark of that night, Marcus heard him get up and collect them from the corner where they had been stacked. He turned on his elbow and spoke into the darkness. ' You are going now? '

A light footfall and a sense of movement told him that Esca was standing at his side. ' Yes, if the Centurion is still sure— quite sure? '

' Perfectly sure. Go and spear your wolf.'

' It is in my heart that I wish the Centurion came too,' Esca said in a rush.

' Maybe I'll come another year,' Marcus said sleepily. ' Good hunting, Esca.'

For an instant a dark shape showed in the lesser darkness of the doorway, and then it was gone, and he lay listening, not at all sleepily now, to the quick, light footfall dying away along the colonnade.

In the grey of the next dawn, he heard the footfall returning, a little heavier than at the setting out, and the dark shape loomed again into the cobweb pallor of the doorway.

' Esca!—How went the hunting? '

' The hunting was good,' Esca said. He stacked the spears with a slight clatter against the wall, and came and bent over the cot; and Marcus saw that there was something curled in the crook of his arm, under the rough cloak. ' I have brought back the fruits of my hunting for the Centurion,' he said, and set the thing down on the blanket. It was alive, and being disturbed, it whimpered: and Marcus's gently exploring hand discovered that it was warm and harshly furry.

'Esca! A wolf cub?' he said, feeling a scrabble of paws and a thrusting muzzle.

Esca had turned away to strike flint and steel and kindle the lamp. The tiny flame sank and then sprang up and steadied; and in the dazzle of yellow light he saw a very small grey cub, who staggered to uncertain paws, sneezing at the sudden light, and pushed in under his hand with the nuzzling thrust of all very young things. Esca came back to the cot and dropped on one knee beside it. And as he did so Marcus noticed that there was a hot look in his eyes, a brightness that he had not seen there before, and wondered with an odd sense of hurt if his return to bondage from a day and night of freedom was the cause.

'In my tribe, when a she-wolf with whelps is killed, we sometimes take the young ones to run with the dog-pack,' Esca said. 'If they are like this one, little, little, so that they remember nothing before; so that their first meat comes from their master's hand.'

'Is he hungry now?' Marcus asked, as the cub's muzzle poked and snuggled into his palm.

'No, he is full of milk—and scraps. Sassticca will not miss them. See, he is half asleep already; that is why he is so gentle.'

The two of them looked at each other, half laughing; but the queer hot look was still in Esca's eyes; while the cub crawled whimpering into the warm hollow of Marcus's shoulder, and settled there. His breath smelled of onions, like a puppy.

'How did you get him?'

'We killed a she-wolf in milk, so I and two others went to look for the whelps. They killed the rest of the litter, those fools of the South; but this one, I saved. His sire came. They are good fathers, the wolf kind, fierce to protect their young. It was a fight: aie! a good fight.'

'It was taking a hideous risk,' Marcus said. 'You should not have done it, Esca!' He was half angry, half humbled, that Esca should have taken such a deadly risk to bring him the cub, for he was enough of a hunter himself to know what the hazard was in robbing a wolf's lair while the sire still lived.

Esca seemed to draw back into himself on the instant. 'I forgot it was my Master's property that I risked,' he said, his voice suddenly hard and heavy as stone.

'Don't be a fool,' Marcus said quickly. 'I didn't mean that, and you know it.'

There was a long silence. The two young men looked at each other, and there was no trace of laughter now in their faces.

'Esca,' Marcus said at last, 'what has happened?'

'Nothing.'

'That is a lie,' Marcus said. 'Someone has been working mischief.'

The other remained stubbornly silent.

'Esca, I want an answer.'

The other moved a little, and some of the defiance went out of him. 'It was my own fault,' he began at last, speaking as though every word was dragged out of him. 'There was a young Tribune; one of those from the transit camp, who I think is taking troops up to Eboracum—a very splendid young Tribune, smooth as a girl, but a skilled hunter. He was one of us who went into the lair; and after the old dog-wolf was dead, and we had come away, and I was cleaning my spear, he laughed and said to me, " So, that was a noble thrust! " And then he saw my clipped ear, and he said, " for a slave ". I was angry, and I let my tongue run away from me. I said: " I am body-slave to the Centurion Marcus Flavius Aquila; does the Tribune Placidus (that was his name) see any cause therein that I should be a worse hunter than himself? " ' Esca broke off for a moment, drawing a harsh breath. 'He said: " None in the world; but at least the Tribune Placidus's life is his own to hazard as he wills. Your Master, having paid good money for his slave, will not thank you for leaving him with a carcass that he cannot even sell to the knacker's yard. Remember that when next you thrust your head into a wolf's lair." And then he smiled, and his smile is a sickness in my belly, still.'

Esca had been speaking in a dull, hopeless monotone, as though he had the bitter lesson by heart; and as he listened, Marcus was filled with a cold anger against the unknown Tribune; and the light of his rage suddenly made clear to him certain things that he had never thought of before.

Abruptly he reached out his free hand and grasped the other's wrist. ' Esca, have I ever, by word or deed, given you to believe that I think of you as that six-month soldier evidently thinks of his slaves? '

Esca shook his head. His defiance was all gone from him, and his face in the paling lamplight was no longer set and sullen, but only wretched. ' The Centurion is not such a one as the Tribune Placidus, to show the whip-lash without need to his hound,' he said drearily.

Marcus, baffled, hurt, and angry, suddenly lost his temper. ' Oh, curse Tribune Placidus! ' he burst out, his grasp tightening fiercely on the other's wrist. ' Does his word strike so much deeper with you than mine, that because of it you must needs talk to me of hounds and whip-lashes? Name of Light! Do I have to tell you in so many words that I really do not imagine a clipped ear to be the dividing-line between men and beasts? Have I not shown you clearly enough all this while? I have not thought of equal or unequal, slave or free in my dealings with you, though you were too proud to do the same for me! Too *proud*! Do you hear me? And now'—forgetful for the moment of the sleeping cub, he made a sudden movement to get on to his elbow, and collapsed again, exasperated but half laughing, his fury gone like a pricked bubble, holding up a bleeding thumb. ' And now your gift has bitten me! Mithras! His mouth is full of daggers! '

' Then you had best pay me a sesterce for the lot of them,' said Esca, and suddenly they were both laughing, the quick light laughter of breaking strain that has very little to do with whether or not there is anything to laugh at, while between them on the striped native blanket the small grey wolf-cub crouched, savage, bewildered, but very sleepy.

The household varied a good deal in their reactions to the sudden appearance of a wolf-cub in their midst. Procyon was doubtful at their first meeting; the new-comer had the wolf smell, the outland smell, and the great hound walked round him on stiff legs, the hair on his neck rising a little, while the cub squatted like a hairy malignant toad on the atrium floor, ears laid back and muzzle wrinkled in his first attempt at a snarl. Uncle Aquila scarcely noticed his arrival, being at the moment too deeply absorbed in the siege of Jerusalem; and Marcipor, the house slave, and Stephanos looked on him rather askance—a wolf-cub that would one day be a wolf, roaming at large about the house. But Sassticca was unexpectedly an ally. Sassticca, her hands on her hips, told them roundly that they should be ashamed of themselves. Who were they, she demanded shrilly, with two sound legs apiece, to begrudge the young Master a pack of wolf-cubs if he wanted them? And she finished her baking in a state of high indignation, and presently brought Marcus three brown honey-cakes in a napkin, and a chipped bowl of castor ware with a hunting scene on it, which she said he might have for the little cub's feeding-bowl.

Marcus, who had overheard her championship—she had a loud voice—accepted both gifts with becoming gratitude, and when she had gone, he and Esca shared the cakes between them. He no longer minded Sassticca quite so desperately as he had done at first.

A few days later, Esca told Marcus about the days before his ear was clipped.

They were in the bath-house when it happened, drying themselves after a cold plunge. The time that he spent in the plunge-bath each day was one of Marcus's greatest pleasures, for it was big enough to splash about in and swim a few strokes; and while he was in the water, unless he was very careless, he could forget about his lame leg. It was a little like his old sense of being born from one kind of life into another, that he had been used

to know in his charioteering days. But the likeness was the
kind that a shadow bears to the real thing, and this morning as
he sat up on the bronze couch, drying himself, he was suddenly
sick with longing for the old splendour. Once more, just once
more, to know that burst of speed as the team sprang forward,
the swoop and the strength of it, and wind of his going singing
by.

And at that moment, as though called up by the intensity of
his longing, a swiftly driven chariot came whirling up the
street beyond the bath-house wall.

Marcus reached out and took his tunic from Esca, saying as
he did so, ' Not often that we hear anything but a vegetable
cart in this street.'

' It will be Lucius Urbanus, the contractor's son,' Esca said.
' There is a back way from his stables which comes through
behind the temple of Sull-Minerva.' The chariot was passing
the house now, and evidently the driver was having trouble,
for the crack of a whip and the loud burst of swearing reached
them through the bath-house wall, and Esca added with disgust,
' It should be a vegetable cart and drawn by an ox. Listen
to him ! He is not worthy to handle horses ! '

Marcus pulled the folds of fine wool over his head and
reached for his belt. ' So Esca also is a charioteer,' he said,
fastening it.

' I was my father's charioteer,' Esca said. ' But that was a
long time ago.'

And suddenly Marcus realized that he could ask Esca, now,
about the time before his ear was clipped. It would no longer
be walking in without leave. He shifted a little, making a
quick gesture towards the foot of the couch, and as the other sat
down, he said : ' Esca, how did your father's charioteer come
to be a gladiator in the Calleva arena ? '

Esca was buckling his own belt; he finished the task very
deliberately, and then, locking his hands round one updrawn
knee, sat silent for a moment, staring down at them. ' My
father was a Clan Chieftain of the Brigantes, lord of five
hundred spears,' he said at last. ' I was his armour-bearer

until such time as I became a warrior in my own right—with
the men of my tribe that happens after the sixteenth summer.
When I had been a year or more a man among men and my
father's charioteer, the Clan rose against our overlords, for the
lust for freedom that was in us. We have been a thorn in the
flesh of the Legions since first they marched north; we, the
bearers of the blue war-shield. We rose, and we were beaten
back. We made our last stand in our strong place, and we
were overwhelmed. Those of the men's side who were left—
there were not many—were sold as slaves.' He broke off,
jerking up his head to look at Marcus. ' But I swear before the
gods of my people, before Lugh the Light of the Sun, that I was
lying for dead in a ditch when they took me. They would not
have taken me, else. They sold me to a trader from the South,
who sold me to Beppo, here in Calleva; and you know the
rest.'

' You alone of all your kin? ' Marcus asked after a moment.

' My father and two brothers died,' Esca said. ' My mother
also. My father killed her before the Legionaries broke
through. She wished it so.'

There was a long silence, and then Marcus said softly:
' Mithras! What a story! '

' It is a common enough story, still. Was it so very different
at Isca Dumnoniorum, do you suppose? ' But before Marcus
could answer, he added quickly, ' None the less, it is not good
to remember too closely. The time before—all the time
before—that is the good time to remember.'

And sitting there in the thin March sunshine that slanted
down through the high window, without either of them quite
knowing how it happened, he began to tell Marcus about the
time before. He told of a warrior's training; of river-bathing
on hot summer days when the midges danced in the shimmering air; of his father's great white bull garlanded with
poppies and moon flowers for a festival; of his first hunt, and
the tame otter he had shared with his elder brother. . . . One
thing led to another, and presently he told how, ten years before,
when the whole country was in revolt, he had lain behind a

boulder to watch a Legion marching north, that never came marching back.

'I had never seen such a sight before,' he said. 'Like a shining serpent of men winding across the hills; a grey serpent, hackled with the scarlet cloaks and crests of the officers. There were queer tales about that Legion; men said that it was accursed, but it looked stronger than any curse, stronger and more deadly. And I remember how the Eagle flashed in the sun as it came by—a great golden Eagle with its wings arched back as I have seen them often stoop on a screaming hare among the heather. But the mist was creeping down from the high moors, and the Legion marched into it, straight into it, and it licked them up and flowed together behind them, and they were gone as though they had marched from one world into—another.' Esca made a quick gesture with his right hand, the first two fingers spread like horns. 'Queer tales there were, about that Legion.'

'Yes, I have heard those tales,' Marcus said. 'Esca, that was my father's Legion. His crest will have been the scarlet hackle next after the Eagle.'

VII

TWO WORLDS MEETING

FROM the open end of Uncle Aquila's courtyard, two shallow steps flanked by a bush of rosemary and a slender bay-tree led down into the garden. It was a rather wild garden, for Uncle Aquila did not keep a full-time garden slave, but a very pleasant one, running down to the crumbling earthworks of British Calleva. In some places the fine stone-faced city walls were already rising. One day they would rise here too, but as yet there was only the curved wave-break of old quiet turf, glimpsed between the branches of wild fruit-trees; and where the bank dipped, stray glimpses over mile upon mile of forest country rolling away into the smoke-blue distance where the Forest of Spinaii became the Forest of Anderida, and the Forest of Anderida dropped to the marshes and the sea.

To Marcus, after being cooped within doors all winter long, it seemed a wonderfully wide and shining place when he reached it for the first time some days later; and when Esca had left him to go off on some errand, he stretched himself out on the bench of grey Purbeck marble, under the wild fruit-trees, his arms behind his head, gazing upwards with eyes narrowed against the brightness, into the blown blue heights of heaven, which seemed so incredibly tall after roof-beams. Somewhere in the forest below him, birds were singing, with that note of clear-washed surprise that belongs to the early spring; and for a while Marcus simply lay letting it all soak into him, the wideness and the shine and the bird-song.

Close beside him, Cub lay curled into a compact ball. Looking at him now, it was hard to believe what a small fury he could be, crouched over his food-bowl with laid-back ears and bared milk-teeth, Marcus thought. Then he took up the task that he had brought out with him. He was one of those people who need something to do with their hands at all times, even if it is only a stick to whittle; and something of the craftsman in him demanded always to have an outlet. If he had not been wounded, he would have turned that craftsmanship to the making of a happy and efficient cohort; things being as they were, he had turned it this spring to overhauling and renovating the Celtic weapons which were the only ornament Uncle Aquila allowed on his walls. Today he had brought out the gem of the small collection, a light cavalry buckler of bull's hide faced with bronze, the central boss exquisitely worked with red enamel; but the straps must have been in a poor state when Uncle Aquila came by it, and now they were ready to tear like papyrus. Laying out his tools and the leather for the fresh straps beside him on the broad seat, he set to work to cut away the old ones. It was a delicate task, needing all his attention, and he did not look up again until he had finished it, and turned to lay the outworn straps aside.

And then he saw that he was no longer alone with Cub. A girl was standing among the wild fruit-trees where the hedge ran up into the slope of the old earthwork, and looking down at him. A British girl, in a pale saffron tunic, straight and shining as a candle-flame; one hand raised to thrust back heavy masses of hair the colour of red baltic amber, which the light wind had blown across her face.

They looked at each other in silence for a moment. Then the girl said in clear, very careful Latin, ' I have waited a long time for you to look up.'

' I am sorry,' Marcus said stiffly. ' I was busy on this shield.'

She came a step nearer. ' May I see the wolf-cub? I have not seen a tame wolf-cub before.'

And Marcus smiled suddenly, and laid aside his defences with the shield he had been working on. ' Surely. Here he is.' And swinging his feet to the ground, he reached down and grabbed the sleeping cub by the scruff of his neck, just as the girl joined him. The wolfling was not fiercer than most hound puppies,

F

save when annoyed, but being bigger and stronger for his age,
he could be very rough, and Marcus was taking no chances.
He set Cub on his feet, keeping a restraining hand under his
small chest. 'Be careful; he is not used to strangers.'

The girl gave him a smile, and sat down on her heels, holding
out her hands slowly to Cub. 'I will not startle him,' she said.
And Cub, who at first had crouched back against Marcus,
ears flattened and hairs bristling, seemed very slowly to change
his mind. Warily, ready to flinch back or snap at any sign
of danger, he began to smell at her fingers; and she held
her hands quite still, to let him. 'What is his name?' she
asked.

'Just Cub.'

'Cub,' she said crooningly. 'Cub.' And as he whimpered
and made a little darting thrust towards her, against Marcus's

74

guarding hand, she began to caress the warm hollow under his chin with one finger. ' See, we be friends, you and I.'

She was about thirteen, Marcus imagined, watching her as she played with Cub. A tall, thin girl, with a pointed face wide at the temples and narrow at the chin; and the shape of her face and the colour of her eyes and hair gave her a little the look of a young vixen. If she were angry, he thought, she would probably look very like a vixen indeed. He had the glimmering of an idea that he had seen her before, but he could not remember where.

' How did you know about Cub? ' he asked at last.

She looked up. ' Narcissa, my nurse, told me—oh, about a moon ago. And at first I did not believe it, because Nissa so often gets her stories wrong. But yesterday I heard a slave on this side of the hedge call to another, " Oh worthless one, thy Master's wolf-whelp has bitten my toe! " And the other called back, " Then the gods grant that the taste of it will not make him sick! " So I knew that it was true.'

Her imitation of Esca and Marcipor the house slave was unmistakable, and Marcus flung up his head with a crow of laughter. ' And it did!—at all events, something did.'

The girl laughed too, joyously, showing little pointed teeth as white and sharp as Cub's. And as though their laughter had unlocked a door, Marcus suddenly remembered where he had seen her before. He had not been interested enough in Kaeso and Valaria to remember that they lived next door, and although he had noticed her so vividly at the time, he had not remembered the girl he had seen with them, because Esca, coming immediately afterwards, had been so much more important; but he remembered her now.

' I saw you at the Saturnalia Games,' he said. ' But your hair was hidden under your mantle, and that was why I did not remember you.'

' But I remember you! ' said the girl. Cub had wandered off after a beetle by that time, and she let him go, sitting back and folding her hands in her lap. ' Nissa says you bought that gladiator. I wish you could have bought the bear too.'

' You minded very badly about that bear, didn't you? ' said Marcus.

' It was cruel! To kill on the hunting trail, that is one thing; but they took away his freedom! They kept him in a cage, and then they killed him.'

' It was the cage, then, more than the killing? '

' I do not like cages,' said the girl in. a small hard voice. ' Or nets. I am glad you bought that gladiator.'

A little chill wind came soughing across the garden, silvering the long grass and tossing the budding sprays of the wild pear- and cherry-trees. The girl shivered, and Marcus realized that her yellow tunic was of very thin wool, and even here in the shelter of the old earthworks it was still very early spring.

' You are cold,' he said, and gathered up his old military cloak which had been flung across the bench. ' Put this on.'

' Do you not want it? '

' No. I have a thicker tunic than that flimsy thing you are wearing. So. Now, come and sit here on the bench.'

She obeyed him instantly, drawing the cloak around her. In the act of doing so, she checked, looking down at the bright folds, then up again at Marcus. ' This is your soldier's cloak,' she said. ' Like the cloaks the centurions from the transit camp wear.'

Marcus made her a quick mocking salute. ' You behold in me Marcus Aquila, ex-Cohort Centurion of Gaulish Auxiliaries with the Second Legion.'

The girl looked at him in silence for a moment. Then she said, ' I know. Does the wound hurt you still? '

' Sometimes,' Marcus said. ' Did Nissa tell you that too? '

She nodded.

' She seems to have told you a deal of things.'

' Slaves! ' She made a quick, contemptuous gesture. ' They stand in doorways and chatter like starlings; but Nissa is the worst of them all! '

Marcus laughed, and a small silence fell between them; but after a little while he said : ' I have told you my name. What is yours? '

'My aunt and uncle call me Camilla, but my real name is Cottia,' said the girl. 'They like everything to be very Roman, you see.'

So he had been right in thinking she was not Kaeso's daughter. 'And you do not?' he said.

'I? I am of the Iceni! So is my Aunt Valaria, though she likes to forget it.'

'I once knew a black chariot team who were descended out of the Royal Stables of the Iceni,' Marcus said, feeling that perhaps Aunt Valaria was not a very safe subject.

'Did you? Were they yours? Which strain?' Her face was alight with interest.

Marcus shook his head. 'They were not mine, and I only had the joy of driving them once; it was a joy too. And I never knew their strain.'

'My father's big stallion was descended from Prydfirth, the beloved of King Prasutogus,' said Cottia. 'We are all horse-breeders, we of the Iceni, from the King downward—when we had a king.' She hesitated, and her voice lost its eager ring. 'My father was killed, breaking a young horse, and that is why I live with my Aunt Valaria now.'

'I am sorry. And your mother?'

'I expect that all is well with my mother,' Cottia said, matter-of-factly. 'There was a hunter who had wanted her always, but her parents gave her to my father. And when my father went West of the Sunset, she went to the hunter, and there was no room in his house for me. It was different with my brother, of course. It is always different with boys. So my mother gave me to Aunt Valaria, who has no children of her own.'

'Poor Cottia,' Marcus said softly.

'Oh no. I did not wish to live in that hunter's house; he was not *my* father. Only . . .' Her voice trailed into silence.

'Only?'

Cottia's changeable face was suddenly as vixenish as he had guessed it could be. 'Only I hate living with my Aunt; I hate living in a town full of straight lines, and being shut up

inside brick walls, and being called Camilla; and I hate—·
hate—*hate* it when they try to make me pretend to be a Roman
maiden and forget my own tribe and my own father!'

Marcus was quickly coming to the conclusion that he did not
like Aunt Valaria. 'If it is any consolation to you, they seem
to have succeeded very ill so far,' he said.

'No! I will not let them! I pretend, outside my tunic. I
answer when they call me Camilla, and I speak to them in
Latin: but underneath my tunic I am of the Iceni, and when I
take off my tunic at night, I say, "There! That rids me of
Rome until the morning!" And I lie on my bed and think—
and think—about my home, and the marsh birds flighting
down from the north in the Fall of the Leaf, and the brood
mares with their foals in my father's runs. I remember all
the things that I am not supposed to remember, and talk to
myself inside my head in my own tongue——' She broke off,
looking at him in quick surprise. 'We are talking in my
tongue now! How long have we been doing that?'

'Since you told me about your real name being Cottia.'

Cottia nodded. It did not seem to strike her that the
hearer to whom she was pouring out all this was himself a
Roman: and it did not strike Marcus either. For the moment
all he knew was that Cottia also was in exile, and his fellowship
reached out to her, delicately, rather shyly. And as though
feeling the touch of it, she drew a little nearer, huddling the
scarlet folds more closely round her.

'I like being inside your cloak,' she said contentedly. 'It
feels warm and safe, as a bird must feel inside its own feathers.'

From beyond the hedge at that moment there arose a voice,
shrill as a peahen before rain. 'Camilla! Ladybird! Oh,
my Lady Camilla!'

Cottia sighed in exasperation. 'That is Nissa,' she said.
'I must go.' But she did not move.

'*Camilla!*' called the voice, nearer this time.

'That is Nissa again,' said Marcus.

'Yes, I—must go.' She got up reluctantly, and slipped off
the heavy cloak. But still she lingered, while the screeching

voice drew nearer. Then with a rush, 'Let me come again! Please let me! You need not talk to me, nor even notice that I am here.'

'Oh, my Lady! Where are you, child of Typhon?' wailed the voice, very near now.

'Come when it pleases you—and I shall be glad of your coming,' Marcus said quickly.

'I will come tomorrow,' Cottia told him, and turned to the old rampart slope, carrying herself like a queen. Most British women seemed to carry themselves like that, Marcus thought, watching her drop out of sight round the hedge; and he remembered Guinhumara in the hut doorway at Isca Dumnoniorum. What had happened to her and the brown baby, after Cradoc lay dead and the huts were burned and the fields salted? He would never know.

The shrill voice was raised in fond scolding on the far side of the hedge; and footsteps came across the grass, and Marcus turned his head to see Esca coming towards him.

'My Master has had company,' Esca said, laying spear-blade to forehead in salute, as he halted beside him.

'Yes, and it sounds as though she is getting a sharp scolding from her nurse on my account,' Marcus said a little anxiously, as he listened to the shrill voice fading.

'If all I hear be true, scolding will not touch that one,' Esca said. 'As well scold a flung spear.'

Marcus leaned back, his hands behind his neck, and looked up at his slave. The thought of Guinhumara and her baby was still with him, standing behind the thought of Cottia. 'Esca, why do all the Frontier tribes resent our coming so bitterly?' he asked on a sudden impulse. 'The tribes of the south have taken to our ways easily enough.'

'We have ways of our own,' said Esca. He squatted on one heel beside the bench. 'The tribes of the south had lost their birthright before ever the Eagles came in war. They sold it for the things that Rome could give. They were fat with Roman merchandise and their souls had grown lazy within them.'

'But these things that Rome had to give, are they not good

things?' Marcus demanded. 'Justice, and order, and good roads; worth having, surely?'

'These be all good things,' Esca agreed. 'But the price is too high.'

'The price? Freedom?'

'Yes—and other things than freedom.'

'What other things? Tell me, Esca; I want to know. I want to understand.'

Esca thought for a while, staring straight before him. 'Look at the pattern embossed here on your dagger-sheath,' he said at last. 'See, here is a tight curve, and here is another facing the other way to balance it, and here between them is a little round stiff flower; and then it is all repeated here, and here, and here again. It is beautiful, yes, but to me it is as meaningless as an unlit lamp.'

Marcus nodded as the other glanced up at him. 'Go on.'

Esca took up the shield which had been laid aside at Cottia's coming. 'Look now at this shield-boss. See the bulging curves that flow from each other as water flows from water and wind from wind, as the stars turn in the heaven and blown sand drifts into dunes. These are the curves of life; and the man who traced them had in him knowledge of things that your people have lost the key to—if they ever had it.' He looked up at Marcus again very earnestly. 'You cannot expect the man who made this shield to live easily under the rule of the man who worked the sheath of this dagger.'

'The sheath was made by a British craftsman,' Marcus said stubbornly. 'I bought it at Anderida when I first landed.'

'By a British craftsman, yes, making a Roman pattern. One who had lived so long under the wings of Rome—he and his fathers before him—that he had forgotten the ways and the spirit of his own people.' He laid the shield down again. 'You are the builders of coursed stone walls, the makers of straight roads and ordered justice and disciplined troops. We know that, we know it all too well. We know that your justice is more sure than ours, and when we rise against you, we see our hosts break against the discipline of your troops, as the sea breaks against a rock. And we do not understand, because all these things are of the ordered pattern, and only the free curves of the shield-boss are real to us. We do not understand. And when the time comes that we begin to understand your world, too often we lose the understanding of our own.'

For a while they were silent, watching Cub at his beetle-hunting. Then Marcus said, ' When I came out from home, a year and a half ago, it all seemed so simple.' His gaze dropped again to the buckler on the bench beside him, seeing the strange, swelling curves of the boss with new eyes. Esca had chosen his symbol well, he thought: between the formal pattern on his dagger-sheath and the formless yet potent beauty of the shield-boss lay all the distance that could lie between two worlds. And yet between individual people, people like Esca, and Marcus, and Cottia, the distance narrowed so that you could reach across it, one to another, so that it ceased to matter.

VIII

THE HEALER WITH THE KNIFE

MARCUS had said 'Come when you like,' and Cottia had said, 'I will come tomorrow.' But it was not so simple as that, after all. Kaeso would have made no particular difficulty, for he was an easy-going and kindly man, very eager to stand well with his Roman fellow-Magistrate. But Aunt Valaria, always so careful to follow the custom of what she called 'civilized Society', was very sure that it was not the custom for gently nurtured Roman maidens to take themselves into other people's gardens and make friends with the total strangers they found there. It was not as though Aquila had ever shown himself in the least friendly.

Marcus of course knew nothing of this; he only knew that Cottia did not come tomorrow, nor the day after. And he told himself that there was no reason why she should. It had been to see Cub that she came in the first place, and having seen him, why should she come again? He had thought that perhaps she wanted to be friends, but it seemed that that had been a mistake, and it did not much matter.

And then on the third day, when he had sworn to himself that he would not look for her coming any more, he heard her calling his name, softly and urgently, and when he looked up from the spear-blade that he had been burnishing, there she was, standing where he had first seen her, among the wild fruit-trees.

'Marcus! Marcus, I could not get free of Nissa before,' she began breathlessly. 'They say that I must not come again.'

Marcus laid down the spear, and demanded, 'Why?'

She glanced quickly over her shoulder into her own garden. ' Aunt Valaria says it is not seemly for a Roman maiden to do as

I have done. But I am not a Roman maiden; and oh, Marcus, you must make her let me come! You *must*!'

She was hovering on the edge of flight, even while she spoke, and clearly it was no time for needless talk or long explanations. 'She *shall* let you come,' Marcus said quickly, 'but it may take time. Now go, before they catch you.' He made her a swift half-laughing obeisance, palm to forehead, and she turned and dropped out of sight.

Marcus returned to his burnishing. The whole incident had come and gone as quickly as the flight of a bird across the garden, but behind it he was suddenly happier that he had been for three days.

That evening, after talking it over with Esca, he laid the whole problem before Uncle Aquila.

'And what,' inquired Uncle Aquila when he had finished, 'do you suggest that I should do about it?'

'If you could make a few neighbourly remarks to the Lady Valaria the next time you cross her path, I think it would help.'

'But Jupiter! I scarce know the woman, save to bow to her as Kaeso's wife.'

'Which is exactly why a few neighbourly remarks seem indicated.'

'And what if she becomes neighbourly in return?' demanded Uncle Aquila in blighting tones.

'She cannot invade you here in your stronghold, at all events, since there are no womenfolk to receive her,' Marcus pointed out, quite unblighted.

'There is truth in that, admittedly. Why do you want the chit to come?'

'Oh—because she and Cub understand each other.'

'And so I am to be thrown to the lions in order that Cub may have his playmate?'

Marcus laughed. 'It is only one lion, or rather lioness.' And then the laughter left him. 'Uncle Aquila, we do need your help. I would contrive to play Perseus for myself, but at this stage nothing I could do would in the least avail to rescue Andromeda. It is a job for the head of the household.'

' It was peaceful in this house before you came,' said Uncle
Aquila with resignation. ' You are an unutterable nuisance,
but I suppose you must have your own way.'

Marcus was never quite sure how it was brought about.
Certainly Uncle Aquila never appeared to bestir himself at all
in the matter, but from that time forward there began to be
more of surface friendliness between the two houses, and before
the woods below the old ramparts had thickened into full leaf,
Cottia had become a part of life in the Aquila household, and
came and went as it pleased her, and as it pleased Marcus.

Esca, who was by nature silent and withdrawn with anyone
save the young Roman, was somewhat prone at first to stand
on his dignity as a slave, where she was concerned; but he
lowered his barriers to her little by little, so far as it was in him
to lower them to anyone who was not Marcus. And Marcus
tyrannized over and laughed at her, and was content in her
company; he taught her to play ' Flash the Fingers ', a game
beloved of Legionaries and gladiators; and told her long
stories about his old home in the Etruscan hills. Telling Cottia
about it, conjuring up for her the sights and sounds and smells,
seemed somehow to bring it all nearer and ease the ache of
exile; and as he told about it, he would catch again that first
glimpse of the farmstead from the corner of the hill track where
the wild cherry-trees grew. ' There were always a lot of
pigeons strutting and fluttering about the courtyards and the
roofs, and their necks would catch the sunlight and shine
iridescent green and purple; little white stock-doves, too, with
coral-pink feet. And when you came into the courtyard they
would all burst upwards with a great deal of fuss, and then
come circling down again round your feet. And then old
Argos would come out of his kennel and bark and wag his tail
at the same time; and there would be a wonderful smell of
whatever was for supper—grilled river trout, perhaps, or fried
chicken if it was a special occasion. And when I came home
in the evening, after being out all day, my mother would come
to the door when she heard Argos barking. . . .'

Cottia never tired of hearing about the farm in the Etruscan hills, and Marcus, homesick as he was, never tired of telling her. One day he even showed her his olive-wood bird.

But towards the summer's end he began to have more and more trouble with the old wound. He had grown so used to the dull ache of it that often he could forget about it altogether, but now there was a jangling sharpness in the old ache, that could not be forgotten, and sometimes the scars were hot to touch and reddened and angry to the sight.

Matters came to a head on a hot August evening, when Marcus and his uncle had just played out their usual game of draughts. It had been a blazing day, and even out here in the courtyard there seemed no air. The evening sky was drained of all colour by the day's heat, a bleached and weary sky, and the scent of the roses and cistus in the courtyard jars hung heavy in the air, as smoke hangs in misty weather.

Marcus had been feeling sick with pain all day, and the heavy sweetness of the flowers seemed to stick in his throat. He had played a thoroughly bad game, and he knew it. He could not lie still. He shifted a little in search of an easier position, and then shifted again, pretending that he had only moved to look at Cub—half grown now, and superbly handsome lying sprawled on the cooling turf beside Procyon, with whom he had long ago made friends.

Uncle Aquila was watching a yellow wagtail on the bath-house roof, and Marcus shifted yet again, hoping that he would not notice.

'Wound troublesome tonight?' inquired Uncle Aquila, his eye still following the yellow wagtail as it scuttled after flies on the warm tiles.

Marcus said, 'No, sir. Why?'

'Oh, I merely wondered. You are quite sure?'

'Perfectly.'

Uncle Aquila brought his eye down from the yellow wagtail, and fixed it on Marcus. 'What a liar you are,' he remarked conversationally. Then, as Marcus's mouth tightened, he leaned forward, crashing a huge hand on the draughts-board and scattering the pieces broadcast. 'This has been going on

long enough! If that fat fool Ulpius does not know his craft,
I have an old friend in practice at Durinum who does. Rufrius
Galarius. He was one of our field surgeons. He shall come
and take a look at that leg.'

'I should not think for a moment that he will,' Marcus said.
'It is a long way from Durinum.'

'He will come,' said Uncle Aquila. 'He and I used to hunt
boar together. Oh yes, he will come.'

And come he did.

Rufrius Galarius, one-time field surgeon of the Second
Legion, was a blue-jowled Spaniard with a merry eye, close
curling black hair scarcely touched with grey, and a chest
like a barrel. But his blunt wrestler's hands were very sure
and gentle, Marcus found, a few evenings later, when he lay
on his narrow cot while his uncle's friend examined the old
wounds.

It seemed a long time before he had finished; and when he
had, he replaced the rug, straightened his back and strode
swearing up and down the little cell. 'Who in the name of
Typhon searched this wound?' he demanded at last, swinging
round on him.

'The camp surgeon at Isca Dumnoniorum,' Marcus said.

'Been there twenty years, and drunk as a mule-driver at
Saturnalia, every night of them,' snapped Galarius. 'I know
these passed-over camp surgeons. Butchers and assassins,
every one!' He made an indescribable and very vulgar
noise.

'Not every night, and he was a very hard-working soul,'
said Marcus, doing his best for the shaggy and rather pathetic
old man whom he remembered with liking.

'Puh!' said Galarius. Then his manner changed abruptly,
and he came and sat himself down on the edge of the cot. 'The
thing is that he did not finish his work,' he said.

Marcus ran the tip of his tongue over uncomfortably dry lips.
'You mean—it is all to do again?'

The other nodded. 'You will have no peace until the wound
has been re-searched.'

'When——' Marcus began, and checked, trying desperately to steady the shameful flinching at the corner of his mouth.

'In the morning. Since it must be done, the sooner it were done the better.' He put a hand on Marcus's shoulder, and kept it there.

For a moment Marcus lay rigid under the blunt, kindly hand, then he drew a long, uneven breath, and relaxed, with a rather crooked attempt at a smile. 'I beg your forgiveness. I think I—am rather tired.'

'It seems possible,' agreed the surgeon. 'You have had rough marching lately. Oh yes, I know. But soon you will have it behind you and better things ahead. I promise you that.'

For a while he sat there, talking of matters that were a long way from tomorrow morning, drifting from the flavour of native oysters to the iniquities of provincial tax-gatherers, yarning about the early days on the Silurian frontier, and long-ago boar hunts with Uncle Aquila. 'We were great hunters, your uncle and I; and now we grow stiff in our joints and set in our ways. Sometimes I think I will pack up and go on my travels again, before it is too late and I am utterly rusted into my socket. But I chose the wrong branch of my calling for that. A surgeon's craft is none so easily picked up and carried about the world. An oculist's, now, that is the craft for a follower of Aesculapius with the itch to wander! Here in the north, where so many have the marsh-blindness, an oculist's stamp is a talisman to carry a man safely where a Legion could not go.' And he launched out into an account of the adventures of an acquaintance who had crossed the Western Ocean and plied his trade through the wilds of Hibernia, a few years before, while Marcus listened with about half his attention, little guessing that the time was to come when that story would be tremendously important to him.

Presently Galarius got up, stretching until the little muscles cracked behind his bull-shoulders. 'Now I go to talk hunting with Aquila until bedtime. Do you lie still, and sleep as well as may be, and I shall be back early in the morning.'

And with a brusque nod, he turned and strode out into the colonnade.

With him, most of Marcus's hard-held courage seemed to go too. He was horrified to find that he was shivering—shivering at the smell of pain as a horse shivers at the smell of fire. Lying with his forearm pressed across his eyes, he lashed himself with his own contempt, but found no help in it. He felt cold in his stomach and very alone.

There came a sudden pattering across the floor, and a cold muzzle was thrust against his shoulder. He opened his eyes to see Cub's grinning head within a few inches of his own. ' Thanks, Cub,' he said, and shifted a little to catch the great head between his hands as Cub put his fore-paws on the cot and blew lovingly in his face. It was near to sunset, and the light of the westering sun was flooding into the cell, splashing like quivering golden water on walls and ceiling. Marcus had not seen it come, and it seemed to break singing on his sight, as a fanfare of trumpets breaks upon the ear. The light of Mithras, springing out of the dark.

Esca, who had come hard behind Cub, appeared in the doorway, sending a great thrust of shadow up the sunlit wall as he came to Marcus's side. ' I have spoken with Rufrius Galarius,' he said.

Marcus nodded. ' He will need your help in the morning. You will do that for me ? '

' I am the Centurion's body-slave; who but I should do it ? ' Esca said, and bent to disentangle the blanket.

As he did so, sounds of a scuffle arose somewhere in the courtyard. Stephanos's old bleating voice was raised in protest, and then a girl's, high, clear, and hard. ' Let me pass. If you do not let me pass, I'll bite ! ' The scuffle seemed to be resumed, and an instant later a howl of anguish from Stephanos told all too clearly that the threat had been carried out. As Marcus and Esca exchanged questioning glances, flying feet came along the colonnade, and Cottia burst into the doorway, a burnished, warlike figure, with the setting sun making a nimbus round her.

Marcus raised himself on one elbow. 'You little vixen! What have you done to Stephanos?'

'I bit his hand,' said Cottia, in the same clear, hard voice. 'He tried to keep me out.'

The scuff-scuff of hurrying sandals sounded behind her even while she spoke, and Marcus said urgently, 'Esca, in the name of Light, go and keep him out of here!' He felt suddenly that he could not deal with a righteously indignant Stephanos at this moment. Then, as Esca strode out to do his bidding, he turned on Cottia. 'And what is it that you suppose you are doing here, my Lady?'

She came close, thrusting in beside Cub, and stood looking down at him accusingly. 'Why did you not tell me?' she demanded.

'Tell you what?' But he knew what.

'About the Healer with the Knife. I saw him come in a mule carriage, through the storeroom window, and Nissa told me why he came.'

'Nissa talks too much,' Marcus said. 'I did not mean that you should know until it was all over and done with.'

'You had no right not to tell me,' she said stormily. 'It was mine to know!' And then in an anxious rush, 'What will he do to you?'

Marcus hesitated an instant, but if he did not tell her, the unspeakable Nissa undoubtedly would. 'I am to have the wound cleaned up. That is all.'

Her face seemed to grow narrower and more sharply pointed while he looked at it. 'When?' she asked.

'In the morning, very early.'

'Send Esca to tell me when it is over.'

'It will be *very* early,' Marcus said firmly. 'You will scarcely be awake by then.'

'I shall be awake,' Cottia said. 'I shall be waiting at the bottom of the garden. And I shall wait there until Esca comes, whoever tries to take me away. I can bite others beside Stephanos, and if anyone tries to take me away, I will, and then I shall be beaten. You would not like to know that I had

G

been beaten because you would not send Esca, would you, Marcus?'

Marcus recognized defeat. 'Esca shall come and tell you.'

There was a long pause. Cottia stood very still, looking down at him. Then she said, 'I wish it could be me instead.'

It was a thing more easily said than meant, but Cottia did mean it. Looking at her, Marcus knew that. 'Thank you, Cottia. I shall remember that. And now you must go home.'

She drew back obediently, as Esca reappeared in the doorway. 'I will go home. When may I come again?'

'I do not know,' Marcus said. 'Esca shall come and tell you that also.'

Without another word she turned and walked out into the golden light. At a sign from Marcus, the slave fell in behind her, and their steps sounded fainter and fainter along the colonnade.

Marcus listened to them until they faded into silence, lying quiet, with the familiar rough warmth of Cub's head under his hand. He was still unpleasantly cold in the pit of his stomach, but he no longer felt alone. In some way that he did not understand, Cub and Esca and Cottia had comforted and steadied him for what was coming.

The golden light was fading, and into the quietness stole a shimmering thread of bird-song, the thin, regretful autumn song of a robin in the wild pear-tree; and he realized that summer was nearly over. Suddenly he knew, with a sense of discovery, that it had been a good summer. He had been homesick, yes, dreaming night after night of his own hills, and waking with a sore heart; but none the less, it had been a good summer. There had been the day that Cub discovered how to bark. Marcus had been almost as surprised as Cub. 'But wolves never bark,' he said to Esca; and Esca had said: 'Rear a wolf with the dog-pack and he will do as the dog-pack does in all things.' And Cub, proud of his new accomplishment, had filled the garden with his shrill puppy clamour for days. Other small sharp-edged memories sprang to meet him: twists of hot pastry brought out by Sassticca and eaten by the four of them as a feast; the hunting-bow which he and Esca had built between them; Cottia holding his olive-wood bird in her cupped hands.

A kind summer, a kingfisher summer; and suddenly he was grateful for it.

He slept that night quietly and lightly as a hunter sleeps, and woke to the call of distant trumpets sounding Cockcrow from the transit camp.

.   .   .   .   .

It was so early that the gossamer still lay thick and dew-grey over the courtyard grass and the smell of the day-spring was cold and fresh in the air when Rufrius Galarius returned; but Marcus had been waiting his coming for what seemed a long time. He returned the surgeon's greeting, and explained, ' My slave is gone to shut up the wolf-cub. He should be back at any moment.'

Galarius nodded. ' I have seen him. He is also fetching sundry things that we shall need,' he said, and opening the bronze case that he had brought with him he began to set out the tools of his trade on the chest top.

Before he had finished, Esca was back, carrying hot water and new linen, and a flask of the native barley spirit which Galarius considered better than wine, though fiercer, for cleansing a wound. ' There will be more hot water when you need it,' he said, setting the things down on the chest top beside the instrument case; and came to stand over Marcus, a little as Cub might have done.

Galarius finished his preparations, and turned. ' Now, if you are ready? '

' Quite ready,' Marcus said, tossing off the blanket, and shut his teeth for what was coming.

A long while later he drifted out of the darkness that had come roaring up over him before the work was finished, to find himself lying under warm rugs, with Rufrius Galarius standing beside him with a square hand set over his heart, as old Aulus had stood in that other waking, just a year ago. For one confused moment he thought that it was still that other waking and he had dreamed in a circle; and then, as his sight and hearing cleared somewhat, he saw Esca standing just behind the surgeon, and a huge shadow in the doorway that could only be Uncle Aquila, and heard the despairing howls of Cub shut in the storeroom: and came back to the present like a swimmer breaking surface.

The ache of the old wound was changed to a jangling throb that seemed to beat through his whole body with a sickening sense of shock, and involuntarily he gave a little moan.

The surgeon nodded. 'Aye, it strikes sharp at first,' he agreed. 'But it will ease presently.'

Marcus looked up rather hazily into the blue-jowled Spaniard's face. 'Have you done?' he mumbled.

'I have done.' Galarius drew up the blanket. There was blood on his hand. 'In a few months' time you will be a sound man again. Lie still and rest now, and this evening I will come back.'

He gave Marcus's shoulder a small brisk pat, and turned to gather up his instruments.

'I leave him in your hands. You can give him the draught now,' he said to Esca, over his shoulder as he went out. Marcus heard him speak to someone in the colonnade. 'Enough splinters to quill a porcupine; but the muscles are less damaged than one might expect. The boy should do well enough now.'

Then he found Esca beside him, holding a cup. 'Cottia— and Cub——' he stammered.

'I will see to them soon, but first you must drink this.'

Esca dropped to one knee beside the cot, and Marcus found that he was lying with his head on his slave's shoulder and the rim of the cup was cool against his mouth as he drank. He remembered the bitter taste from last year. Then, as the cup was withdrawn, he turned his head contentedly on Esca's arm. There was a pinched greyness in the other's face, he realized, an odd wryness about his mouth, like the look of a man who wishes to be sick but has nothing in his stomach to be sick with.

'Was it as bad as that?' he asked with a weak attempt at laughter.

Esca grinned. 'Go to sleep.'

IX

TRIBUNE PLACIDUS

A MILE or two south of Calleva, where the forest opened suddenly to a steep drop of bracken-clad hillside, two men were standing: a Roman and a Briton; and between them, head up and muzzle quivering into the wind, a young brindled wolf.

Abruptly, the Roman stooped to unbuckle the heavy bronze-studded collar from the wolf's neck. Cub was full grown now, though not yet come to his full strength, and the time had arrived when he must have his choice of returning to the wild. You could tame a wild thing, but never count it as truly won until, being free to return to its own kind, it chose to come back to you. Marcus had known that all along, and he and Esca had made their preparations with infinite care, bringing Cub to this spot again and again, that he might be sure of the way home if he wished to take it. If he wished to take it. With his fingers on the buckle, Marcus wondered whether he would ever feel the hairy living warmth of Cub's neck again.

The collar was off now, and he thrust it into the breast of his tunic. For a lingering moment he fondled the pricked ears. Then he stood erect. 'Go free, brother. Good hunting.' Cub looked up into his face, puzzled; then, as a fresh burst of woodland smells reached his quivering nose, trotted off down the woodshore.

The other two watched him go in silence, a brindled shadow slipping away into the undergrowth. Then Marcus turned and made for the trunk of a fallen birch-tree a little way down the slope, moving quickly but awkwardly over the rough ground with a sideways lurch of the shoulders at every step. Rufrius Galarius had done his work well, and now, some eight months later, Marcus was to all intents and purposes as sound

as ever, just as the surgeon had promised. He would carry
the scars to his dying day, and a twisted leg that would bar him
from the Legions, but that was all; indeed, after a winter
spent with Esca's help in training as though for the arena, he
was now as hard as a gladiator. He reached the fallen tree-
trunk and sat down on it, and an instant later Esca was
squatting at his feet.

This was a favourite vantage point of theirs. The tree-
trunk made a convenient seat, and the steep drop of the hillside
gave a clear view of wooded hills and the blue lift of the downs
beyond. He had seen these rolling woods in their winter
bareness, dappled like a partridge's breast. He had seen
the first outbreaking of the blackthorn foam; and now the full
green flame of spring was running through the forest and the
wild cherry-trees stood like lit candles along the woodland ways.

The two in their vantage point sat talking lazily, with long
silences between, of many things under the sun, including the
guest whom Uncle Aquila was expecting that evening; no
less a person than the Legate of the Sixth Legion on his way
down from Eburacum to Regnum, and thence to Rome.

'He is a very old friend of your uncle's?' asked Esca idly.

'Yes. I believe they served together in Judaea when my
uncle was First Cohort of the Fretensis and this man was doing
his year as a Tribune on the Staff. He must be a great deal
younger than Uncle Aquila.'

'And now he goes home, to his own place?'

'Yes, but only on some business with the Senate, Uncle
Aquila says; then back to the Eagles again.'

After a time they fell silent altogether, each busy with his
own thoughts. Marcus's were mainly concerned, as they had
been for some time past, with the question of what he was going
to do with himself and his life, now that he was well again.
The Legions were closed to him, and that left just one other way
of life that he would have turned to as a bird flies home.
Farming was in the blood of most of his race, from the Senator
with his estate in the Alban Hills to the time-expired Legionary
with his pumpkin patch; and to Marcus, born and bred as he

had been, farming and soldiering were yoke-mates, the two natural ways of life. But to start anything of that sort, one needed money. It was all right for the time-expired Legionary with his government grant of land. It would have been all right for Marcus if he had served his twenty years—even though he never became Prefect of an Egyptian Legion—and had savings from his pay and a centurion's gratuity behind him. But as it was, he had nothing. He might have turned to Uncle Aquila for help, he knew, but he would not do that. His uncle, although he had sufficient for his needs, was not a rich man, and had done enough for him already. He should have set about finding some way to earn his living before now, he supposed, but there were so few ways open to a free man, and the frightful conviction was growing on him that he would end up as somebody's secretary. There were people who preferred a free secretary to a slave, here—or even at home in Etruria. But even as that thought touched his mind, he knew that for him to drift home, rootless, and without any stake in the country that had bred him, nor any hope of such, would be only the shadow and none of the substance of homecoming. He would have carried his exile with him into his own hills and spoiled them; and that was all. No, he must look for his secretaryship here in Britain.

Only this morning he had made up his mind to lay the secretary idea before Uncle Aquila tonight, but the Legate's message had arrived, and now of course it would have to wait until the sudden guest had gone on his way. And part of him —a part of which he was rather ashamed—caught at the delay as a breathing-space; one day's grace in which something might happen, though what was likely to happen he would have been hard put to it to say.

In their silence, the wild had drawn close in to the two in the vantage point. Presently a red glint slipping through the uncurling bracken and young foxgloves at the lower end of the clearing told them where a vixen passed. She paused an instant in full view, her pointed muzzle raised, the sun shining with almost metallic lustre on her coat; then she turned in among the trees. And watching the russet glint of her flicker out of sight, Marcus found himself thinking of Cottia.

The closer friendliness between her house and his had continued. He knew Kaeso quite well now, and even Valaria a little; Valaria, plumpish and prettyish and foolish, floating with pale-coloured mist-linen, clanking with bracelets, her hair closely curled as a ram's fleece. He was for ever meeting her in her litter, as he came and went about Calleva, to the baths or the gymnasium or the Golden Vine, from whose stables he and Esca had lately hired ponies once or twice for a trip into the outback; and always he had to stop and talk. But of Cottia herself, he suddenly realized, he had seen less and less as the months went by.

With life opening to him again, he had had less need of her, and she had drawn back little by little, without a shadow of reproach. Yet he did not feel in the least guilty, and all at once, realizing how very easily Cottia could have made him feel guilty if she had chosen to, he felt a quick rush of warmth towards her. The odd thing was that now he came to think of it he did need Cottia as much as ever; he often forgot her altogether with the surface of his mind, but he knew that if he were never to see her again he would be very unhappy, perhaps as unhappy as he would if Cub never came back. . . .

And would Cub ever come back? Would the call of his own kind prove stronger than the tie that bound him to his master? Either way, Marcus hoped that it would be quick and easy and final; no tearing of the heart in two, for Cub. He stirred, and looked down at Esca. 'We have been roosting here long enough.'

The other tipped back his head, and for a moment their eyes met. Then Esca got up, and reached a helping hand to Marcus. 'Let the Centurion whistle once, in case he is near; then we will go home.'

Marcus gave the shrill, broken whistle he had always used to summon Cub, and stood listening. A magpie, startled by the sound, scolded sharply from the woods behind them, and nothing more. After a few moments he whistled again. Still no answering bark, no brindled shape trotting out of the wood-shore.

'He is out of hearing,' said Esca. 'Well, he knows the way home, and there'll be no harm come to him.'

No, there would be no harm come to Cub. He was well known in and around Calleva, and since he had long since lost his wolf-smell, the dog-pack accepted him for one of themselves, and one to be respected. No harm would come to him from his own kind, either, for save when man took a hand, there was little war between wolf-pack and dog-pack, who indeed mated together often enough to make it sometimes hard to tell which was which. Only, if he went back to his own kind, the day might come when men would hunt Cub as they had hunted his mother.

Marcus longed to look back once, as they turned in among the hazel scrub of the forest verge, in case, even now, Cub might be coming uphill at a canter. But looking back was not in the bargain, and with his slave beside him he turned resolutely homeward.

They came to the South Gate of Calleva and passed through, Esca immediately falling the usual three paces to the rear. They made their way round by the short cut behind the temple of Sull-Minerva and entered the house by the nearest door, which gave on to the slaves' quarters and the garden. Cub, if he came at all, would likely come over the old earthworks at the foot of the garden, for he was used to that road, but Marcus had had word with the City gatekeepers in case he came the other way.

They reached the courtyard without meeting anyone, and while Esca went to set out a fresh tunic for his master, Marcus turned off along the colonnade towards the atrium. As he neared the doorway, a strange voice sounded behind it. The guest had arrived already, then.

'You are sure?' said the voice, a harsh, clipped voice, but pleasant. 'It would be a simple matter to send him up to the transit camp.'

And Uncle Aquila's voice replied: 'When I have not the

space to lodge two guests at the same time, I will tell you. You are a fool, Claudius.'

There were two strangers in the long room with Uncle Aquila, both in uniform: one, resplendent under his coating of dust in the gilded bronze of a Legate; the other, standing a little behind him, evidently a Staff Officer. It seemed that they had only just arrived, for they had done no more than lay aside cloak and crested helmet. That much Marcus saw as he hesitated an instant on the threshold before his uncle looked round and saw him.

' Ah, you are back, Marcus,' said Uncle Aquila; and then, as he came forward to join the group, ' Claudius, I present to you my nephew Marcus. Marcus, this is my very old friend Claudius Hieronimianus, Legate of the Sixth Legion.'

Marcus raised his hand in salute to his uncle's friend, and found himself looking into a pair of long, jet-black eyes that seemed to have the sun behind them. The Legate was an Egyptian, and, he judged, of the old strain, for there was none of the Syrian softness in his face that he had seen so often in the faces of the men of the Nile. ' I am very much honoured to meet the Legate of Victrix,' he said.

The Legate's face crinkled into a smile that sent a thousand fine lines deepening about his mouth and eyes. ' And I am very glad to meet a kinsman of my ancient friend, all the more so because until today he might have been hatched out of a turtle's egg in the sand, for all the kith and kin that he had to my knowledge.' He indicated his companion. ' I make known to you Tribune Servius Placidus, of my staff.'

Marcus turned to the young officer, and instantly became painfully conscious of his twisted leg. Once or twice before he had met people who made him feel like that, and he did not find that it endeared them to him. The two greeted each other as custom demanded, but without warmth. The Staff Officer was about Marcus's own age, an extremely beautiful young man, with the graceful carriage, the oval face, and clustering hair that suggested Athenian ancestry. ' Smooth as a girl,' Marcus thought with quick dislike; and the phrase seemed vaguely familiar. So did the name, Placidus, for that matter; but it was a common enough name, and anyhow, this was no time to be trailing marsh-light memories. Marcus supposed that until the guests went to wash off the dust of the journey, it was for him to hold the Tribune in conversation, leaving Uncle Aquila free to talk to his old friend.

Marcipor had brought in wine for the travellers, and when it has been poured, the two young men turned from their elders and drifted over to a sunlit window. For a while they made casual small-talk to each other; but as the moments went by, Marcus found it harder and harder to think of anything to say, while the Tribune appeared to have been born bored. At last Marcus, at his wits' end for another word, asked: 'You return to Rome with the Legate, or only as far as Regnum?'

'Oh, to Rome. Praise be to Bacchus, I am done with Britain once and for all when I board the galley in two days' time.'

'You have not, I take it, found Britain much to your taste?'

The other shrugged, and took a gulp of his wine. 'The girls are well enough, and the hunting. For the rest—Roma Dea! I can bear to leave it behind me!' A doubt seemed to strike him. 'You are not native born to this benighted province?'

'No,' Marcus said. 'I am not native born.' And then, feeling that he had been over abrupt, he added: 'Indeed, I have been out less than three years.'

'What possessed you to come out at all? You must have found the long journey very trying.'

There was nothing so very much in the words, but the tone in which they were spoken made Marcus, who was rather on edge because of Cub, feel his hackles rising. 'I came out to join my Legion,' he said coldly.

'Oh.' Placidus was slightly put out. 'A wound, then?'

'Yes.'

'I do not think that I have ever met you in the Tribune's Club, at home?'

'It would be strange if you had. I was a mere cohort

centurion.' Marcus smiled, but all the contempt that the professional soldier could feel for the aristocrat playing at soldiers for a year was politely but thinly veiled behind his quiet words.

Placidus flushed a little. 'Really? Do you know, I should scarce have guessed it.' He returned the thrust, with the silken suggestion in his tone that really Marcus seemed almost civilized. 'Do I salute a brother of the Victrix? Or was it Capricorn or the charging boar with you?'

Before Marcus could answer, a low chuckle came from the Legate, whose back was towards them. 'For one who considers himself—I believe not without the right—a somewhat skilled hunter, you can be singularly unobservant of small things, my Placidus.' He said over his shoulder, 'I have mentioned the fact to you before. You will find the Signum of his Legion on his left wrist,' and he returned to his conversation with Uncle Aquila.

At his words, something had clicked in Marcus's mind, and as the Tribune's glance jerked down to the heavy gold bracelet that he always wore, he remembered. 'Smooth as a girl, but a skilled hunter,' Esca had said; and the name had been Placidus. His mouth felt dry with disgust, and the flicker of discomfiture—yes, and something very like envy—that showed for an instant in the other's face, gave him a quick satisfaction that was on Esca's account rather than his own.

Placidus recovered himself at once, and looked up with his faintly supercilious air. 'See what it is to serve under a Legate renowned for his appreciation of his junior officers,' he murmured. 'My dear Marcus, I do congratulate——' His eyes widened suddenly, and the soft, drawling voice sharpened into life. 'Roma Dea! A wolf!'

Before the words were out, Marcus had swung round. There in the colonnade doorway stood a brindled shape, savage head alertly raised, and eyes wary of the strangers within, whose unfamiliar scent had halted him on the threshold.

'Cub!' Marcus called, 'Cub!' and crouched down as, with a joyful bark, the brindled shape hurled itself upon him, fawning against his breast and singing as a crock sings on the boil. Cub's flanks were heaving with the speed that he had made to find his master, and he was frantically apologetic for having somehow lost him. And Marcus caught the great head in his hands, rubbing his thumbs into the hollows behind the pricked ears. 'So you have come back, brother,' he said. 'You have come back, Cub.'

'It is a wolf! It really *is* a wolf—and the brute behaving like a puppy!' said Placidus, in tones of disgusted unbelief above him.

'It seems that we are witnesses to a reunion. Surely we have come in a happy hour,' said the Legate.

Marcus freed himself from Cub's embraces and got to his feet. 'A reunion—yes, you could call it so,' he said.

Then Cub did a thing that he had never done before. He thrust his lowered head between Marcus's knees, as a dog will sometimes do with someone he perfectly trusts; and stood there contentedly, in the one position in which he was utterly defenceless and at his master's mercy.

And while he stood like that with slowly swinging tail, Marcus brought out the bronze-studded collar from the breast of his tunic, and bent to put it round his neck again.

'How long have you had him?' Placidus asked, watching with a gleam of interest as, his collar safely buckled on again, the young wolf shook himself violently, and sat down with lolling tongue and eyes half closed, propped against his master's leg.

'Since he was a very small cub, more than a year ago,' Marcus said, fondling a twitching ear.

'Then, if I am not mistaken, I saw him taken from the lair after his dam was killed! The painted barbarian who fetched him out claimed to be slave to a Marcus Aquila. I remember now.'

'You are not mistaken,' Marcus said quietly. 'The painted barbarian told me that story.'

Rather fortunately Stephanos appeared at that moment hovering in the doorway; and Uncle Aquila took the Legate's

empty wine-cup from him. ' You will be wishing to soak off
the dust of the road,' he said. ' We may live at the world's
end, but the bath-water could not be hotter in Rome itself.
Your own slaves will be awaiting you in your quarters, no
doubt. That is so, Stephanos? Good. I look forward to
our next meeting at dinner.'

X

MARCHING ORDERS

PRESENTLY, having bathed and changed, the four came together again in the small dining recess which opened from the atrium. This room was as austere as the rest of the house; the lime-washed walls bare of ornament save for the bronze-faced cavalry buckler with a pair of crossed javelins behind it, hanging opposite the entrance; the three couches about the table spread with beautifully dressed deerskins instead of the usual quiltings and embroideries. And, ordinarily, the meals which Marcus and his uncle ate there were as austere as the room. But tonight was an occasion, and Sassticca had bestirred herself to produce a dinner worthy of it.

To Marcus, because Cub had come back, the whole room seemed to shimmer with a faint air of festival, as he glanced about him by the soft yellow light of the palm-oil lamps on the table. The future and the question of finding a livelihood could wait for the moment; he was pleasantly tired after a long day in the open; he had had a cold plunge and changed his rough tunic for one of soft white wool; and he was prepared even to keep a truce with Placidus, since Esca had only laughed when told of his arrival.

The main part of dinner was over. Uncle Aquila had just poured the second libation to the household gods, whose little bronze statues stood with the salt-cellars at the corners of the table; and Esca and the other slaves had gone their way. The soft, uncertain lamplight cast a delicate web of radiance over the table, making the red Samian bowls glow like coral, turning the withered yellow apples of last year's harvest to the fruit of the Hesperides, casting here a bloom of light over the fluted curve of a glass cup, kindling there a pointed scarlet flame in the heart of a squat flask of Falernian wine, strangely intensifying the faces of the men who leaned each on a left elbow round the table.

So far the two older men had had most of the conversation to themselves, talking over old days, old skirmishes, old frontier camps, old friends and enemies, while Marcus and Placidus put in a word from time to time, spoke to each other occasionally —the truce was holding quite well—but for the most part ate their dinner in silence.

And then, splashing water into the Falernian in his cup, Uncle Aquila asked, ' Claudius, how long since you left the Fretensis? '

' Eighteen years in August.'

'Jupiter!' said Uncle Aquila, reflectively. Suddenly he glared at his old friend. ' Eighteen years in August since you and I last sat at meat in the same mess; and yet you have been in Britain almost three, and made no attempt—not the faintest attempt—to come near me! '

' Nor you to come near me,' said Claudius Hieronimianus, helping himself to one of Sassticca's honey cakes and topping it with a cluster of raisins. He looked up from his plate, his strange face breaking into a winged, eager smile. ' Is it not most often so, when we follow the Eagles? We make a friend here and there, in Achaea, in Caesarea or Eburacum; and our ways part again, and we take remarkably few pains to keep in touch one with another. But if the gods who rule the destinies of men bend our paths to cross again—why then . . .'

' Why then we take up the old threads very much where we laid them down,' said Uncle Aquila. He raised his re-charged cup. ' I drink to the old threads. No, I don't. It is only old men who look backward all the time. I drink to the *renewing* of old threads.'

' Do you come and renew them at Eburacum, after I return,' said the Legate, as he set down his own cup.

' It may be that I will even do that—one day. It is all of five-and-twenty years since I was last at Eburacum, and I should be interested to see the place again.' Suddenly, bethinking himself of his manners, Uncle Aquila turned to

H

include the young Tribune. ' I took a contingent of the Second
up there in one of the Troubles; it was thus that I came to
know the Station a little.'

' So?' Placidus contrived to sound bored and polite at the
same time. ' That would be in the Hispana's time, of course.
You would scarce recognize the Station now. It is really
almost habitable.'

' The new generally build in stone where the old cleared the
forest and built in wood,' said Uncle Aquila.

The Legate was staring reflectively into the heart of his
wine. ' Sometimes at Eburacum it seems to me that the
foundations of that old building lie uneasy beneath the new,'
he said.

Marcus turned on him quickly. ' You mean, sir?'

' Eburacum is still—how shall I put it?—still more than a
little ghost-ridden by the Ninth Legion. Oh, I do not mean
that their spirits have wandered back from the fields of Ra, but
the place is haunted, none the less. By the altars to Spanish
gods that they set up and worshipped at; by their names and
numbers idly scratched on walls; by British women whom they
loved and children with Spanish faces whom they fathered.
All this lying, as it were, like a sediment under the new wine of
another Legion. Also they linger strongly, almost terrifyingly,
in the minds of the people.' He made a small gesture with his
open hand. ' It sounds little enough, put into words, and yet
it can create an atmosphere which is unpleasantly strong. I am
not an imaginative man, but I tell you that there have been
times, when the mist comes down from the high moors, when I
have more than half expected to see the lost Legion come
marching home.'

There was a long silence, and a little shiver ran through the
room like a little wind through long grass. Uncle Aquila's
face was unreadable. Placidus's showed clearly his opinion
of such vapourings. Then Marcus said: ' Have you any idea
—any theory—as to what became of the Hispana, sir?'

The Legate looked at him shrewdly. ' Their fate has some
importance for you?'

'Yes. My father was their First Cohort—Uncle Aquila's brother.'

The Legate turned his head. 'Aquila, I never knew that.'

'Oh yes,' said Uncle Aquila. 'Did I never mention him to you? He never came much in my way; we were at opposite ends of the family, with twenty years between us.'

The Legate nodded, and after seeming to consider a moment, gave his attention back to Marcus. 'There is, of course, the possibility that somewhere they were cut off and annihilated so completely that no survivors were left to carry back word of the disaster.'

'Oh, but surely, sir,' put in Placidus with a great show of deference, 'in a Province the size of Valentia, even in the whole of Caledonia, upward of four thousand men could not be destroyed without trace? Is it not far more likely that having had their fill of the Eagles, they merely butchered such of their officers as would not join with them, and deserted to the Tribes?'

Marcus said nothing; the Tribune was his uncle's guest; but his mouth shut into a hard, hot line.

'No, I do not think it particularly likely,' said the Legate.

But Placidus had not yet finished planting his sting. 'I stand corrected,' he said silkily. 'I was led to think it was the only possible explanation to the mystery, by the extremely unsavoury reputation the Hispana left behind them. But I am happy to find that I was at fault.'

'I am sure you are,' said the Legate, with a glint of humour.

'But you do not find the ambush theory a very likely one, either, I think, sir?' Marcus helped himself carefully to a cluster of raisins which he did not want.

'I do not greatly care to believe that any Legion of the Empire could have fallen so low, could have become such rotten fruit, as the other explanation would prove them.' The Legate hesitated, and his face seemed to grow keener; no longer the face of a man enjoying a pleasant meal, Marcus thought, but that of a soldier. He began to speak again, abruptly. 'There has been a rumour quite lately, along the Wall—incidentally giving me cause to wish profoundly that the Senate had not chosen this moment to recall me, though I leave behind a Camp Commandant and a First Cohort both knowing more of the game than I shall ever do—a rumour which, if it were true, would suggest that the Hispana did indeed go down fighting. Only market talk, but in such there is often a core of truth. The story runs that the Eagle has been seen; that it is receiving divine honours in some tribal temple in the far north.'

Uncle Aquila, who had been playing with his wine-cup, set it down so sharply that a drop splashed over on to his hand. 'Go on,' he said, as the other halted.

'That is all; there is no more to add, no more to work on, which is the cursed part of it. But you take my point?'

'Oh yes, I take your point.'

'But I am afraid that I do not, not with any clearness,' Marcus said.

'A Legion which went rogue would probably hide its Eagle or hack it to pieces, or simply topple it into the nearest river. It would be most unlikely to have either the wish or the chance to set it up in the temple of some local godling. But an Eagle taken in war is in a very different case. To the Outland Tribes it must seem that they have captured the god of the Legion: and so they carry it home in triumph, with many torches and perhaps the sacrifice of a black ram, and house it in the temple of their own god to make the young men strong in war and help the grain to ripen. You see now?'

Marcus saw. 'What do you intend doing about it, sir?' he asked, after a moment.

'Nothing. For all the evidence that I can gather, there may be no shred of truth in the story.'

'But if there is?'

'There is still nothing that I can do about it.'

'But, sir, it is the Eagle; the Hispana's lost *Eagle*!' Marcus said, as though trying to drive an idea into the head of one half-witted.

'Eagle lost—honour lost; honour lost—all lost,' the Legate quoted. 'Oh yes, I know.' The regret in his voice sounded very final.

'More than that, sir.' Marcus was leaning forward, almost stammering in his sudden desperate eagerness. 'If the Eagle could be found and brought back, it—it might even mean the re-forming of the Legion.'

'That also I know,' said the Legate. 'And I know a thing which interests me even more. If trouble were to break out again in the north, a Roman Eagle in the hands of the Painted People might well become a weapon against us, owing to the power it would undoubtedly have to fire the minds and hearts of the Tribes. The fact remains that on a mere wind-blown rumour, I can take no action. To send an expeditionary force would mean open war. A whole Legion would scarcely win through, and there are but three in Britain.'

'But where a Legion could not get through, one man might; at least to find out the truth.'

'I agree, if the right man came forward. It would have to be one who knew the Northern Tribes and would be accepted by them and allowed to pass; and it would have, I think, to be one who cared very deeply for the fate of the Hispana's Eagle, else he would not be madman enough to thrust his head into such a hornet's nest.' He set down the cup that he had been turning between his fingers while he spoke. 'If I had had such a one among my young men, I would have given him his marching orders. The matter seems to me serious enough for that.'

'Send me,' Marcus said deliberately. His glance moved from one to another of the men round the table; then he turned to the curtained entrance and called, 'Esca! Hi! Esca!'

'Now by the——' began Uncle Aquila, and broke off, for once at a loss for words.

No one else spoke.

Quick footsteps came through the atrium, the curtain was drawn aside, and Esca appeared on the threshold. 'The Centurion called?'

In as few words as might be, Marcus told him what was toward. ' You will come with me, Esca? '

Esca moved forward to his master's side. His eyes were very bright in the lamplight. ' I will come,' he said.

Marcus turned back to the Legate. ' Esca was born and bred where the Wall runs now: and the Eagle was my father's. Between us we fulfil your conditions finely. Send us.'

The queer silence that had held the other men was shattered abruptly as Uncle Aquila banged an open hand on the table. ' This is lunacy! Sheer, unmitigated lunacy! '

' No, but it is not! ' Marcus protested urgently. ' I have a perfectly sane and workable plan. In the name of Light, listen to me.'

Uncle Aquila drew breath for a blistering reply, but the Legate put in quietly, ' Let the boy speak, Aquila,' and he subsided with a snort.

For a long moment Marcus stared down at the raisins on his plate, trying to get the rough plan in his head into some sort of order. Trying also to remember exactly what Rufrius Galarius had told him that would help him now. Then he looked up and began to speak, eagerly, but with great care and long pauses, rather as though he were feeling his way, as indeed he was.

' Claudius Hieronimianus, you say that it would have to be one whom the Tribes would accept and allow to pass. A travelling oculist would be such a one. There are many sore eyes here in the north, and half the travellers on the roads are quack-salvers. Rufrius Galarius, who used to be a field surgeon with the Second ' (he glanced at his uncle with a half smile), ' once told me of a man well known to him, who even crossed the Western Waters and plied his trade through the length and breadth of Hibernia, and came back with a whole hide to tell the tale. And if an oculist's stamp will carry a man safely through Hibernia, of a surety it will carry Esca and me through what was once, after all, a Roman Province! ' He sat up on the couch, almost glaring at the two older men. Placidus he had forgotten. ' It may be that we shall not be able to bring back the Eagle; but the gods willing, we will at least find out the truth or untruth of your rumour for you.'

There was a long pause. The Legate was looking at Marcus searchingly. Uncle Aquila broke the silence. ' An enterprising plan, but with one trifling objection to it, which you would appear to have overlooked.'

' And what is that? '

" You know rather less than an addled egg about the doctoring of sore eyes.'

' The same could be said for three out of four quack-salvers on the roads; but I shall go on a visit to Rufrius Galarius. Oh yes, he is a surgeon and not an oculist, I have not forgotten that; but he will know enough of the craft to put me in the way of getting a few needful salves, and give me some idea how to use them.'

Uncle Aquila nodded, as conceding the point.

And then, after a moment, the Legate asked abruptly, ' How serviceable is that leg of yours? '

Marcus had been expecting the question. ' Save that it would not do for the parade ground, very near as serviceable as ever it was,' he said. ' If we should have to run for it, it would load the dice against us, I grant you, but in strange country we should not stand a dog's chance on the run, anyway.'

Again the silence settled. And he sat with his head up, gazing from the Legate to his uncle and back again. They were summing up his chances, and he knew it: his chances of coming through, his chances of doing the thing that he went out to do. Moment by lengthening moment it became more desperately urgent to him that he should win his marching orders. The very life or death of his father's Legion was at stake; the Legion that his father had loved. And because he had loved his father with all the strength of his heart, the matter was a personal quest to him and shone as a quest shines. But beneath that shining lay the hard fact of a Roman Eagle in hands that might one day use it as a weapon against Rome; and Marcus had been bred a soldier. So it was in no mood of high adventure alone, but in a soberer and more purposeful spirit that he awaited the verdict.

'Claudius Hieronimianus, you said just now that had you had the right man among your young men, you would have sent him,' he said at last, able to keep silent no longer. 'Do I get my marching orders?'

It was his uncle who answered first, speaking to the Legate as much as to Marcus. 'The gods of my fathers forbid that I should hold back any kinsman of mine from breaking his neck in a clean cause, if he has a mind to.' His tone was distinctly caustic; but Marcus, meeting the disconcertingly shrewd eyes under his fierce jut of brow, realized that Uncle Aquila knew and understood very much more of what all this was meaning to him than he would somehow have expected.

The Legate said, 'You understand the position? The Province of Valentia, whatever it once was, whatever it may be again, is not worth an outworn sandal-strap today. You will be going out alone into enemy territory, and if you run into trouble, there will be nothing that Rome can or will do to help you.'

'I understand that,' Marcus said. 'But I shall not be alone. Esca goes with me.'

Claudius Hieronimianus bent his head. 'Go then. I am not your Legate, but I give you your marching orders.'

Later, after certain details had been thrashed out round the brazier in the atrium, Placidus said an unexpected thing. 'I almost wish that there was room for a third in this insane expeditionary force! If there were, Bacchus! I would leave Rome to fend for itself awhile, and come with you!'

For the moment his face had lost its weary insolence, and as the two young men looked at each other in the lamplight Marcus was nearer to liking him than he had been since they first met.

But the faint fellowship was short-lived, and Placidus killed it with a question. 'Are you sure that you can trust that barbarian of yours in a venture of this kind?'

'Esca?' Marcus said in surprise. 'Yes, quite sure.'

The other shrugged. 'Doubtless you know best. Personally I should not care to let my life hang by so slender a thread as the loyalty of a slave.'

'Esca and I——' Marcus began, and broke off. He was not going to make a circus show of his innermost feelings and Esca's for the amusement of such as Tribune Servius Placidus. 'Esca has been with me a long time. He nursed me when I was sick; he did everything for me, all the while that I was laid by with this leg.'

'Why not? He is your slave,' said Placidus carelessly.

Sheer surprise held Marcus silent for a moment. It was a long time since he had thought of Esca as a slave. 'That was not his reason,' he said. 'It is not the reason that he comes with me now.'

'Is it not? Oh, my Marcus, what an innocent you are; slaves are all—slaves. Give him his freedom and see what happens.'

'I will,' said Marcus. 'Thanks, Placidus, I will!'

.   .   .   .   .   .

When Marcus, with Cub at his heels, entered his sleeping-quarters that night, Esca, who was waiting for him as usual, laid down the belt whose clasps he had been burnishing, and asked: 'When do we start?'

Marcus closed the door and stood with his back against it. 'Probably the morn's morning—that is, for myself, at least. The details can wait awhile; but first you had best take this,' and he held out a slim papyrus roll he had been carrying.

Esca took it with a puzzled glance at his face, and unrolling it, he held it to the lamplight. And watching him, Marcus remembered suddenly and piercingly the moment that afternoon when he had taken off Cub's collar. Cub had come back to him; but Esca?

Esca looked up from the papyrus, and shook his head. 'Capitals are one thing,' he said, 'but I can make nothing of this script. What is it?'

'Your manumission—your freedom,' Marcus said. 'I

made it out this evening, and Uncle Aquila and the Legate witnessed it. Esca, I ought to have given it to you long ago ; I have been a completely unthinking fool, and I am sorry.'

Esca looked down to the thing in his hands once more, and again back to Marcus, as though he was not sure that he understood. Then he let the roll spring back on itself, and said very slowly : 'I am free? Free to go?'

'Yes,' Marcus said. 'Free to go, Esca.'

There was a long dragging silence. An owl cried somewhere afar off, with a note that seemed at once desolate and mocking. Cub looked from one to the other, and whined softly in his throat.

Then Esca said, 'Is it that you are sending me away?'

'No! It is for you to go, or stay, as you wish.'

Esca smiled, the slow grave smile that always seemed to come a little unwillingly to his face. 'Then I stay,' he said, and hesitated. 'It is perhaps not only I who think foolish thoughts because of the Tribune Placidus.'

'Perhaps.' Marcus reached out and set both hands lightly on the other's shoulders. 'Esca, I should never have asked you to come with me into this hazard when you were not free to refuse. It is like to prove a wild hunt, and whether or no we shall come back from it lies on the knees of the gods. No one should ask a slave to go with him on such a hunting trail ; but—he might ask a friend.' He looked questioningly into Esca's face.

Esca tossed the slender papyrus roll on to the cot, and set his own hands over Marcus's. 'I have not served the Centurion because I was his slave,' he said, dropping unconsciously into the speech of his own people. 'I have served Marcus, and it was not slave-service . . . My stomach will be glad when we start on this hunting trail.'

.   .   .   .   .

Next morning, promising to pay his old friend another visit on his way north again in the autumn, the Legate departed with Placidus, escorted by half a squadron of Cavalry. And

Marcus watched them ride away down the long road to Regnum and the waiting galleys, without quite the heart-ache that the sight would once have given him, before he set about his own preparations.

Esca's freedom caused less interest, and certainly less ill-feeling in the household than might have been expected. Sassticca, Stephanos, and Marcipor had all been born slaves, the children of slaves; and Esca, the freeborn son of a free chieftain, had never been one with them, even while he ate at their table. They were old and well content with things as they were; they had a good master, and slavery sat easy on them, like an old and familiar garment. Therefore they did not greatly begrudge freedom to Esca, accepting it as something that was likely to have happened one day or another—he and the young master having been, as Sassticca said, the two halves of an almond these many moons past, and only grumbled a little among themselves, for the pleasure of grumbling.

And anyhow, with Marcus going off—as the household had been told—about some sudden business for his uncle next day, and Esca going with him, no one, including Esca, had much time for raising difficulties or even for feeling them.

That evening, having made the few preparations that were needful, Marcus went down to the foot of the garden and whistled for Cottia. Lately she had always waited to be whistled for; and she came out to him among the wild fruit-trees under the old ramparts, with one end of her damson-coloured mantle drawn over her head against the heavy spring shower that had come with her.

He told her the whole story as briefly as might be, and she heard him out in silence. But her face seemed to grow sharper and more pointed in the way that he knew of old, and when he had finished, she said, ' If they want this Eagle back; if they fear that it may harm them, where it is, let them send someone else for it! Why need *you* go? '

' It was my father's Eagle,' Marcus told her, feeling in-stinctively that that would make sense to her as the other reasons behind his going would never do. A personal loyalty needed no explaining, but he knew that it was quite beyond him to make Cottia understand the queer, complicated, wider loyalties of the soldier, which were as different from those of the warrior as the wave-break curve of the shield-boss was from the ordered pattern of his dagger sheath. 'You see, with us, the Eagle is the very life of a Legion; while it is in Roman hands, even if not six men of the Legion are left alive, the Legion itself is still in being. Only if the Eagle is lost, the Legion dies. That is why the Ninth has never been re-formed. And yet there must be more than a quarter of the Ninth who never marched north that last time at all, men who were serving on other frontiers, or sick, or left on garrison duty. They will have been drafted to other Legions, but they could be brought together again to make the core of a new Ninth. The Hispana was my father's first Legion, and his last, and the one he cared for most of all the Legions he served in. So you see . . .'

'It is to keep faith with your father, then?'

'Yes,' Marcus said, 'amongst other things. It is good to hear the trumpets sounding again, Cottia.'

'I do not think that I quite understand,' Cottia said. 'But I see that you must go. When will you start?'

'Tomorrow morning. I shall go down to Rufrius Galarius first, but Calleva will not come in my way again as I go north.'

'And when will you come back?'

'I do not know. Maybe, if all goes well, before winter.'

'And Esca goes with you? And Cub?'

'Esca,' Marcus said. 'Not Cub. I leave Cub in your charge, and you must come and see him every day and talk to him about me. In that way neither of you will forget about me before I come back.'

Cottia said, 'We have good memories, Cub and I. But I will come every day.'

'Good.' Marcus smiled at her, trying to coax a smile in return. 'Oh, and Cottia, do not mention the Eagle to anyone. I am supposed to be going on business for my uncle; only—I wanted you to know the truth.'

The smile came then, but it was gone again at once. ' Yes, Marcus.'

' That is better. Cottia, I cannot stay any longer, but before I go, there is one thing else that I want you to do for me.' As he spoke he pulled off the heavy gold bracelet with its engraved signum. The skin showed almond white where it had been, on the brown of his wrist. ' I cannot wear this where I am going; will you keep it safe for me until I come back to claim it? '

She took it from him without a word, and stood looking down at it in her hands. The light caught the Capricorn badge and the words beneath. ' *Pia Fidelis* '. Very gently she wiped the rain-drops from the gold, and stowed it under her mantle. ' Yes, Marcus,' she said again. She was standing very straight and still, very forlorn, and with the darkness of her mantle covering her bright hair as it had done when he first saw her.

He tried to think of something to say; he wanted to thank her for the things that he was grateful for; but with everything that was in him reaching out to what lay ahead, somehow he could not find the right words, and he would not give Cottia words that meant nothing. At the last moment he would have liked to tell her that if he never came back, she was to keep his bracelet; but maybe it were better that he told Uncle Aquila. ' You must go now,' he said. ' The Light of the Sun be with you, Cottia.'

' And with you,' said Cottia. ' And with you, Marcus. I shall be listening for you to come back—for you to come down here to the garden foot and whistle for me again, when the leaves are falling.'

Next instant she had put aside a dripping blackthorn spray and turned from him; and he watched her walking away without a backward glance, through the sharp thin rain.

XI

ACROSS THE FRONTIER

FROM Luguvallium in the west to Segedunum in the east, the Wall ran, leaping along with the jagged contours of the land; a great gash of stone-work, still raw with newness. Eighty miles of fortresses, mile-castles, watch-towers, strung on one great curtain wall, and backed by the vallum ditch and the coast-to-coast Legionary road; and huddled along its southern side, the low sprawl of wine shops, temples, married quarters, and markets that always gathered in the wake of the Legions. A great and never-ceasing smother of noise: voices, marching feet, turning wheels, the ring of hammer on armourer's anvil, the clear calling of trumpets over all. This was the great Wall of Hadrian, shutting out the menace of the north.

On a morning in early summer, two travellers who had been lodging for some days in a dirty and dilapidated inn close under the walls of Chilurnium presented themselves at the Praetorian gate of the fortress, demanding to pass through to the north. There was not much coming and going across the frontier, save for the military patrols; but such as there was,

hunters for the most part, or trappers with chained wild beasts
for the arena, or a stray fortune-teller or quack-salver, had all
to pass through the great fortresses of the Wall.

They were a faintly disreputable couple, mounted on small
ex-cavalry mares of the Arab type which had certainly seen
better days. The Legions could always find a steady market
for their old mounts, cheap and well trained, and with several
years of working life in them. They were to be seen everywhere along the Empire's roads, and there was nothing about
these two to suggest that they had been bought, not for money,
but by a few words signed by the Legate of the Sixth Legion,
on a sheet of papyrus.

Esca had made very little real difference to his appearance,
for he had no need; he had returned to the dress of his own
people, and that was all. But with Marcus it was quite otherwise. He also had taken to British dress, and wore long
bracco of saffron wool, cross-gartered to the knee, under a tunic
of faded and distinctly dirty violet cloth. Bracco were comfortable in a cold climate, and many of the wandering herbalists
and suchlike wore them. But the dark cloak flung back over
his shoulders hung in folds that were foreign and exotic, and he
wore a greasy Phrygian cap of scarlet leather stuck rakishly on
the back of his head. A small silver talisman shaped like an
open hand covered the brand of Mithras on his forehead, and he
had grown a beard. Being little over a month old, it was not a
very good beard; but such as it was, he had drenched it in
scented oils. He looked much like any other wandering quack-
salver, though somewhat young, despite the beard; and there
was certainly no trace about him of the Centurion of the Eagles
he had once been. His box of salves, provided for him by Rufrius Galarius, was stowed in the pack behind Esca's saddlepad,
and with it his oculist's stamp, a slab of slate on which the
hardened salves were ground, which proclaimed in engraved
letters round the edge, ' The Invincible Anodyne of Demetrius
of Alexandria, for all kinds of defective eyesight '.

The sentries passed them through without trouble into the
fortress of Chilurnium, into the world of square-set barrack

lines, and life ordered by trumpet calls that was familiar as a home-coming to Marcus. But at the Northern Gate, as they reached it, they met a squadron of the Tungrian Cavalry Cohort that formed the garrison coming up from exercise. They reined aside and sat watching while the squadron trotted by; and that was when the pull of long-familiar custom laid hold of Vipsania, Marcus's mare, and as the tail of the squadron passed she flung round with a shrill whinny, and tried to follow. Because of the old wound, Marcus had little power in his right knee, and it was a few trampling and sweating moments before he could master her and swing her back to the gate, and when he finally managed it, it was to find the decurion of the gate guard leaning against the guard-house wall, holding his sides and yelping with laughter, while his merry men stood grinning in the background.

'Never bring a stolen cavalry nag into a cavalry barracks,' said the decurion amiably, when he had had his laugh out. 'That's good advice, that is.'

Marcus, still soothing his angry and disappointed mare, demanded with a cool hauteur that Aesculapius himself could scarcely have bettered, had he been accused of being a horse-thief, 'Do you suggest that I, Demetrius of Alexandria, *the* Demetrius of Alexandria, am in the habit of stealing cavalry horses? Or that if I were, I should not have had the wisdom to steal a better one than this?'

The decurion was a cheerful soul, and the small grinning crowd that had begun to gather spurred him on to further efforts. He winked. 'You can see the brand on her shoulder, as plain as a pilum shaft.'

'If you cannot also see as plain as a pilum shaft that the brand has been cancelled,' Marcus retorted, 'then you must be in dire need of my Invincible Anodyne for all kinds of defective eyesight! I can let you have a small pot for three sesterces.'

There was a roar of laughter. 'Better have two pots, Sextus,' somebody called out. 'Remember the time you didn't see that Pict's legs sticking out from under the furze bush?'

The decurion evidently did remember the Pict's legs, and

would rather not, for though he laughed with the rest, his laughter rang a trifle hollow, and he made haste to change the subject. ' Are there not enough sore eyes for your salving in the Empire, that you must needs go jaunting beyond the Pale to look for more? '

' Maybe I am like Alexander, in search of fresh worlds to conquer,' said Marcus modestly.

The decurion shrugged. ' Every man to his own taste. The old world is good enough for me—with a whole hide to enjoy it in! '

' Lack of enterprise. That is the trouble with you.' Marcus sniffed. ' If I had been so lacking, should I now be *the* Demetrius of Alexandria, the inventor of the Invincible Anodyne, the most celebrated oculist between Caesarea and——'

' *Cave !* Here's the Commander,' somebody said. Instantly such of the group who had no business there melted away, and the rest straightened themselves on their feet and became painfully efficient. And Marcus, still discoursing loudly on his own importance and the healing powers of the Invincible Anodyne, was hustled out through the dark crowded arch of the gatehouse, with Esca, solemn-faced, in his wake.

The Frontier was behind them, and they rode out into the one-time Province of Valentia.

Chilurnium must be a pleasant place for the garrison, Marcus thought, as his quick glance took in the shallow wooded vale, the quiet river. There would be fishing and bathing here—when no trouble was brewing—and good hunting in the forest; a very different life from that of the upland fortresses farther west, where the Wall crossed bare moorland, leaping from crest to crest of the black hills. But his own mood just now was for the high hills, the tearing wind, and the curlews crying, and as soon as Chilurnium was well behind, he was glad to swing westward following the directions given them by a hunter before they set out, leaving the quiet vale for the distant lift of damson-dark uplands that showed through a break in the oakwoods.

Esca had ranged up alongside him, and they rode together in

1

companionable silence, their horses' unshod hooves almost soundless on the rough turf. No roads in the wilderness and no shoe-smiths, either. The country south of the Wall had been wild and solitary enough, but the land through which they rode that day seemed to hold no living thing save the roe-deer and the mountain fox; and though only the man-made wall shut it off from the south, the hills here seemed more desolate and the distances darker.

It was almost like seeing a friendly face in a crowd of stran-gers when, long after noon, they came dipping down over a shoulder of the high moors into a narrow green glen through which a thread of white water purled down over shelving stones, where the rowan-trees were in flower, filling the warm air with the scent of honey. A good place to make a halt, it seemed to them, and they off-saddled accordingly, and having watered the horses, and seen them begin to graze, they drank from their cupped hands and sprawled at their ease on the bank. There was wheaten biscuit and dried fish in the saddle-pack, but they left it there, having long since learned—Marcus on the march and Esca on the hunting trail—that morning and evening were the times for food.

Esca had stretched himself full length, with a sigh of content, under the leaning rowan-trees; but Marcus lay propped on one elbow to watch the little torrent out of sight round the shoulder of the glen. The silence of the high hills was all about them, made up of many small sounds: the purling of the water, the murmur of wild bees among the rowan blossom overhead, the contented cropping of the two mares. It was good to be up here, Marcus thought, after the long contriving of ways and means, the days of hanging along the Wall, kicking one's heels and listening for the faintest breath of a rumour that had evidently died as a stray wind dies, since it came to the Legate's ears. Up here in the silence of the hills, the strivings and im-patiences of the past few weeks that had seemed to web him round all fell away, leaving him face to face with his task.

They had worked out a rough plan of campaign weeks ago, in Uncle Aquila's study, which now seemed a whole world away. It was very simple: merely to work their way north in a series of casts that would take them from coast to coast each time, in the manner of a hound cutting across a scent. In that way they must cut the trail of the Eagle—and the Legion, too, for that matter—at every cast; and surely somewhere, if they kept their eyes and ears open, they must pick it up. It had all seemed fairly simple in Uncle Aquila's study, but out here in the great emptiness beyond the Frontier it seemed a gigantic task.

And yet its seeming hopelessness was a challenge that he took up joyously. For the moment he forgot the sober facts of his search, and remembered only the personal quest. And sitting there in the little sun-warmed glen, his heart lifted suddenly and almost painfully to the crowning moment when he would carry the lost Eagle back into Eburacum, knowing that his father's Legion would live again, its name clean before the world; and surely, surely, no god worth the serving would be so unjust as not to see that his father knew that he had kept faith.

Esca broke the silence presently. 'So the contriving is done with,' he said, speaking apparently into the bee-loud rowan branches above his head, ' and the hunting is begun at last.'

'The hunting-ground is a wide one,' Marcus said, and turned to look down at his companion. 'And who knows into what strange covers the hunt may lead us? Esca, you know this sort of country better than I can do, and if the people are not of your tribe, at least they are nearer to you than to me. They are people of the shield-boss, and not of the pattern on my dagger sheath. Therefore, if you tell me to do a thing, I will do it, without clamouring to know why.'

'There may be wisdom in that,' Esca said.

Presently Marcus shifted, looking up at the sun. ' Soon we must be moving on, I suppose, lest we sleep in the woods tonight, seeing that we have not yet found this village that the man at the inn spoke of '; for even south of the Wall one did not go to a strange village after dark, unless one was tired of life.

'We shall not have far to seek,' Esca said, 'if we follow the stream downward.'

Marcus quirked an eyebrow at him. 'What tells you that?'

'Smoke. Over the shoulder of the hill yonder; I caught the blur of it against the birch-trees, a while back.'

'It could be heath fire.'

'It was hearth fire,' Esca said with simple conviction.

Marcus relaxed again on the grass. Then, as though on a sudden impulse, he drew his dagger and fell to cutting small square turfs from the fine burnside grass, loosening and lifting them with infinite care. Having cut as many as he wanted, he drew the arching briars and the hemlock leaves back over the scars, and shifting farther up the bank, began to build them one a-top the other.

'What is it that you do?' Esca asked, after watching him in silence for a while.

'I build an altar,' Marcus said, 'here in the place of our first halt.'

'To what god?'

'To my own god. To Mithras, the Light of the Sun.'

Esca was silent again. He did not offer to help with this altar to Marcus's god, who was not his; but he drew closer and sat hugging his knees and looking down at the work. Marcus went on trimming and shaping the sods; the crumbling soil was faintly warm under his fingers, and a low-hanging rowan branch cast ring-streaked shadows over his intent hands. When the altar was finished and squared to his satisfaction, he cleaned and sheathed his dagger, and brushed away the scatter of loose soil from the surrounding grass with his palms. Then with scraps of birch bark and dry sticks and sprigs of dead heather—Esca helped him gather these—he built a small fire on the altar top. He built it very carefully, hollowing it slightly in the middle, as though to make a nest for something that he loved, and breaking a creamy curd of blossom from the rowan spray, nipped floweret from floweret, and scattered them over all. Lastly, he took from the breast of his tunic his olive-wood bird—his olive-wood bird. It was polished smooth and dark with years of carrying; rather a clumsy and ridiculous little bird, now that he came to look at it, but dear to him; and its dearness made it a fitting sacrifice. It had been part of his life, something that continued back from him to the wild olive-tree in the loop of the stream, and the life and places and things and people that the wild olive-tree belonged to. And suddenly, as he laid it in the hollow among the tiny stars of the rowan blossom, it seemed to him that with it—in it—he was laying the old life down too.

He held out his hand to Esca for the flint and steel which he always carried on him.

The golden sparks that he struck out dropped on to the tinder-dry scraps of birch bark, and hung there an instant like jewels; then, as he blew on them, nursing them to life, they flared up into crackling flame; a flower of flame with the olive-wood bird sitting at its heart like a dove on her nest.

He fed the fire carefully, with bits of wood from a fallen branch that Esca brought him.

XII

THE WHISTLER IN THE DAWN

ALL that summer Marcus and Esca wandered through the abandoned Province of Valentia, crossing and re-crossing from coast to coast, and making steadily north-ward. They ran into no serious trouble, for Rufrius Galarius had spoken the truth when he said that the oculist's stamp was a talisman that would carry its owner anywhere. In Valentia, as in the rest of Britain, there were many people with marsh ophthalmia, and Marcus did his best for those who came to him for help, with the salves which the old field surgeon had shown him how to use. They were good salves, and Marcus had common sense and gentle hands and the craftsman's dislike of a job ill done, and so he succeeded better than most of

the few quack-salvers who had passed that way. The tribesmen were not exactly friendly; it was not in them to be
friendly towards men not of their own tribe, but they were
certainly not unfriendly. There was generally somebody in
each village who would give them food and shelter at the day's
end; and always, if the way was difficult to find or dangerous
to follow, a hunter from one village would act as their guide to
the next. They would have paid well, too, for Marcus's skill,
with a palmful of jet beads, a fine javelin-head or a dressed
beaver skin—things which would have fetched many times the
value of the salves, south of the Wall. But Marcus was not in
this adventure to make a fortune, nor did he wish to jingle
round the country loaded like a trader, and he shelved the
difficulty by saying to each offer, ' Keep it for me until I come
again on my way south.'

Late summer came, and the rowan-trees that had been in
new flower when Marcus built his altar in the glen of their first
halt were heavy now with flaming bosses of berries; and on an
August noon they sat side by side, looking down through the
birch-woods to the great firth which half cut Valentia from
what lay beyond. It was a day like a trumpet blast, the
wooded hills swimming in the heat, and at their backs the mares
stamped and fretted, swishing their tails against the cloud of
flies that beset them. Marcus sat with his hands locked round
his updrawn knees and stared out across the firth. The sun
was hot on the nape of his neck, scorching his shoulders
through the cloth of his tunic, and he would have dearly liked
to copy Esca, lying on his stomach beside him, who had
discarded his tunic altogether and now went stripped to the
waist like the Painted People. But to ride round the country
in his bracco would have been beneath the dignity of Demetrius of Alexandria, and he supposed that he must continue to
stew in his woollen tunic.

He heard the bees zooming among the bell-heather of the
clearing, smelled the warm aromatic scents of the sun-baked
birch-woods overlaying the cold saltiness of the sea; singled
out one among the wheeling gulls and watched it until it

became lost in a flickering cloud of sun-touched wings. But he was not really conscious of any of these things.

'We have missed the trail somehow,' he said abruptly. 'It is in my mind that we have come too far north. We are all but up to the old frontier now.'

'The Eagle is surely more likely to be found beyond the northern wall,' said Esca. 'The tribesmen would scarcely leave it in territory that was even in name a Roman province. They will have carried it away into one of their holy places.'

'I know,' Marcus said. 'But the traces should be in Valentia; and if the accounts of Caledonia that we have heard are true, we stand small chance of sighting our quarry among the mountains, unless we have some trail to follow. We shall simply wander up through Caledonia until we fall into the sea off the northernmost headland.'

'A holy place is apt to spread signs of itself abroad, for those, having eyes to see, who come even a little near,' Esca suggested.

Marcus sat silent for a moment, still hugging his knees. Then he said, 'When there is nothing, nothing at all, to guide a man in his choice, then it is time to lay the choice on the gods,' and fishing in the breast of his tunic, he brought out a small leather bag, and from the bag, a sesterce.

Esca rolled over and sat up, the blue warrior patterns moving on arms and breast as the muscles slid under his brown skin.

The disc of silver lay in Marcus's palm, showing the head of Domitian crowned with laurel; a small thing to hold their destinies. 'Heads we push on, ships we try a cast back,' Marcus said, and sent the coin spinning into the air. He caught it on the back of his hand, clapping the other over it, and for an instant their eyes met, questioningly. Then Marcus lifted the covering hand and they looked down at the winged victory on the obverse side of the coin, which had been called 'Ships' from the days of the Republic, when the design had been the prow of a galley.

'We turn south again,' Marcus said.

Turn south they did; and a few nights later they encamped

in the old fort which Agricola had raised at Trinomontium, the Place of Three Hills.

Thirty years ago, when Valentia was a Roman province in more than name, before Agricola's work had been all undone by meddling from the Senate, Trinomontium had been a busy fort. A double cohort had drilled in the wide forum and slept in the barrack rows; there had been many horses in the stables, cavalry manoeuvres on the gentle southern slope below the ramparts, with the riders crested with tossing yellow plumes, the usual baths and wine-shops and the turf bothies of the women's quarters; and over all, the crested sentries marching to and fro. But now the wild had flowed in again; grass covered the cobbles of the streets, timber roofs had fallen in, and the red sandstone walls stood gaunt and empty to the sky. The wells were choked with the debris of thirty autumns, and an elder-tree had taken root in one corner of the roofless shrine where once had stood the cohort's standard and the altars of its gods, and had thrust a jagged gap in the wall to make room for itself. In all that desolation the only living creature that Marcus and Esca found as they wandered through it in the heavy stillness of the summer evening, was a lizard basking on a fallen block of stone, which darted off like a whip-lash at their approach. Looking down at the stone, Marcus saw roughly carved on it the charging boar of the Twentieth Legion. Somehow the sight brought the desolation home to him very sharply.

' If ever the Legions come north again, they will have a fine building job on their hands,' he said.

The hoof-beats of their led mounts sounded unnaturally loud in the silence; and when they halted at a crossways, the silence that came rushing in on them seemed almost menacing.

' It is in my heart that I wish we had pushed on to the next village,' Esca said, half under his breath. ' I do not like this place.'

' Why not? ' Marcus asked. ' You did not mind it when we were here before.' For they had turned aside to look at the derelict fort on their way north, hoping against hope that it might hold some clue for them.

'That was at noon. Now it is evening, and soon the light will go.'

'We shall do well enough with a fire,' Marcus said in surprise. 'We have slept out time and again since we started on this venture, and had no trouble while the fire burned. And surely the only creatures likely to lair in these ruins are wild pig, and we have seen no signs of any such.'

'I have not been a hunter since first I could hold a spear, without growing used to sleeping in the wild,' Esca said, in the same suppressed voice. 'It is not the forest folk that make me cold between my shoulders.'

'What, then?'

Esca laughed, and broke off his laughter midway. 'I am a fool. Maybe the ghosts of a lost Legion.'

Marcus, who had been gazing out over the grass-grown forum, looked round quickly. 'It was a cohort of the Twentieth that served here, never the Ninth.'

'How do we know where the Ninth served,' Esca said, 'after they marched into the mist?'

Marcus was silent for a moment. He came of a breed that did not trouble unduly about ghosts, but he knew that with Esca it was quite otherwise. 'I do not think that they would bring us any harm, if they did come,' he said at last. 'It seemed to me that this would be a good place to sleep, especially with the curlews calling rain as they are this evening; but if you say the word, we will find a sheltered place among the hazel woods, and sleep there.'

'I should be ashamed,' Esca said simply.

Marcus said, 'Then we had best set about choosing our quarters.'

They settled finally on one end of a barrack row, where the roof had not fallen in, and the few feet of timber and rotten thatch made a shelter from the coming rain. There they unloaded the mares, rubbed them down and turned them loose in the long building, in the British fashion; after which

Esca went off to gather a few armfuls of fodder, and bracken for bedding, while Marcus collected a stock of the rotten timber which lay about, and got a fire going, watched with close attention by Vipsania and Minna.

Later that evening the tumble-down shelter bore a much more cheerful aspect; a small fire burned brightly at its entrance, the smoke finding its own way round the bat-wing edge of the rotten thatch, into the darkening sky; and the piled bracken in the far corner spread with the sheepskins which by day were folded to serve as saddles. Marcus and Esca ate some of the food which they had brought with them from last night's village, coarse barley bannock and strips of strong part-smoked deer meat, which they broiled over the fire; and afterwards Esca lay down at once to sleep.

But Marcus sat for a while beside the fire, watching the sparks fly upward, hearing nothing but the occasional shifting of the mares in the farther shadows. From time to time he bent forward to put more wood on the fire; otherwise he sat quite unmoving, while, on the piled bracken against the wall, Esca slept the quiet, light sleep of the hunter. Looking at him, Marcus wondered whether he would have had the courage to lie quietly down to sleep on what he believed to be haunted ground. With the full dark, the rain came up, soft, heavy swathes of rain; and the swish and whisper of it on the rotten thatch seemed to deepen the utter desolation of this place that had once been living and was now dead. Marcus found himself listening with straining ears to the silence, his thoughts growing full of crowding ghosts that came and went along the rampart walls and through the forsaken forum, until it was all he could do to make himself bank the fire and lie down beside Esca.

Normally when they camped in the wild they took turns to sit up and keep the fire in while the other slept, but here, with four walls round them and a pile of thorn branches across the door to keep the horses in, there could be no need for that. For a while he lay wakeful, every nerve jumping with a queer expectancy; but he was tired, and the spread skins and the fragrant, high-piled bracken were very comfortable. And before long he fell asleep, and dreamed that he was watching Legionaries at pilum practice, quite ordinary Legionaries, save that between their chin-straps and the curves of their helmets—they had no faces.

He woke to a sense of light, steady pressure below his left ear, woke quietly and completely as people roused in that way always do, and opened his eyes to see that the fire had sunk to a few red embers and Esca was crouching beside him in the first faint pallor of the dawn. The evil taste of the dream was still in his mouth. 'What is it?' he whispered.

'Listen.'

Marcus listened and felt a small unpleasant chill trickling up his spine. His own eerie fancies of last night returned to him uncomfortably. Maybe Esca had been right about this place, after all. For somewhere in the abandoned fort, somebody—or some *thing*—was whistling the tune of a song that he knew well. He had marched to it more than once, for though an old song, it was a favourite with the Legions, and for no particular reason had outlived many and many that they picked up and marched to for a few months and then forgot.

> 'Oh when I joined the Eagles,
> (As it might be yesterday)
> I kissed a girl at Clusium
> Before I marched away.'

The familiar words joined themselves to the tune in Marcus's head, as he rose silently, and stood getting his stiffened leg into marching order. The whistling was drawing nearer, becoming every moment more clearly recognizable:

> 'A long march, a long march, and twenty years in store,
> When I left my girl at Clusium, beside the threshing-floor.'

There were many more verses, all describing girls that the maker of the song had kissed in different parts of the Empire; but as Marcus went purposefully to the doorway, and Esca stooped to drag aside the thorn branches, the whistling ceased, and a voice—a husky voice with a queer, brooding quality in it, as though the singer's thoughts were turned inward and backward—took up the song at the last verse of all:

> ' The girls of Spain were honey-sweet,
> And the golden girls of Gaul:
> And the Thracian maids were soft as birds
> To hold the heart in thrall.
>
> > ' But the girl I kissed at Clusium
> > Kissed and left at Clusium,
> > The girl I kissed at Clusium
> > I remember best of all.
>
> ' A long march, a long march, and twenty years behind,
> But the girl I kissed at Clusium comes easy to my mind.'

Rounding the end of the barrack row, they came face to face with the singer, who was standing in the Sinister Gate. Marcus had not known what he had expected to see—perhaps nothing, which would have been worst of all. But what he did see pulled him up in astonishment, for the man—it was no ghost —standing with his hand on the bridle of a rough-coated pony, was one of the Painted People, such as he had lived among all summer.

The man had checked at sight of Marcus and Esca, and stood looking at them warily, with upflung head, like a stag when it scents danger; his hunting-spear held as though for instant attack. For a moment they surveyed each other in the dawn light, then Marcus broke the silence. By now he could make himself understood without much trouble in the dialect of the Northern Tribes. ' It has been a good hunting, friend,' he said, pointing to the carcass of a half-grown roe-buck that was slung across the pony's back.

' Good enough until I can do better,' said the man. ' There is none to spare.'

' We have food of our own,' Marcus said. ' Also we have a fire, and unless it seems good to you to build your own or eat your meal raw, you are welcome to share it.'

' What do you here, in the Place of Three Hills? ' asked the man suspiciously.

' Camp for the night. Not knowing how far we might be from a village, and judging that rain was on the way, it seemed to us a better sleeping-place than the open moor. Is not the Place of Three Hills free to all, or only to the raven and the lizard—and yourself? '

For an instant the man did not answer, then slowly and deliberately he reversed the spear in his hand, so that he was carrying it with head trailing, as a man carries his spear when he comes in peace. ' I think that you will be the Healer of sore eyes, of whom I have heard? ' he said.

' I am.'

' I will come and share your fire.' He turned and whistled, and in answer to the summons, two swift brindled hunting dogs came springing up through the bracken to join him.

A few moments later they were back in their shelter, and the small, shaggy pony, free of his burden now, was hitched to a fallen beam beside the door. Esca threw a birch branch on to the red embers, and as the silver bark blackened and flared up, Marcus turned for a better look at the stranger. He was a middle-aged man, lean and powerful, his eyes wary and a little furtive under the wild hair that was coarse and grey as a badger's pelt; he wore nothing but an ochre-coloured kilt, and in the light of the fire his body and arms were covered all over with bands of tattooing, after the manner of the Painted People. Even on his cheeks and forehead and the wings of his nostrils the blue curves and spandrils showed. The dogs were nosing at the body of the deer which lay at his feet, and as their master stooped to cuff them away, the firelight fell strongly slantwise across his forehead, throwing into relief the scar of a curiously shaped brand, just between the brows.

Esca squatted down by the fire and put more strips of smoked meat to broil in the hot ash, then sat with his arms across his knees and his spear within easy reach, watching the stranger under his brows; while the stranger, kneeling over the flattened carcass of the buck—which had been gralloched already—began to skin it with the long hunting-knife which he drew from his raw-hide belt. Marcus also watched him, though less obviously. He was puzzled. The man seemed a tribesman like any other of his kind; yet he had sung ' The Girl I Kissed at Clusium ' in good Latin; and at some time, years ago to judge by the faintness of the scar, he had been initiated into the Raven Degree of Mithras.

He might of course have learned the song from the Legionaries who had served here; he was fully old enough for that. Mithra sometimes found followers in unexpected places. But taking the two things together, it was unusual, to say the least of it, and Marcus had been looking for something unusual all summer.

The hunter had laid back a large flap of hide from the flank and haunch of the buck. He cut thick collops of meat from it, and a shapeless lump with the hair still on, which he flung to the dogs who crouched beside him. And while they fought over it, snarling and worrying, he heaved up what remained of the carcass and flung it across a half-rotten tie-beam, where it hung, the dangling legs out of reach of the hounds. He put the collops that he had cut for his own eating to broil in the hot ash, rubbed his hands on his kilt, for they were juicy, and sitting back on his heels, peered from Marcus to Esca and back again with a strange intent look, as though their faces—Marcus's at all events—had some meaning for him which he could not fathom.

' I thank you for the heat of your fire,' he said, speaking less roughly than he had done before. ' It is in my heart that I might have been swifter to reverse my spear; but I had not thought to find any before me, here in the Place of Three Hills.'

' I can well believe that,' Marcus said.

' Aye, in all the years that I have come here on the hunting trail, never until now have I found any man here before me.'

' And now you have found two. And since we share the same fire,' said Marcus with a smile, ' surely we should know each other's names. I am Demetrius of Alexandria, a travelling oculist, as you seem to know, and this, my friend and spear-bearer, is Esca Mac Cunoval, of the tribe of the Brigantes.'

' The Bearers of the blue war-shield. You have heard maybe of my tribe, if not of me,' added Esca, and his teeth flashed white in his tanned face as he lifted his head and smiled.

'I have heard of your tribe—a little, yes,' said the stranger, with, as it seemed to Marcus, a hint of grim amusement in his voice, though there was no amusement in his gaunt face, as he blinked at the fire. 'For myself, I am called Guern, and I am a hunter, as you see. My rath lies upwards of a day's trail to the west, and I come here sometimes for the sake of the fat deer to be had in the hazel woods yonder.'

Silence fell between the three, while the daylight grew around them, and the dogs snarled and tussled over their lump of meat. Then Marcus, idly peeling a bit of stick, began half under his breath to whistle the tune that had so startled him an hour before. Out of the corner of his eyes he was aware that Guern had started and looked towards him. For a few moments he continued with the peeling and the whistling, and then, seeming suddenly to tire of his pastime, tossed the stick into the fire and looked up. 'Where did you learn that song, friend Guern the Hunter?'

'Where else but here?' said Guern. For an instant his face took on a look of blank stupidity, but Marcus had an idea that behind it he was thinking furiously. 'When this was a Roman fort there were many Roman songs sung here. That one I learned from a centurion who used to hunt boar with me. I was only a boy, but I have a good memory.'

'Did you pick up any Latin, other than the words of the song?' Marcus shot at him, speaking in that language.

The hunter made as if to answer, checked, and looked at him an instant slantwise, under down-twitched brows. Then he spoke in Latin, very slowly, like a man fumbling back across the years for a speech that comes half-forgotten to his tongue. 'A few words I remember still, such words as soldiers use.' Then, dropping back into the Celtic speech, 'Where did *you* learn that song?'

'I have followed my trade in fortress towns before now,' Marcus said, 'and ones that were not deserted to the wild boar, as the Place of Three Hills. I have a quick ear for a tune.'

Guern leaned forward to turn the cooking meat with his hunting-knife. 'Yet surely you can have been but a short while at this trade you practise. There are not many years under that beard of yours.'

'Maybe there are more than there seem,' Marcus said, and stroked the beard tenderly. It had grown well in the months since he came north, though it was still very clearly a young beard. 'Moreover, I began early, following my father's footsteps in the way of sons. . . . And talking of this trade of mine, are there any that have sore eyes in your village?'

Guern poked experimentally at the meat. He seemed to be making up his mind about something; and after a few moments he looked up as though he had made it. 'I am an outdweller, living to myself and my family,' he said, 'and we have no sore eyes for your healing. None the less, if you wait until my hunting is done, you are very welcome to come with me; and we will eat salt together, and later I will set you on your way to another village. That is for the place that you have given me at your fire.'

For an instant, Marcus hesitated; then, with the instinct still strong upon him that this man was not what he seemed, he said, 'All ways are alike to us. We will come, and gladly.'

'There is more flesh on my kill than I had thought,' said Guern, suddenly and shamefacedly, and stood up, knife in hand.

So the three of them ate fresh broiled buck together, in good fellowship; and a day later, when Guern's hunting was done, they set out, Marcus and Esca riding, and the hunter leading his own pony, across whose back was bound the carcass of a great red stag, and the dogs cantering ahead. Swishing through the rain-wet bracken they went, over the heathery shoulder of three-headed Eildon and away into the west, leaving the red sandstone fort deserted once again to the creatures of the wild.

XIII

THE LOST LEGION

GUERN'S homestead, when they reached it, proved to be a bleak huddle of turf huts high among the dark moors. A small boy herding wild-eyed cattle up from the drinking-pool to the night-time shelter of the cattle-yard greeted their appearance with a kind of fascinated dismay. Evidently strangers were not in his scheme of things, and while stealing constant sly peeps at them, he took care to keep the great herd bull, which he managed with casual pokes and slaps, between him and danger, as they went on towards the rath together.

'This is my house,' said Guern the Hunter, as they reined in before the largest of the huts. 'It is yours for so long as it pleases you.'

They dismounted, while the yelling small boy and the lowing herd pelted by in the direction of the cattle-yard, and, tossing the reins over a hitching-post, turned to the doorway. A girl child of perhaps eighteen months old, wearing nothing but a red coral bead on a thong round her neck to ward off the Evil Eye, sat before the door, busily playing with three dandelions, a bone, and a striped pebble. One of the hounds poked a friendly muzzle into her face as he stalked past her into the darkness, and she made a grab at his disappearing tail, and fell over.

The doorway was so small that Marcus had to bend double under the heather thatch, as he stepped over the little sprawling figure and followed his host steeply down into the firelit gloom. The blue peat-smoke caught him by the throat and made his eyes smart, but he was used to that by now: and a woman rose from beside the central hearth.

'Murna, I have brought home the Healer of sore eyes and his

138

spear-bearer,' said Guern. ' Do you make them welcome while
I tend to their horses and the fruits of my hunting.'

' They are very welcome,' said the woman, ' though praise be
to the Horned One, there are no sore eyes here.'

' Good fortune on the house, and on the women of the house,'
Marcus said courteously.

Esca had followed their host out again, trusting no one but
himself to see to the mares, and Marcus sat down on the roe
deerskin that the woman spread for him on the piled heather
of the bed-place, and watched her as she returned to whatever
she was cooking in the bronze cauldron over the fire. As his
eyes grew used to the peat-smoke and to the faint light which
filtered down through the narrow doorway and the smoke-hole
in the roof, he saw that she was much younger than Guern:
a tall, raw-boned woman with a contented face. Her tunic
was of coarse reddish wool, such as only a poor woman would
have worn in the south; but clearly she was not a poor woman,
or rather her husband was not a poor man, for there were
bracelets of silver and copper and blue Egyptian glass on her
arms, and the mass of dull-gold hair knotted up behind her head
was held in place with amber-headed pins. Above all, she
was the proud possessor of a large bronze cauldron: Marcus
had been long enough in the wilderness to know that a bronze
cauldron, more than anything else, brought a woman the envy
of her neighbours.

After a short while footsteps sounded outside, and Esca and
Guern came ducking in, followed almost at once by the small
herdsman and an even younger boy, both very like Guern in
face, and already tattooed as he was, against the day when they
would be warriors. They watched the strangers warily under
their brows, and drew back against the far wall of the hut,
while their mother brought bowls of black pottery from some
inner place, and served the steaming stew to the three men
sitting side by side on the bed-place. She poured yellow mead
for them into the great ox-horns, and then went to eat her own
meal on the far side of the fire, the woman's side, with the small
girl child in her lap. The younger boy sat with her, but the

elder, suddenly overcoming his distrust, came edging round to examine Marcus's dagger, and finished up by sharing his bowl.

They were a pleasant small family, yet oddly isolated in a land where most people lived in groups for greater safety; and it seemed to Marcus that here was another hint of the unusual to add to the song and the brand of Mithras. . . .

It was next morning that he got the final proof of his suspicions.

That morning, Guern decided to shave. Like many of the British tribesmen, he went more or less clean shaven save for his upper lip, and he was certainly in need of a shave. As soon as he announced his intention, preparations began as though for a solemn festival. His wife brought him a pot of goose-fat to soften his beard, and the whole family gathered to watch their lord and master at his toilet; and so, amid an enthralled audience of three children and several dogs, sitting in the early light before the hut-place door, Guern the Hunter set to work, scraping away at his chin with a heart-shaped bronze razor. How little difference there was between children, all the world over, Marcus thought, looking on with amusement, or fathers, or shaving, for that matter; the small patterns of behaviour and relationship that made up family life. He remembered the fascination of watching his own father on such occasions. Guern squinted at his reflection in the polished bronze disc his patient wife was holding for him, cocked his head this way and that, and scraped away with an expression of acute agony, that made Marcus look forward with foreboding to the day when he and Esca would have to rid themselves of their own beards.

Guern had begun to shave under his chin, tipping his head far back, and as he did so, Marcus saw that just under the point of his jaw, the skin was paler than elsewhere, and had a thickened look, almost like the scar of an old gall. It was very faint, but still to be seen; the mark made by the chin-strap of a Roman helmet, through many years of wearing it. Marcus had seen that gall too often to be mistaken in it, and his last doubt was gone.

Something forbade him to tax Guern with his old life, here at the heart of the new life that he had made. And so a little later, while preparing to take the trail once more, he reminded the hunter of his promise, to set them on their way to the next village. He had a mind to go westward, he said, and Guern replied willingly enough, that since westward there were no more villages for two days' trail, if they were set on going that way, he would ride with them the first day and share their camp that night.

So presently they set out. And in the long-shadowed evening, many miles to the west, the three of them ate their evening meal in the curved lee of a rocky outcrop, and afterwards sat together round their small fire. Their three mounts, each hobbled by a rein from the head to the left foreleg to prevent them straying, cropped contentedly at the short hill-turf that spread here and there like green runnels among the bell-heather. Below them the hills rolled away north-westward, falling gradually to a blue haze of low ground, maybe forty miles away, and Marcus followed the fall of them with his eyes, knowing that somewhere in that blueness the wreck of Agricola's northern wall slashed across the land, severing Valentia from the country beyond that the Romans called Caledonia and the Celts Albu; knowing that somewhere beyond the blueness was the lost Eagle of his father's Legion.

In all the world there seemed no sound but the dry soughing of the wind through the heather, and the sharp yelp of a golden eagle circling the blue spirals of the upper air.

Esca had drawn back a little into the heather, and sat polishing his spear, and Marcus and Guern were alone by the fire, save for the hunter's favourite hound, who lay, nose on paws, with his flank against his master's thigh. Presently Marcus turned to his companion. 'Soon, very soon now, our ways part,' he said, ' but before you go your way and I go mine, there is a question that I have in my heart to ask you.'

'Ask, then,' said the other, playing with his dog's ears.

Marcus said slowly, 'How did you come to be Guern the Hunter who once served with the Eagles? '

There was a sudden flicker in the other's eyes; and then for
a long moment he became very still, with a sullen stillness,
peering at Marcus under his brows, in the way of the Painted
People. 'Who told you such a thing?' he asked at last.

'No one. I go by a song, and the scar between your brows.
But most of all by the gall-mark under your chin.'

'If I were—what you say,' Guern growled, 'what need have
I to tell you of it? I am a man of my tribe, and if I was not
always so, there is none among my sword-brethren who would
speak of that to a stranger. What need, then, have I to tell?'

'None in the world,' said Marcus, 'save that I asked you in
all courtesy.'

There was another long silence, and then his companion
said, with a queer mingling of sullen defiance and a long-
forgotten pride, 'I was once Sixth Centurion of the Senior
Cohort of the Hispana. Now go and tell it to the nearest
Commander on the Wall. I shall not stop you.'

Marcus took his time, sitting quiet and searching the fierce
face of the man before him. He was looking for any trace that
might be left under the painted hunter of the Roman centurion
of twelve years ago; and presently he thought he had found it.
'No patrol could reach you, and you know it,' he said. 'But
even if it were not so, still there is a reason that I should keep
my mouth shut.'

'And that reason?'

Marcus said, 'That I bear on my forehead a mark which is
brother to the mark that you bear on yours,' and with a quick
movement he freed the crimson riband that bound the silver
talisman in place, and jerked it off. 'Look!'

The other bent forward swiftly. 'So,' he said lingeringly.
'Never before have I known one of your trade who made his
evening prayer to Mithras.' But even as he spoke, his gaze
narrowed into a new intentness, became like a dagger-thrust.
'Who are you? What are you?' he demanded; and suddenly
his hands were on Marcus's shoulders, wrenching him round
to face the last windy gold of the sunset. For a long moment
he held him so, kneeling over him and glaring into his face;

while Marcus, with his lame leg twisted under him, stared back, his black brows frowning, his mouth at its most disdainful.

The great hound crouched watchfully beside them, and Esca got quietly up, fingering his spear; both man and hound ready to kill at a word.

' I have seen you before,' said Guern in a rasping voice. ' I remember your face. In the Name of Light, who are you? '

' Maybe it is my father's face that you remember. He was your Cohort Commander.'

Slowly Guern's hands relaxed and dropped to his side. ' I should have known,' he said. ' It was the talisman—and the beard. But none the less, I should have known.' He sat rocking himself a little, almost as if he were in pain, his eyes never leaving Marcus's face. ' What is it that you do, your father's son, here in Valentia? ' he said at last. ' You are no Greek of Alexandria, and I think that you are no eye doctor.'

' No, I am no eye doctor. Nevertheless, the salves that I carry are good, and I was shown how to work with them by one skilled in their use. When I told you that I had followed my father's trade, that at least was the truth. I followed it until I got me this leg and my discharge, two years ago. As to what I do, here in Valentia——' he hesitated, but only for an instant. He knew that in this one matter, at least, he could trust Guern utterly.

And so, very briefly, he told him what it was he did in Valentia, and why. ' And when it seemed to me that you were not as the other hunters of the Painted People,' he finished, ' it seemed to me also that from you I might learn the answer to my questions.'

' And could you not have asked me at the first? Because I was drawn to you, not knowing why, and because you spoke the Latin tongue that I had not heard these twelve years, I brought you to my own place, and you slept under my roof and ate of my salt; with this hidden in your heart concerning me. It would have been better that you asked me at the first! '

' Much better,' Marcus agreed. ' But all that I had in my heart concerning you was a guess, and a wild guess enough!

If I had spoken out to you without first being sure, and found too late that you were, after all, no other than you seemed, would there not have been Ahriman the Dark One to pay?'

'What is it that you want to know?' Guern said dully, after a moment.

'What became of my father's Legion. Where is the Eagle now?'

Guern looked down at his own hand, on the head of the great dog who was once more lying quiet beside him; then up again. 'I can answer the first of your questions, at least in part,' he said, 'but it is a long story, and first I will mend the fire.'

He leaned forward as he spoke, and fed the sinking flames from the pile of thorn branches and heather snarls beside him. He did it slowly, deliberately, as though holding off the moment when he must begin his story. But even when the flames sprang up again, he still squatted silent on his haunches, staring into the smoke.

Marcus's heart had begun to race, and suddenly he felt a little sick.

'You never knew your father's Legion,' Guern began at last. 'No, and if you had, you would have been too young to read the signs. Too young by many years.' He had changed his tongue to Latin, and with the change, all that was of the tribes in him seemed to have dropped away. 'The seeds of death were in the Hispana before ever it marched north that last time. They were sown sixty years ago, when men of the Legion carried out the Procurator's orders to dispossess the Queen of the Iceni. Boudicca her name was; maybe you have heard of her? She cursed them and their whole Legion, it is said, for the treatment that she had at their hands, which was hardly just, for they had their orders: if she was minded to curse anyone, it had better have been the Procurator himself. But a woman who thinks herself wronged is seldom over particular where her thrust lands, so that it draws blood. Me, I am not one to set much store by cursings, or I was not in the old days. But be that as it may, the Legion was cut to pieces in the rising that followed. When at last the rising failed, the Queen took poison, and maybe her death gave potency to her cursing.

'The Legion was re-formed and brought up to strength again, but it never prospered. Perhaps if it had been moved elsewhere it might have been saved, but for a Legion to serve year after year, generation after generation, among tribes who believe it to be accursed is not good for that Legion. Small misfortunes bloat into large ones, outbreaks of sickness are set down to the working of the curse, instead of the marsh mists; the Spaniards are a people quick to believe in such things. So it became harder to find recruits, and the standard of those taken grew lower, year by year. It was very slow at first—I have served with men no older than myself, who remembered the Ninth when it was only a little rough and run to seed. But at the last it was terribly swift, and when I joined the Legion as a centurion, two years before the end—I was promoted from the ranks of the Thirtieth, which was a proud Legion—the rind seemed sound enough, but the heart was rotten. Stinking rotten.'

Guern the Hunter spat into the fire.

' I strove to fight the rot in my own Century at first, and then —the fighting grew to be too much trouble. The last Legate was a hard and upright man without understanding—the worst man to handle such a Legion—and soon after his coming the Emperor Trajan withdrew too many troops from Britain for his everlasting campaigns; and we who were left to hold the Frontier began to feel the tribes seethe under us like an over-ripe cheese. Then Trajan died, and the tribes rose. The whole North went up in flames, and barely had we settled with the Brigantes and the Iceni when we were ordered up into Valentia to hammer the Caledonians. Two of our cohorts were serving in Germany; we had suffered heavy casualties already, and leaving a cohort to garrison Eburacum and be cut to shreds by the Brigantes if they happened to feel like it, that left well under four thousand of us to march north. And when the Legate took the omens in the usual way, the sacred chickens

had gone off their feed and would not touch the pulse he threw
to them.   After that we gave ourselves up for doomed, which is
a bad state of mind for a Legion to march in.

'It was autumn, and almost from the start the mountain
country was blanketed in mist, and out of the mist the tribesmen harried us.   Oh, it never came to a fight; they hung
about our flanks like wolves; they made sudden raids on our
rearguard and loosed their arrows into us from behind every
tuft of sodden heather, and disappeared into the mist before
we could come to grips with them; and the parties sent out
after them never came back.

'A Legate who was also a soldier might have saved us; ours
had seen no more of soldiering than a sham fight on Mars Field,
and was too proud to listen to his officers who had, and by the
time we reached Agricola's old headquarters on the Northern
Wall, which was to be our base, upward of another thousand
of us had gone, by death or desertion.   The old fortifications
were crumbling, the water supply had long since given out, and
the whole North had gathered in strength by then.   They sat
round the walls and yelled, like wolves howling to the moon.
We stood one attack in that place.   We rolled the dead down
the scarp into the river; and when the tribes drew off to lick
their wounds, we chose a spokesman and went to the Legate
and said: "Now we will make what terms we can with the
Painted People, that they may let us march back the way we
came, leaving Valentia in their hands, for it is no more than a
name, and a name that tastes sour on the tongue at that."   And
the Legate sat in his camp chair, which *we* had had to carry
for him all the way from Eburacum, and called us evil names.
Doubtless we deserved the names, but they did not help.
Then more than half of us mutinied, many of my own Century
among them.'

Guern turned from the fire to face Marcus.   'I was not one
of them.   Before the Lord of the Legions I swear it.   My full
shame was not yet come upon me and I held the few men left
to me in leash yet awhile.   Then the Legate saw where his
mistake had lain, and he spoke more gently to his Legion in

revolt than ever he had done before, and that was not from fear. He bade the mutineers lay down the arms that they had taken up against their Eagle, and swore that there should be no summary punishment, even of the ringleaders; swore that if we did our duty from thenceforth, he would make fair report of it, the good with the bad, on our return. As though we should ever return! But even had the way back been clear, it was too late for such promises. From the moment that the cohorts mutinied it was too late. There could be no turning back for them, knowing all too well what the word of the Senate would be.'

' Decimation,' Marcus said quietly, as the other halted.

' Aye, decimation. It comes hard, to draw lots out of a helmet, knowing that one in every ten means death by stoning to the man who draws it.

' So the thing ended in fighting. That was when the Legate was killed. He was a brave man, though a fool. He stood out before the mob, with his hands empty, and his Eagle-bearer and his beardless Tribunes behind him, and called on them to remember their oath, and called them curs of Tiber-side. Then one struck him down with a pilum, and after that there was no more talking. . . .

' The tribesmen came swarming in over the barricades to help the red work, and by dawn there were barely two full cohorts left alive in the fort. The rest were not all dead, oh no; many of them went back over the ramparts with the tribesmen. They may be scattered about Caledonia now, for all I know, living even as myself, with a British wife, and sons to come after them.

' Just after dawn, your father called together the few that were left in the open space before the Praetorium, and there, every man with his sword ready in his hand, we took hurried counsel, and determined to win out of the old fort, which was become a death-trap, and carry the Eagle back to Eburacum as best we might. It was no use by then to think of making terms with the tribesmen, for they had no longer any cause to fear us. And besides, I think there was the thought in all of us that if we won through, the Senate could scarcely count us as disgraced. That night the fools feasted—so low had we sunk in their contempt—and while they drank, baying to the moon, we got out, all that were left of us, by the southern scarp, and passed them by in the darkness and the mist—the first time ever the mist had seemed our friend—and began the forced march back, heading for Trinomontium.

'The tribes picked up our trail at dawn and hunted us as though it had been for sport. Have you ever been hunted? All that day we struggled on, and the sorest wounded, who dropped out, died. Sometimes we heard them die, in the mist. Then I dropped out too.' Guern rubbed his left flank. 'I had a wound that I could put three fingers in, and I was sick. But I could have gone on. It was being hunted—the being—hunted. I took my chance at dusk, when the hunters drew off a space; I slipped into some long furze-cover, and hid. One of the Painted People nearly trod on me presently, but they did not find me, and after dark, when the hunt had passed far away, I stripped off my harness and left it. I look like a Pict, do I not? That is because I am from Northern Gaul. Then I suppose I wandered all night. I do not know, but in the dawn I came to a village and fell across the door-sill of the first hut.

'They took me in and tended me. Murna tended me. And when they found that I was a Roman soldier, they did not greatly care. I was not the first of my kind to desert to the tribes; and Murna spoke for me, like a lioness whose cub is threatened.' For an instant, a glint of laughter sounded in his voice, and then it grew harsh and heavy again. 'A few nights later I saw the Eagle carried by on its way north again, with a great triumph of torches following behind.'

There was a long, strained silence. Then Marcus said in a quiet, hard voice, 'Where did they make an end?'

'I do not know. But they never reached Trinomontium. I have looked there again and again, and found no sign of fighting.'

'And my father?'

' He was with the Eagle when I dropped out.   There were no captives with it when they carried it north again.'

' Where is the Eagle now? '

Guern reached out and touched the dagger in the other's belt, looking at him steadily.   ' If you are minded to die, here is the means to your hand.   Save yourself the further journey.'

' Where is the Eagle now? '   Marcus repeated his question, as though the other had not spoken.

For a moment he held the hunter's eyes with his own; then Guern said, ' I do not know.   But tomorrow, when there is light to see by, I will give you what direction I can.'

And Marcus realized suddenly that he was seeing the other's face by firelight, and all beyond him was blurred into the blue dusk.

He did not sleep much that night, but lay rigid with his head in his arms.   All these months he had followed a dream; in a way, he realized now, he had followed it since he was eight years old.   It had been bright and warm, and now it was broken, and without it he felt very cold, and suddenly older than he had been a few hours ago.   What a fool he had been!   What a blind fool!   Clinging to the stubborn faith that because it had been his father's, there had been nothing much wrong with the Ninth Legion, after all.   He knew better now.   His father's Legion had been putrid, a rotten apple that fell to pieces when it was struck by a heel.   And God of the Legions! what his father must have suffered!

Out of the ruin, one thing stood up unchanged: that the Eagle was still to be found and brought back, lest one day it became a menace to the Frontier.   There was something comforting about that.   A faith still to be kept.

Next morning when the early meal had been eaten, and the fire quenched and scattered, Marcus stood beside his mare, looking away north-west, along the line of Guern's pointing finger.   The light wind whipped his face, and his morning shadow ran away downhill as though eager to be off before him, and he heard the wild, sweet calling of the green plover that seemed to be the voice of the great loneliness.

'Yonder where the vale opens,' Guern was saying. 'You will know the ford by the leaning pine that grows beside it. You must cross there, and follow the right bank, or you will find yourself at the last with the whole broad Firth of Cluta between you and Caledonia. Two days' march, three at the most, will bring you to the old northern line.'

'And then?' Marcus said, not turning his narrowed gaze from the blue hazed distance.

'I can tell you only this: that the men who carried the Eagle north were of the tribe of the Epidaii, whose territory is the deep firths and the mountains of the west coast, running from the Cluta.'

'Can you hazard any guess as to where in this territory their holy place may be?'

'None. It may be that if you find the Royal Dun, you will find the Holy Place not far off; but the Epidaii is divided into many clans, so I have heard, and the Royal Clan may not be the guardians of the Holy Place and the holy things of the tribe.'

'You mean—it might be some quite small and unimportant clan?'

'Not unimportant; it would be as powerful as the Royal Clan, maybe more so. But small, yes. There is no more help that I can give you.'

They were silent a moment until there sounded behind them the faint jink of a bridle-bit, as Esca brought up the other mare. Then Guern said hurriedly, 'Do not follow that trail; it leads into the mouth of death.'

'I must take my chance of that,' Marcus said. He turned his head. 'And you, Esca?'

'I go where you go,' said Esca, busy with a buckle.

'Why?' Guern demanded. 'Now that you know the truth? They will not re-form the Legion. Why should you go on? Why?'

'There is still the Eagle to be brought back,' Marcus said.

Another silence, and then Guern said almost humbly, 'You have said nothing about all this that I have told you; no more than if it had been a story told to while away an idle evening.'

'What should I say?'

The other laughed, shortly and harshly. 'Mithras knows! But my belly would be the lighter if you said it.'

'Last night I felt too sick in my own belly to care over much for yours,' Marcus said wearily. 'That is passed now, but if I cursed the Hispana with every foul Tiber-side word that I could lay my tongue to, it would not serve my father, nor sweeten the stink of the Legion's name.' He looked for the first time at the man beside him. 'As for you, I have never been hunted, and the Lord of the Legions forbid that I should be your judge.'

The other said defiantly, 'Why did you come? I was happy with my woman; she is a good woman to me. I am a great man in my tribe, though an outdweller. Often I forget— almost—that I was not born into my tribe, until once again Trinomontium draws me back for a little while. And now I shall be ashamed to my dying day, because I let you go north on this trail alone.'

'No need that you should carry a new shame,' Marcus said. 'This is a trail that three can follow better than four, and two better than three. Go back to your tribe, Guern. Thank you for your salt and your shelter, and for answering my questions.'

He turned away to mount his horse, and a few moments later was heading down the stream-side with Esca close behind.

XIV

THE FEAST OF NEW SPEARS

ON an evening more than a month later, Marcus and
Esca reined in to breathe their tired horses, on the
crest of a steep ridge above the Western Ocean. It
was an evening coloured like a dove's breast; a little wind
feathered the shining water, and far out on the dreaming
brightness many scattered islands seemed to float lightly as
sleeping sea-birds. In the safe harbourage inshore, a few
trading-vessels lay at anchor, the blue sails that had brought
them from Hibernia furled as though they, too, were asleep.
And to the north, brooding over the whole scene, rose Cruachan,
sombre, cloaked in shadows, crested with mist; Cruachan,
the shield-boss of the world.

Mountain and islands and shining sea were all grown
familiar to Marcus. For a month now he had seldom been
out of sight of one or other of them, as he came and went among
the mist-haunted glens where the Epidaii had their hunting
grounds. It had been a heartbreaking month. So often, since
he crossed the northern line, it had seemed to him that he was
at last on the trail of what he sought, and always he had been
wrong. There were so many holy places along the coast.
Wherever the Ancient People, the little Dark People, had left
their long barrows, there the Epidaii, coming after, had made a

holy place at which to worship their gods; and the Ancient
People had left so many barrows. Yet nowhere could Marcus
hear any whisper of the lost Eagle. These people did not speak
of their gods, nor of the things which had to do with their
gods. And suddenly, this evening, looking out over the
shining sea, Marcus was heart-sick and not far from giving up
hope.

He was roused from his bleak mood by Esca's voice beside
him. 'Look, we have companions on the road.' And following
the direction of his friend's back-pointing thumb, he turned to
look down the deer-path by which they had come, and saw a
party of hunters climbing towards them. He wheeled Vipsania, and sat waiting for them to come up. Five men in all,
two of them carrying the slung carcass of a black boar; and
the usual pack of wolfish hounds cantering among them. How
different they were from the men of Valentia: darker and more
slightly built. Maybe that was because the blood of the Dark
People ran more strongly in them than in the lowland tribes;
less outwardly fierce than the lowlanders too, but in the long
run, Marcus thought, more dangerous.

'The hunting has been good.' He saluted them as they
came up at a jog-trot.

'The hunting has been good,' agreed the leader, a young man
with the twisted gold torc of a chieftain round his neck. He
looked inquiringly at Marcus, forbidden by courtesy to ask his
business, but clearly wondering what this stranger, who was not
one of the traders from the blue-sailed ships, was doing in his
territory.

Almost without thinking, Marcus asked him the question
which had become a habit with much asking. 'Are there any
in your dun who have the eye sickness?'

The man's look grew half eager, half suspicious. 'Is it that
you can cure the eye sickness?'

'Can I cure the eye sickness?—I am Demetrius of Alexandria. *The* Demetrius of Alexandria,' said Marcus, who had
long since learned the value of advertisement. 'Speak my
name south of the Cluta, speak it in the Royal Dun itself, and

men will tell you that I am indeed a healer of all sickness of the eye.'

'There are several that I know of in the dun, who have the eye sickness,' said the man. 'None of your trade ever came this way before. You will heal them?'

'How should I know, even I, until I see them?' Marcus turned his mare into the way. 'You are for the dun now? Let us go on together.'

And on they went, Marcus with the Chieftain loping at his horse's shoulder, then Esca and the rest of the hunting party with the slung boar in their midst and the hounds weaving to and fro among them. For a while they followed the ridge, then turned inland, and came looping down through thin birch-woods towards a great loch that lay, pearl-pale with evening, among the hills. Marcus and Esca knew that loch—they had touched its further shores more than once. The Loch of Many Islets it was called, from the little islands scattered in it, some of them steep and rocky, or low and willow-fringed where the herons nested.

It was twilight when they reached the dun on its hill shoulder above the still waters of the loch; the soft mulberry twilight of the west coast, through which the firelit doorways of the living-huts bloomed like yellow crocus flowers dimly veined with red. The cluster of huts that made up the rath of the Chieftain was at the head of the dun, in a sharp curve of the turf ramparts, and they turned aside to it, while the other hunters, after arranging for the sharing of the boar, scattered to their own houses.

At the sound of their arrival, a lad who Marcus took to be the Chieftain's brother ducked out from the firelit doorway and came running to meet them. 'How went the hunting, Dergdian?'

'The hunting was good,' said the Chieftain, 'for see, beside a fine boar, I have brought home a healer of sore eyes; also his spear-bearer. Look to their horses, Liathan.' He turned quickly to Marcus, who was rubbing his thigh. 'You are saddle-stiff? You have ridden over-far today?'

' No,' said Marcus. ' It is an old hurt which still cramps me sometimes.'

He followed his host into the great living-hut, ducking his head under the low lintel. Inside it was very hot, and the usual blue peat-reek caught at his throat. Two or three hounds lay among the warm fern. A little, wizened woman, evidently a slave, bent over the raised hearth, stirring the evening stew in a bronze cauldron, and did not look up at their coming in; but a gaunt old man who sat beyond the fire peered at them through the eddying peat-smoke with bright, masterful eyes. That was in the first instant; then the curtain of beautifully worked deerskins over the entrance to the women's place was drawn aside, and a girl appeared on the threshold; a tall girl, dark even for a woman of the Epidaii, in a straight green gown, clasped at the shoulder with a disc of red-gold as broad and massive as a shield-boss. She had been spinning, it seemed, for she still carried spindle and distaff.

' I heard your voice,' she said. ' Supper is ready and waiting.'

' Let it wait a while longer, Fionhula my heart,' said Derg-dian the Chieftain. ' I have brought home a healer of sore eyes; therefore do you bring out to him the little cub.'

The woman's long dark eyes moved quickly, with a kind of startled hope in them, to Marcus's face, then back to the Chieftain's. She turned without a word, letting the curtain fall behind her, and a few moments later she was back, holding a little boy of about two in her arms. A brown pleasant infant, dressed in the usual coral bead, but as the light fell on his face, Marcus saw that his eyes were so swollen and red and crusted that they would scarcely open.

' Here is one for your healing,' said the Chieftain.

' Yours? ' Marcus asked.

' Mine.'

' He will be blind,' said the old man by the fire. ' All along, I have said that he will be blind, and I am never wrong.'

Marcus ignored him. ' Give the little cub to me,' he commanded. ' I will not hurt him.' He took the little boy from his mother with a quick reassuring smile, and slipped down awkwardly on to his sound knee beside the fire. The child whimpered, turning away from the fire; evidently the light hurt him. Not blind already, then. That was something. Very gently, he turned the little boy's face back to the firelight. 'There, cubling, it is but for a moment. Let me look. What is this you have been putting in the child's eyes?'

'Toad's fat,' said the old man. 'With my own hands I salved them, though it is women's work, for my grandson's wife is a fool.'

'Have you found it do any good?'

The old man shrugged his gaunt shoulders. 'Maybe not,' he said grudgingly.

'Then why use it?'

'It is the custom. Always our womenfolk put toad's fat on such places; but my grandson's wife——' The old man spat juicily to express his opinion of his grandson's wife. 'But all along, I have said the child will be blind,' he added, in the satisfied tone of a true prophet.

Marcus heard the girl behind him catch her breath in agonized protest, and felt his own temper flash up in him, but he had the sense to know that if he made an enemy of the old devil he might as well give up any hope of saving the child's sight. So he said peaceably enough, 'We will see. Toad's fat is doubtless good for sore eyes, but since it has failed, this time, I shall try my own salves; and it may be that they will do better.' And before the old man could get in another word he turned to Fionhula. 'Bring me warm water and linen rags,' he said, 'and light a lamp. I must have light to work by, not this flickering fire-glow. Esca, do you bring in my medicine box.'

And there and then, while the mother held the sick child in her lap, he set to work, bathing, salving, bandaging, by the light of the lamp which the slave woman deserted the stew to hold for him.

Marcus and Esca remained many days in the dun of Dergdian. Always before, Marcus had merely started the good work, left a lump of salve and instructions how to use it, and moved on. But this time it was different. The child's eyes were worse than any that he had had to tend before, and there was grandfather and his toad fat to be reckoned with. This time he would have to stay. Well, he might as soon stay here as in any other place, since he was as likely, or as unlikely, to be near finding the Eagle here as anywhere else.

So he stayed, and a weary stay it seemed. The days went very slowly, for he had long empty stretches of time on his hands, and after the first sharp battle for the little cub's sight had been won, and it was only a question of waiting, they seemed to crawl more slowly still.

Most of the time he sat in the hut-place doorway, watching the womenfolk at work, or grinding sticks of dried salves for the small leaden pots that needed replenishing, while Esca went off with the hunters, or joined the herdsmen in the steep cattle-runs. In the evening he talked with the men round the fire; exchanged travellers' tales with the dark Hibernian traders who came and went through the dun (for there was a constant trade in gold-work and weapons, slaves and hunting dogs, between Hibernia and Caledonia); listening patiently to old Tradui, the Chieftain's maternal grandfather, telling inter-minable stories of seal hunts when he and the world were young and men and seals stronger and fiercer than they were now.

But all the while, listen as they might, neither he nor Esca heard anything to suggest that the place and the thing they were looking for was nearby. Once or twice, during those days, Marcus glimpsed a black-cloaked figure passing through the dun, remote from the warm and crowded humanity of the tribe and seeming to brood over it as Cruachan brooded over the land. But Druids were everywhere, up here beyond the reach of Rome, just as holy places were everywhere. They did not live among the people, but withdrawn into themselves, in the misty fastnesses of the mountains, in the hidden glens, and among the forests of birch and hazel. Their influence lay heavy on the duns and villages, but no one spoke of them, any more than they spoke of their gods and the prowling ghosts of their forefathers. Neither did anyone ever speak of a captured Eagle. But still Marcus waited, until he knew that the little cub's sight was safe.

And then one evening, returning with Esca from a plunge in the deep water below the dun, he found the Chieftain squatting in his hut-place doorway with his hunting dogs around him, lovingly burnishing a heavy war-spear with a collar of eagles' feathers. Marcus folded up beside him and watched, vividly remembering another war-spear whose collar had been the blue-grey feathers of a heron. Esca stood leaning one shoulder against the rowan-wood doorpost, watching also.

Presently the Chieftain looked up and caught their gaze. 'It is for the Feast of New Spears,' he said. 'For the warrior dancing that comes after.'

'The Feast of New Spears,' Marcus echoed. 'That is when your boys become men, is it not? I have heard of such a feast, but never seen it.'

'You will see in three nights from now; on the Night of the Horned Moon,' Dergdian said, and returned to his burnishing. 'It is a great feast. From all over the tribe, the boys come, and their fathers with them. If it were the King's son, still he must come to us, when it is time for him to receive his weapons.'

'Why?' Marcus asked, and then hoped that he had not sounded too eager.

'We are the keepers of the Holy Place, we, the Seal People,' said Dergdian, turning the spear on his knee. 'We are the guardians of the Life of the Tribe.'

After a long pause, Marcus said casually, 'So. And it is allowed to anyone to witness this mystery of the New Spears?'

'Not the mystery, no; that is between the New Spears and the Horned One, and none save the priest-kind may see and live; but the ceremonies of the forecourt, they are for any who choose to be there. They are not hidden, save from the women's side.'

'Then with your leave I shall most assuredly choose to be

there. We Greeks—we are born asking questions,' Marcus said.

Next day began a bustle of preparation that reminded Marcus of his own Etruscan village on the eve of Saturnalia; and by evening the first inflow of the New Spears had begun; boys and their fathers from the farthest fringes of the tribal lands, riding fine small ponies, wearing their brightest clothes, and many of them with their hounds cantering along beside. Odd, he thought, watching them, odd that people so poor in many ways, hunters and herdsmen who do not till the soil, and live in mud hovels in acute discomfort, should enrich the bridles of their superbly bred ponies with silver and bronze and studs of coral, and clasp their cloaks with buckler-brooches of red Hibernian gold. There was an in-swarming of another kind too, of merchants and fortune-tellers, harpers and horse-dealers, who encamped with the tribe on the level shores of the loch until the whole stretch below the dun was dark with them. It was all warm and gay and human, a market crowd on a large scale, and nowhere any sign of the strangeness that Marcus had expected.

But there was to be strangeness enough before the Feast of New Spears was over.

It began on the second evening, when suddenly the boys who were to receive their weapons were no longer there. Marcus did not see them go; but suddenly they were gone, and behind them the dun was desolate. The men daubed their foreheads with mud; the women gathered together, wailing and rocking in ritual grief. From within the dun and from the encampment below the ramparts the wailing rose as the night drew on, and at the evening meal a place was left empty and a drinking-horn filled and left untouched for every boy who had gone, as for the ghosts of dead warriors at the feast of Samhain; and the women made the death chant through the long hours of darkness.

With morning, the wailing and the lamentation ceased, and in its place there settled on the dun a great quietness and a great sense of waiting. Towards evening the tribe gathered on the level ground beside the loch. The men stood about in groups, each clan keeping to itself. Wolf Clan to Wolf Clan, Salmon to Salmon, Seal to Seal; skin-clad or cloaked in purple or saffron or scarlet, with their weapons in their hands and their dogs padding in and out among them. The women stood apart from the menfolk, many of the young ones with garlands of late summer flowers in their hair: honeysuckle, yellow loose-strife, and the wild white convolvulus. And men and women alike turned constantly to look up into the south-western sky.

Marcus, standing with Esca and Liathan, the Chieftain's brother, on the outskirts of the throng, found himself also looking again and again to the south-west, where the sky was still golden, though the sun had slipped behind the hills.

And then, quite suddenly, there it was, the pale curved feather of the new moon, caught in the fringes of the sunset. Somewhere among the women's side a girl saw it at the same instant, and raised a strange, haunting, half-musical cry that was caught up by the other women, then by the men. From somewhere over the hills, seaward, a horn sounded. No braying war-horn, but a clearer, higher note that seemed per-fectly akin to the pale feather hanging remote in the evening sky.

As though the horn had been a summons, the crowd broke up, and the men moved off in the direction from which it had sounded; a long, ragged train of warriors moving quietly, steadily, leaving the dun to the women, to the very old, and the very young. Marcus went with them, keeping close to Liathan, as he had been told, and suddenly very glad to know that Esca was walking at his shoulder in this strange multitude.

They climbed steadily to the mountain saddle, and came dropping down on the seaward side. They traversed a steep glen and swung out along a ridge. Down again, and another steep climb, and suddenly they were on the lip of a wide upland valley running at an angle to the sea. It lay at their feet, already brimmed with shadows under a sky still webbed and washed with light that seemed to burst upward from the hidden sun; but at its head a great turf mound rose steeply, catching still a faint glow from the sunset on its thorn-crowned crest and the tips of the great standing stones that ringed it round like a bodyguard. Marcus had seen the long barrows of the Ancient People often enough before, but none had caught and held his awareness as this one did, at the head of its lonely valley, between the gold of the sunset and the silver of the new moon.

'Yonder is the Place of Life!' said Liathan's voice in his ear. 'The Life of the Tribe.'

The many-coloured throng had turned northward, winding along the valley towards the Place of Life. The great mound rose higher on their sight, and presently Marcus found himself standing among the Seal People, in the shadow of one of the great standing stones. Before him stretched the emptiness of a wide, roughly paved forecourt, and beyond the emptiness, in the steep mass of the bush-grown mound, a doorway. A doorway whose massive uprights and lintel were of age-eaten granite. A doorway from one world into another, Marcus thought with a chill of awe, closed seemingly by nothing but a skin apron enriched with bosses of dim bronze. Was the lost Eagle of the Hispana somewhere beyond that barbaric entrance? Somewhere in the dark heart of this barrow that was the Place of Life?

There was a sudden hiss and flare of flame, as somebody kindled a torch from the fire-pot they had brought with them.

 The fire seemed to spread almost of its own accord from torch to torch, and several young warriors stepped out from the silent waiting crowd, into the vast emptiness within the standing stones. They carried the flaming brands high above their heads, and the whole scene, which had begun to blur with the fading light, was flooded with a flickering red-gold glare that fell most fiercely on the threshold of that strange doorway, showing the uprights carved with the same curves and spirals that swirled up the standing stones, flashing on the bronze bosses of the sealskin apron so that they became discs

of shifting fire. Sparks whirled upward
on the light, sea-scented wind, and by
contrast with their brightness, the hills
and the dark thorn-crowned crest of the
mound seemed to sink back into the sudden twilight. A man's shape showed for
an instant high among the thorn-trees,
and again the horn sounded its high clear
note; and before the echoes had died
among the hills, the sealskin curtain was
flung back, its bronze discs clashing like
cymbals.

A figure stooped out under the low
lintel into the torchlight. The figure of
a man, stark naked save for the skin of a
grey dog-seal, the head drawn over his
own. The Seal Clan greeted his coming
with a quick, rhythmic cry that rose and
fell and rose again, setting the blood
jumping back to the heart. For an
instant the man—Seal-priest or man-seal—stood before them,
receiving their acclamation, then with the clumsy scuffling
motion of a seal on dry land, moved to one side of the
doorway; and another figure sprang out of the darkness,
hooded with the snarling head of a wolf. One after another
they came, naked as the first had been, their bodies daubed with
strange designs in woad and madder, their head-dresses of
animal pelts or bird-feathers, the wings of a swan, the pelt of
an otter with the tail swinging behind the wearer's back, the
striped hide of a badger shining black and white in the torch-
light. One after another, prancing, leaping, shuffling; men
who were not merely playing the part of animals, but who in
some strange way, impossible of understanding, actually *were*
for the moment the animals whose skins they wore.

One after another they came, until for every clan of the
tribe, a totem priest had joined the grotesque dance—if dance
it could be called, for it was like no dance that Marcus had ever

seen before, and none that he wanted ever to see again. They had swung into a chain, into a circle, hopping, scuffling, bounding, the animal skins swinging behind them. There was no music—indeed music of any sort, however weird, however discordant, seemed worlds away from this dancing; but there seemed to be a pulse beating somewhere—perhaps a hollow log being struck with an open palm—and the dancers took their time from it. Quicker and quicker it beat, like a racing heart, like the heart of a man in fever; and the wheel of dancers spun faster and faster, until, with a wild yell, it seemed to break of its own spinning, and burst back to reveal someone —something—that must have come unnoticed into its midst from the blackness of that doorway in the barrow.

Marcus's throat tightened for an instant as he looked at the figure standing alone in the full red glare of the torches, seeming to burn with its own fierce light. An unforgettable figure of nightmare beauty, naked and superb, crested with a spreading pride of antlers that caught the torch-light on each polished tip, as though every tine bore a point of flame. A man with the antlers of a stag set into his head-dress so that they seemed to grow from his brow—that was all. And yet it was not all; even for Marcus, it was not all. The people greeted him with a deep shout that rose and rose until it was like a wolf-pack howling to the moon; and while he stood with upraised arms, dark power seemed to flow from him as light from a lamp. 'The Horned One! The Horned One!' They were down on their faces, as a swathe of barley going down before the sickle. Without knowing that he did so, Marcus stumbled to his knee; beside him Esca was crouching with his forearm covering his eyes.

When they rose again, the priest-god had drawn back to the threshold of the Place of Life, and was standing there, his arms fallen to his sides. He burst into a spate of speech, of which Marcus could understand just enough to gather that he was telling the tribe that their sons who had died as boys were now reborn as warriors. His voice rose into pealing triumph, passing little by little into a kind of wild chant in which the tribesmen joined. Torches were springing up all along the close-packed throng, and the standing stones were reddened to their crests and seemed to pulse and quiver with the crashing rhythm of the chant.

When the triumphal chanting was at its height, the priest-god turned and called, then moved from before the doorway; and again someone stooped out from the darkness of the entrance into the glare of torches. A red-haired boy in a chequered kilt, at sight of whom the tribesmen sent up a welcoming shout. Another followed, and another, and many more, each greeted with a shout that seemed to burst upward and break in a wave of sound against the standing stones, until fifty or more New Spears were ranged in the great forecourt. They had a little the look of sleep-walkers, and they blinked dazzled eyes in the sudden blaze of torches. The boy next to Marcus kept running his tongue over dry lips, and Marcus could see the quick panting of his breast, as though he had been running—or very much afraid. What had happened to them in the dark, he wondered, remembering his own hour, and the smell of bull's blood in the darkened cave of Mithra.

After the last boy, came one last priest, not a totem priest, as the others had been. His head-dress was made of the burnished feathers of a golden eagle, and a long roar burst from the crowd, as the curtain dropped clashing into place behind him. But to Marcus everything seemed for the moment to have grown very still. For the last comer was carrying something that had once been a Roman Eagle.

XV

VENTURE INTO THE DARK

A MAN stepped out from the ranks of the tribe, stripped and painted as for war, and carrying shield and spear; and at the same instant a boy started forward. The two—they were clearly father and son—came together in the centre of the open space, and the boy stood with shining pride to take shield and spear from his father's hand. Then he turned slowly on his heel, showing himself to the tribe for their acceptance; turned to the place where Cruachan was hidden by the darkness; turned last of all to the new moon, which had strengthened from a pale feather to a sickle of shining silver in a deep-green sky; and brought his spear crashing down across his shield in salute, before following his father, to stand for the first time among the warriors of his tribe.

Another boy stepped out, and another, and another; but Marcus was aware of them only as moving shadows, for his eyes were on the Eagle; the wreck of the Ninth's lost Eagle. The gilded wreaths and crowns that the Legion had won in the days of its honour were gone from the crimson-bound staff; the furious talons still clutched the crossed thunderbolts, but where the great silver wings should have arched back in savage pride, were only empty socket-holes in the flanks of gilded bronze. The Eagle had lost its honours, and lost its wings; and without them, to Demetrius of Alexandria it might have seemed as commonplace as a dunghill cock; but to Marcus it was the Eagle still, in whose shadow his father had died; the lost Eagle of his father's Legion.

He saw very little of the long-drawn ritual that followed, until at last the Eagle had been carried back into the dark, and he found himself part of a triumphal procession led by the New Spears, heading back for the dun: a comet-tail of tossing

torches, a shouting like a victorious army on the homeward march. As they came down the last slope they were met by the smell of roasting meat, for the cooking-pits had been opened. Great fires burned on the open turf below the dun, flowering fiercely red and gold against the remote, sheeny pallor of the loch below, and the women linked hands and came running to join their returning menfolk and draw them home.

Only a few men who were not of the tribe had cared to go with the warriors to the Place of Life. But now the ceremonies were over and it was time for feasting; and traders and soothsayers and harpers had thronged in from the encampment, a party of seal-hunters from another tribe, even the crews of two or three Hibernian ships; they crowded with the warriors of the Epidaii around the fire and feasted nobly on roast meat, while the women, who did not eat with their lords, moved among them with great jars of fiery yellow metheglin, to keep the drinking-horns brimming.

Marcus, sitting between Esca and Liathan at the Chieftain's fire, began to wonder if the whole night was going to be spent like this, in eating and drinking and shouting. If it was, he should go raving mad. He wanted quiet; he wanted to think; and the joyous uproar seemed to beat inside his head, driving all thought out of it. Also he wanted no more metheglin.

Then quite suddenly the feasting was over. The noise and the vast eating and deep drinking had been, maybe, only a shield raised against the too-potent magic that had gone before. Men and women began to draw back, leaving a wide space of empty turf amid the fires; dogs and children were gathered in. Again torches flared up, casting their fierce light on to the empty space. Again there came that sense of waiting. Marcus, finding himself beside the Chieftain's grandfather, turned to the old man, asking under his breath, ' What now? '

' Dancing now,' said the other without looking round. ' See. . . .'

Even as he spoke, the flaming brands were whirled aloft,

and a band of young warriors sprang into the torch-lit circle and began to stamp and whirl in the swift rhythm of a war-dance. And this time, strange and barbaric as it might be, Marcus found this was dancing as he understood the word. Dance followed dance, blending into each other so that it was hard to tell where one ended and another began. Sometimes it would seem that the whole men's side was dancing, and the ground would tremble under their stamping heels. Some-times it would be only a chosen few who leapt and whirled and crouched in mimic hunting or warfare, while the rest raised the terrifying music of the British before battle by droning across their shield-rims. Only the women never danced at all, for the Feast of New Spears had nothing to do with womenkind.

The moon had long since set, and only the fierce light of fire and torches lit the wild scene, the twisting bodies and brandished weapons, when at last two rows of warriors stepped out on to the trampled turf and stood facing each other. They were stripped to the waist like the rest of the men's side, and carried shield and feathered war spear; and Marcus saw that one rank was made up of the boys who had become men that day, and the other of their fathers who had armed them.

'It is the Dance of the New Spears,' Esca told him as the two lines swept together with upraised shields. 'So, we dance it, too, we the Brigantes, on the night our boys become men.'

On his other side Tradui leaned towards him, asking, 'Do not your people hold the Feast of New Spears?'

'We hold a feast,' Marcus said, 'but it is not like this. All this is strange to me, and I have seen many things tonight that make me wonder.'

'So?—and these things?' The old man, having got over his first annoyance with Marcus over the toad's fat, had gradually become more friendly as the days went by; and tonight, warmed still further by the feasting and the metheglin, he was eager to enlighten the stranger within his gates. 'I will explain them to you, these things at which you wonder; for you are young and doubtless wish to know, and I am old and by far the wisest man in my tribe.'

M

If he went warily, Marcus realized, here might be a chance to gather certain information that he needed. 'Truly,' he said, 'wisdom shines from Tradui the Chieftain's grandsire, and my ears are open.' And he settled himself, with a most flattering show of interest, to ask and listen. It was slow work, but little by little, drawing the old man on with all the skill he possessed, listening patiently to a great deal that was of no use to him whatever, he gathered the scraps of knowledge that he needed. He learned that the priest-kind had their living-place in the birchwoods below the Place of Life, and that no guard was kept over the holy place, no watch of attendant priests.

'What need?' said the old man when Marcus showed surprise at this. 'The Place of Life has guardians of its own, and who would dare to meddle with that which is of the Horned One?' He broke off, abruptly, as though catching himself in the act of speaking of forbidden things, and stretched out an old thick-veined hand with the fingers spread horn-wise.

But presently he began to talk again. Under the influence of the metheglin and the torch-light and the dancing, he, too, was remembering his own night: the long-ago night when he had been a New Spear, and danced for the first time the warrior dances of the tribe. Never taking his eyes from the whirling figures, he told of old fights, old cattle-raids, long-dead heroes who had been his sword-brothers when the world was young and the sun hotter than it was now. Pleased at finding an attentive listener who had not heard the story before, he told of a great hosting of the tribes, no more than ten or twelve autumns ago; and how he had gone south with the rest— though some fools had said that he was too old for the war-trail, even then—to stamp out a great army of the Red Crests. And how, having given them to the wolf and to the raven, they had brought back the Eagle-god that the Red Crests carried before them, and given it to the gods of his own people in the Place of Life. The Healer of sore eyes must have seen it tonight when it was carried out and shown to the men's side?

Marcus sat very still, his hands linked round his updrawn knees, and watched the sparks fly upward from the whirling torches.

'I saw it,' he said. 'I have seen such Eagle gods before, and I wondered to see it here. We are always curious, we Greeks; also we have small cause to love Rome. Tell me more of how you took this Eagle-god from the Red Crests; I should like to hear that story.'

It was the story that he had heard once already, from Guern the Hunter; but told from the opposite side; and where Guern's story had ended, this one went on.

Much as he might tell of a bygone hunting that had been good, the old warrior told how he and his sword-brethren had hunted down the last remnants of the Ninth Legion, closing round them as a wolf-pack closes round its prey. The old man told it without a shadow of pity, without a shadow of understanding for the agony of his quarry; but with a fierce admiration that lit his face and sounded in every word.

'I was an old man even then, and it was my last fight, but *what* a fight! Ayee! Worthy to be the last fight of Tradui the Warrior! Many a night when the fire sinks low, and even the battles of my youth grow thin and cold, I have kept warm thinking of that fight! We brought them to bay at last in the bog country a day north of the place they call the Three Hills; and they turned like a boar at bay. We were flushed with easy triumph, for until that day it had been very easy. They crumbled at a prick, but that day it was not so. Those others had been but the flakings of the flint, and these were the core; a small core, so small. . . . They faced outward all ways, with the winged god upreared in their midst; and when we broke their shield-wall, one would step over his fallen brother, and lo, the shield-wall would be whole as before. We pulled them down at last—aye, but they took a goodly escort of our warriors with them. We pulled them down until there were left but a knot—as many as there are fingers on my two hands—and the winged god still in their midst. I, Tradui, I slew with my last throw-spear the priest in the spotted hide who held the staff; but another caught it from him as he fell, and held it so that the winged god did not go down, and rallied the few who were left, yet again.   He was a chieftain among the rest, he had a taller crest, and his cloak was of the warrior scarlet. I wish that it had been I who killed him, but one was before me. . . .

'Well, we made an end.   There will be no more Red Crests going to and fro in our hunting grounds.   We left them to the raven and the wolf, and also to the bog.   Bog country is swift to swallow the traces of fighting.   Yes, and we brought back the winged god; we, the Epidaii, claiming it as our right because it was the warriors of the Epidaii who were First Spear at the killing.   But there was heavy rain later, and the rivers coming down in spate; and at a ford the warrior who carried the god was swept away, and though we found the god again (three lives it cost us, in the finding), the wings, which were not one with it but fitted into holes in its body, were gone from it, and so were the shining wreaths that hung from its staff; so that when we brought it to the Place of Life it was as you saw it tonight.   Still, we gave it to the Horned One for tribute, and surely the Horned One was well pleased, for have not our wars gone well for us ever since, and the deer waxed fat in our hunting runs?   And I will tell you another thing concerning the Eagle-god; it is ours now, ours, the Epidaii's; but if ever the day comes when we host against the Red Crests again, when the Cran-tara goes out through Albu, calling the tribes to war, the Eagle-god will be as a spear in the hand of all the tribes of Albu, and not of the Epidaii alone.'

The bright old eyes turned at last, consideringly, to Marcus's face.   'He was like you, that Chieftain of the Red Crests; yes. And yet you say that you are a Greek.   Surely that is strange?'

Marcus said, 'There are many of Greek blood among the Red Crests.'

'So.   That might be it.'   The old man began to fumble under the shoulder-folds of the chequered cloak he wore.   'They were truly warriors, and we left them their weapons, as befits warriors. . . .   But from that chieftain I took this for the virtue in it, as one takes the tush from a boar who was fierce and valiant above others of his kind; and I have worn it ever since.' He had found what he wanted now, and slipped a leather thong from about his neck. ' It will not go on my hand,' he added, almost fretfully. ' It must be that the Red Crests had narrower hands than we have. Take it and look.'

A ring swung on the end of the thong, sparkling faintly with green fire in the torch-light. Marcus took it from him and bent his head to examine it. It was a heavy signet-ring; and on the flawed emerald which formed the bezel was engraved the dolphin badge of his own family. He held it for a long moment, held it very gently, as if it were a living thing, watching the torch-light play in the green heart of the stone. Then he gave it back into the old man's waiting hand with a casual word of thanks, and turned his attention again to the dancers. But the fierce whirl of the dance was blurred on his sight, for suddenly, across twelve years and more, he was looking up at a dark, laughing man who seemed to tower over him. There were pigeons wheeling behind the man's bent head, and when he put up his hand to rub his forehead, the sunlight that rimmed the pigeons' wings with fire caught the flawed emerald of the signet-ring he wore.

All at once, with over much finding-out for one day, Marcus was tired to the depths of his soul.

．　　　．　　　．　　　．　　　．

Next morning, sitting on an open hill-shoulder where they could not be overheard, Marcus laid his plans very carefully with Esca.

He had already told the Chieftain that he was for starting south again next day, and the Chieftain, and indeed the whole dun, were loath to let him go. Let him stay until spring; maybe there would be more sore eyes for him to salve.

But Marcus had remained firm, saying that he wished to be in the south again before the winter closed in, and now, with the great gathering for the Feast of New Spears breaking up and going its separate ways, was surely the time for him to be going too.   The friendliness of the tribesmen gave him no sense of guilt in what he was going to do.   They had welcomed and sheltered him and Esca, and in return Esca had hunted and herded with them, and he had doctored their sore eyes with all the skill that he possessed.   In all that there was no debt on either side, no room for guilt.   In the matter of the Eagle, they were the enemy, an enemy worthy of his steel.   He liked and respected them; let them keep the Eagle if they could.

That last day passed very quietly.   Having laid their plans and made what few preparations were needful, Marcus and Esca sat in the sun, doing—to all outward seeming—nothing in particular, save watch the delicate flight of the sand-pipers above the still waters of the loch.   Towards evening they bathed; not their usual plunge and splash about for pleasure, but a ritual cleansing in readiness for whatever the night might bring.   Marcus made his sunset prayers to Mithras, Esca made them to Lugh of the Shining Spear; but both these were Sun Gods, Light Gods, and their followers knew the same weapons against the dark.   So they cleaned themselves for the fight, and ate as little as might be at the evening meal, lest a full stomach should blunt their spirits within them.

When the time came for sleep, they lay down as usual with Tradui and the dogs and Liathan in the great living-hut; lay down in the places nearest to the door, which also was usual with them, for they had always had it in mind that a time might come when they would wish to leave quietly in the night. Long after the rest were asleep, Marcus lay watching the red embers of the fire, while every nerve in his body twanged taut as an overdrawn bowstring; and beside him he could hear Esca breathing quietly, evenly, as he always breathed in sleep. Yet it was Esca, with a hunter's instinct for the passing of the night, who knew when midnight was gone by—the time at which the priest-kind would be making the nightly offering— and the Place of Life would be deserted again; and told Marcus so with a touch.

They got up silently, and slipped out of the hut.   The

hounds raised no outcry, for they were used to night-time comings and goings. Marcus dropped the deerskin apron silently into place behind him, and they made for the nearby gateway. They had no difficulty in getting out, for with the dun full of guests and so many of the tribe encamped outside, the thorn-trees that usually blocked the gate at night had not been set in place. They had counted on that.

Turning away from the camp-fires, the sleeping men, and the familiar things of this world, they struck off uphill, and the night engulfed them. It was a very still night, with a faint thunder haze dimming the stars, and once or twice as they walked a flicker of summer lightning danced along the sky-line. The moon had long since set, and in the darkness and the brooding quiet the mountains seemed to have drawn closer than by day; and as they dropped downward into the valley of the Place of Life, the blackness rose around them like water.

Esca had brought them into the valley from its head, behind the Place of Life, where the sun-dried turf would make no sound at their passing, and carry no track afterwards. But in one place the heather came down almost to the foot of the standing-stones, and he stooped and broke off a long switch of it, and thrust it into the strap about his waist. They reached the lower end of the temple, and stood for what seemed a long time to listen for any sound; but the silence was like wool in their ears; not a bird cried, even the sea was silent tonight. No sound in all the world save the quickened drubbing of their own hearts. They passed between the standing stones and stood in the paved forecourt.

The black mass of the barrow rose above them, its crest of thorn-trees upreared against the veiled stars. The massive granite uprights and lintel were a faint pallor against the surrounding turf; it swelled on their sight as they walked towards it. They were on the threshold.

Marcus said softly but very clearly, ' In the Name of Light,' and feeling for the edge of the sealskin curtain, lifted it back. The bronze discs on it grated and chimed very faintly as he did

so. He ducked under the low lintel, Esca beside him, and the
curtain swung back into place. The black darkness seemed to
press against his eyes, against his whole body, and with the
darkness, the atmosphere of the place. The atmosphere:
it was not evil, exactly, but it was horribly personal. For
thousands of years this place had been the centre of a dark
worship, and it was as though they had given to it a living
personality of its own. Marcus felt that at any moment he
would hear it breathe, slowly and stealthily, like a waiting
animal. . . . For an instant sheer panic rose in his throat, and
as he fought it down, he was aware of a rustle and a faint glow,
as Esca fetched out from under his cloak the fire-pot and glim
they had brought with them. Next instant a tiny tongue of
flame sprang up, sank to a spark, and rose again, as the wick
in its lump of beeswax caught. Esca's bent face grew suddenly
out of the dark as he tended the little flame. As it steadied,
Marcus saw that they were in a passage, walled, floored, and
roofed with great slabs of stone. How long it might be there
was no guessing, for the little light could find no end to it. He
held out his hand for the glim. Esca gave it to him, and holding
it high he walked forward, leading the way. The passage was
too narrow for two to walk abreast.

A hundred paces, the darkness giving back unwillingly
before them, crowding hungrily in behind, and they stood on
the threshold of what must once have been the tomb chamber,
and saw, set close before them on the slightly raised flagstone
at the entrance, a shallow and most beautifully wrought amber
cup filled to the brim with something that gleamed darkly and
stickily red in the light of the glim. Deer's blood, maybe, or
the blood of a black cock. Beyond, all was shadow, but as
Marcus moved forward with the light, past the midnight
offering, the shadows drew back, and he saw that they were
standing in a vast circular chamber, the stone walls of which
ran up out of the candle-light and seemed to bend together
high overhead into some kind of dome. Two recesses at either
side of the chamber were empty, but there was a third in the
far wall, opposite the entrance. In it, too far off for any spark

of light to catch its gilded feathers, something was propped a little drunkenly, blotted dark against the stones; that must surely be the Eagle of the Ninth Legion.

Otherwise the place was empty, and its emptiness seemed to add a hundredfold to its menace. Marcus did not know what he had expected to find here, but he had not expected to find nothing—nothing at all, save that in the exact centre of the floor lay a great ring of what appeared to be white jadite, a foot or more across, and a superbly shaped axehead of the same material, arranged so that one corner of the blade very slightly overlapped the ring.

That was all.

Esca's hand was on his arm, and his voice whispering urgently in his ear: ' It is strong magic. Do not touch it! '

Marcus shook his head. He was not going to touch it.

They made their way round the thing, and reached the recess in the far wall. Yes, it was the Eagle all right.

' Take the glim,' Marcus whispered.

He lifted it from its place, realizing as he did so that the last Roman hand to touch the stained and battered shaft had been his father's. An odd, potent link across the years, and he held to it as to a talisman, as he set about freeing the Eagle from its staff.

' Hold the light this way—a little higher. Yes, keep it so.'

Esca obeyed, steadying the shaft with his free hand that Marcus might have both hands free to work with. It would have been easier to have lain the thing on the ground and knelt down to it, but both of them had a feeling that they must remain on their feet, that to kneel down would put them at a disadvantage with the Unknown. The light fell on the heads of the four slim bronze pegs that passed through the Eagle's talons, securing them through the crossed thunderbolts to the shaft. They should have drawn out easily enough, but they had become corroded into their holes, and after trying for a few moments to shift them with his fingers, Marcus drew his dagger, and began to lever them up with that. They came, but they came slowly. It was going to take some time—some time here in this horrible place that was like a crouching animal waiting to spring at any moment. The first peg came out, and he slipped it into his belt and began on the second. Panic began to whimper up from his stomach again, and again he thrust it down. No good hurrying; once he started to hurry he would never get these pegs out. For a moment he turned over in his mind the idea of taking the whole standard outside and finding some hide-out among the heather, and doing the job in the clean open air. But the job would have to be done, for the whole standard was too big to hide in the place that they had in mind; time was limited, and he could not work quickly without light, and light, anywhere outside, might betray them, however carefully they shielded it. No, this was the one place where they might be safe from interruption (for unless something went wrong, the priest-kind would not return until the next midnight)—from the interruption of men, that was.

Marcus begun to feel that he could not breathe. ' Quietly,' he told himself. ' Breathe quietly; don't hurry.' The second pin came out, and he thrust it into his belt with the other; and as Esca turned the shaft over, began on the third. It came more easily, and he had just started on the fourth and last, when it seemed to him that he could not see as clearly as he had done a few moments ago. He looked up, and saw Esca's face shining with sweat in the upward light of the glim; but surely the glim was giving less light than it had done? Even as he looked, the tiny flame began to sink, and the dark came crowding on.

It might be only bad air, or a fault in the wick—or it might not. He said urgently, ' Think Light! Esca, *think Light*! " And even as he spoke, the flame sank to a blue spark. Beside him he heard Esca's breath, whistling through flaring nostrils; his own heart had begun to race, and he felt not only the many-fingered dark, but the walls and roof themselves closing in on him, suffocating him as though a soft cold hand was pressed over his nose and mouth. He had a sudden hideous conviction that there was no longer a straight passage and a leather curtain between them and the outer world, only the earth-piled mountain high over them, and no way out. No way out! The darkness reached out to finger him, softly. He braced himself upright against the cold stones, putting out his will to force the walls back, fighting the evil sense of suffocation. He was doing as he had told Esca to do, thinking Light with all the strength that was in him, so that in his inner eye, the place was full of it: strong, clear light flowing into every cranny. Suddenly he remembered the flood of sunset light in his sleeping-cell at Calleva, that evening when Esca and Cub and Cottia had come to him in his desperate need. He called it up now, like golden water, like a trumpet call, the Light of Mithras. He hurled it against the darkness, forcing it back—back—back.

How long he stood like that he never knew, until he saw the blue spark strengthen slowly, sink a little, and then lick up suddenly into a clear, small flame. It might have been only a fault in the wick. . . . He realized that he was breathing in great shuddering gasps, and the sweat was running down his face and breast. He looked at Esca, and Esca returned his look; neither of them spoke. Then he started again on the fourth pin. It was the most stubborn of the lot, but it yielded at last, and Eagle and thunderbolts came loose in his hands. He lifted them off with a long, shaken breath, and sheathed his dagger. Now that it was done, he wanted to fling the staff aside and make a blind dash for the open air, but he schooled himself to take the staff from Esca and return it to its place in the recess, to lay the thunderbolts and the four bronze pegs on the floor beside it, before he turned at last to go, carrying the Eagle in the crook of his arm.

Esca had taken the branch of heather from his belt, and, still carrying the glim, followed him, moving backward to brush out any recognizable tracks they might have left in the dust. His own tracks, Marcus knew, were all to easily recognizable, because, however hard he tried not to, he dragged his right leg a little.

It seemed a long way round to the other side of the tomb chamber, and every few instants Esca glanced hastily aside to the ring and the axehead, as though they were a snake about to strike. But they gained the mouth of the entrance passage at last, and began to make their way down it; Esca still switching out their trail. Marcus moved sideways along the wall, guarding his own back and his friend's. Esca's crouching figure blotted out most of the light from the glim he carried, save where it fell on the dusty flag-stones and the flicking heather-switch, and his shadow swallowed up their way, so that every step Marcus took was into the edge of the darkness. The passage seemed much longer than it had done when they fóllowed it inward; so long that a new nightmare grew on Marcus that either there were two passages and they had chosen the wrong one, or the only one had ceased, since their coming in, to have any end.

But the end was still there. Suddenly Esca's giant shadow ran on to the sealskin curtain, and they had reached it.

'Get ready to douse the light,' Marcus said.

The other glanced round without a word. Marcus's hand was on the curtain when they were plunged in darkness. He drew it back slowly, with infinite care, ears and eyes straining for any hint of danger, and the two of them ducked out under the lintel. He let the curtain ease back into place behind them, and stood with his hand on Esca's shoulder, drawing in great gasps of the clean night air with its scent of bog myrtle and its salt tang of the sea, and gazing up at the veiled stars. It seemed to him that they had been many hours in the dark; but the stars had swung only a little way on their courses since he saw them last. The summer lightning was still flickering along the hills. He realized that Esca was shuddering from head to foot, like a horse that smells fire, and tightened his hand on his friend's shoulder.

'We are out,' he said. 'We are through. It is over. Steady, old wolf.'

Esca answered him with a shaken breath of laughter. ' It is that I want to be sick.'

'So do I,' Marcus said. 'But we have no time, just now. This is no place to wait in until we are discovered by the priest-kind. Come.'

Some while later, having recrossed the hills and fetched a wide half-circle round the dun and encampment, they emerged from the steeply falling woods on to the bleak shores of the loch, just where a spit of rough turf and boulders laced together with alder scrub ran out from the grey shingle beach. Just above the beach they halted, and Esca hurriedly stripped. 'Now give me the Eagle.' He took it, handling it reverently, though it had been no Eagle of his; and a moment later Marcus was alone. He stood with one hand on a low-hanging rowan branch, and watched the pale blur that was Esca's body slip down through the alder scrub, and come out on the spit of land below. There was the tiniest splash as of a fish leaping, then silence; only the water lapping on the lonely shore, and then the faint mutter of thunder a long way off, and a night bird cried eerily in the heavy silence. For what seemed a long time, he waited, eyes straining into the darkness, and then suddenly a pale blur moved again on the spit, and a few moments later Esca was beside him once again, wringing the water out of his hair.

'Well?' Marcus murmured.

'It fits into the place under the bank like a nut into a nut-shell,' Esca told him. 'They might search till the loch runs dry, and never find it; but I shall know the place when I come again.'

The next danger was that their absence would have been noticed; but when they came to the dun again, and passed unseen through the gateway, all was quiet. They were none too soon. The sky was still black—blacker than at their setting out, for the cloud had thickened, blotting out the stars. But the smell of the day-spring was in the air, unmistakable as that other smell of thunder. They slipped in through the hut-place doorway. In the darkness only the embers of the fire glowed like red jewels, and nothing moved. Then a dog growled, half sleepily, green-eyed in the gloom, and there was a sudden stirring and an equally sleepy murmur of inquiry from Liathan, who lay nearest to the door.

' It is only I,' Marcus said. ' Vipsania was restless; it's the thunder in the air. Always it makes her restless.'

He lay down. Esca also lay down, curled close to the fire, that he might not have damp hair to explain in the morning. Silence settled again over the sleeping-hut.

XVI

THE RING-BROOCH

A FEW hours later Marcus and Esca took their leave of the Dun, and started out, riding through a world that was clear-washed and as deeply coloured as a purple grape, after the thunderstorm which had finally broken over them at dawn. Southwards they went at first, following the shores of the loch to its foot, then north-east by a herding path through the mountains that brought them down towards evening to the shores of another loch, a long sea-loch this time, loud with the crying of shore-birds. That night they slept in a village that was no more than a cluster of turf bothies clinging to the narrow shore between the mountains and the grey water, and next morning set out again for the head of the loch, where there was a village through which they had passed before.

All that day they rode easily, breathing the horses often. Marcus was eager to be out of this land of sea lochs, through which one had to zigzag like a snipe, in which one could so easily become trapped and entangled, but it was no good getting too far from the Place of Life before the next move in the game could be played. The loss of the Eagle would have been discovered at midnight, when the priest went to renew the offering, and suspicion, though it would be widespread over all outside the tribe who had gathered to the Feast of New Spears, would certainly fall most heavily on himself and Esca. So the tribe would be up and after them long before now. Knowing the way that they had taken, Marcus reckoned that their pursuers could be up with them not long after noon if they crossed the loch by coracle and commandeered ponies on the near shore, as they undoubtedly would do. But he had forgotten to allow for the difficulties of the few mountain passes, and it was much later than he had expected when at last his ear caught the soft drumming of unshod hooves a long way off; and looking back, he saw a ragged skein of six or seven horsemen coming at break-neck speed down a steep side-glen towards them. He drew a quick breath that was almost of relief, for it had been a nerve-racking business waiting for them. ' Here they come at last,' he said to Esca; and then as a distant yell echoed down the mountainside, ' hear how the hounds give tongue.'

Esca laughed quietly, his eyes bright with the excitement of danger. ' Sweff! Sweff! ' he encouraged them softly. ' Do we ride on, or rein in and wait for them? '

' Rein in and wait,' Marcus decided. ' They will know that we have seen them.'

They wheeled the mares, and sat waiting while the skein of wild riders swept towards them, the ponies sure-footed as goats among the rocks of the steep glen. ' Mithra! What cavalry they would make! ' Marcus said, watching them. Vipsania was uneasy; she fidgeted and side-stepped, blowing down her nose, her ears pricked forward, and he patted her neck reassuringly. The tribesmen had reached the low ground now, and swung into the long curve of the lochside; and a few moments later they were up with the two who waited for them, and reining back their ponies in full gallop, dropped to the ground.

Marcus looked them over as they crowded in on him, seven warriors of the tribe, Dergdian and his brother among them. He took in their ugly looks, and the war-spears they carried, and his face was puzzled and inquiring. ' Dergdian? Liathan? What is it that you want with me, in so much haste? '

' You know well enough what it is that we want with you,' Dergdian said. His face was set like a stone, and his hand tightened on the shaft of his spear.

' But I fear that I do not,' Marcus said in a tone of rising annoyance, pretending not to notice that two of the tribesmen, leaving their own mounts standing, had gone to Vipsania's and Minna's heads. ' You will have to tell me.'

' Yes, we will tell you,' an older hunter cut in. ' We come

to take back the winged god; also for blood to wash out the insult that you have put upon us and upon the gods of our tribe.'

The others broke into a threatening outcry, pressing in on the two, who had by now dismounted also. Marcus faced them with a pucker of bewilderment between his black brows. ' The winged god? ' he repeated. ' The Eagle-god that we saw carried at the Feast of New Spears? Why, you——' Light seemed to dawn on him. ' You mean that you have lost it? '

' We mean that it is stolen, and we are come to take it back from those who robbed us,' Dergdian said very softly; and the softness was as though a cold finger gently stroked Marcus's spine.

He looked into the other's face with slowly widening eyes. ' And it must needs be I who stole it? ' he said, and then flared out at them. ' Why in the name of the Thunderer should I want a wingless Roman Eagle? '

' You might have had your reasons,' said the Chieftain in the same soft voice.

' I cannot think of any.'

The tribesmen were growing impatient; there were shouts of ' Kill! kill! ' And they crowded closer; fierce, rage-darkened faces were thrust into Marcus's and a spear was shaken before his eyes. ' Kill the thieves! There has been enough of talking! '

Startled by the angry turmoil, Vipsania was flinging this way and that, showing the whites of her eyes, and Minna squealed, going up in a rearing turn as she tried to break from the man who held her, and was forced down again by a blow between the ears.

Marcus raised his voice above the tumult. ' Is it the custom of the Seal People to hunt down and slay those who have been their guests? Well do the Romans call the men of the North barbarians.'

The shouting sank to a sullen, menacing mutter, and he went on more quietly.

' If you are so sure that we have stolen the Red Crests' god
N

you have but to search our gear, and you will surely find it. Search, then.'

The muttering grew fiercer, and Liathan had already turned to Esca's mare, stretching out his hand to the fastening of the pack. Marcus moved distastefully aside, and stood watching. Esca's hand tightened for an instant on the shaft of his spear, as though he longed to use it; then he shrugged, and swung away to join Marcus. Together they watched their few possessions tumbled on the grass; a couple of cloaks, a cooking-pot, some strips of smoked deer-meat flung out with rough haste. The lid of the bronze medicine box was wrenched back, and one of the hunters began to rummage inside like a little dog after a rat. Marcus said quietly to the Chieftain, who stood beside him with folded arms, also looking on, ' Will you bid your hounds be less rough with the tools of my trade. It may be that there are still sore eyes in Albu, though your small son's eyes are well.'

Dergdian flushed at the reminder, and glanced aside at him for an instant, with a kind of sullen half-shame; then he spoke sharply to the man who was delving among the salves. ' Softly, you fool; there is no need that you should break the medicine sticks.'

The man growled, but handled the things more carefully thereafter. Meanwhile the others had unfolded and shaken out the sheepskin saddle-pads, and all but torn the bronze ring-brooch out of a violet-coloured cloak by their rough handling.

' Are you satisfied now?' Marcus asked, when everything had been turned inside out, and the tribesmen stood about, baffled and empty-handed, staring down at the chaos they had made. ' Or is it that you would search us to the skin?' He held out his arms, and their eyes ran over him, over Esca. It was perfectly obvious that they could have nothing a tenth the size and weight of the Eagle hidden on them.

The Chieftain shook his head. 'We must cast our net wider, it seems.'

The tribesmen were all known to Marcus, at least by sight; they looked bewildered, sullen, a little shamed, and they found it hard to meet his eyes. At a gesture from the Chieftain they began to gather up the scattered objects and bundle them, with the torn cloak with its dangling ring-brooch, into the pack-cloth. Liathan stooped to the disembowelled medicine box, glancing up at Marcus, and then away again.

They had offended against their own laws of hospitality. They had hunted down two who had been their guests, and not found the winged god, after all. 'Come back with us,' said the Chieftain. 'Come back with us, lest our hearths are shamed.'

Marcus shook his head. 'We are for the South, before the year closes in. Go and cast your net wider for this wingless winged god of yours. We shall remember that we have been your guests, Esca and I.' He smiled. 'The rest we have already forgotten. Good hunting to you on the game trails this winter.'

When the tribesmen had whistled up their own ponies, who had stood quietly by all this while with their reins over their heads, and, remounting, set off back the way they had come, Marcus did not move at once. He stood gazing after the dwindling specks up the glen, with a queer regret, while his hand mechanically soothed and fondled his upset and angry mare.

'Do you wish the Eagle yet in the place we took it from?' Esca asked.

Marcus was still watching those dwindling specks, almost out of sight now. 'No,' he said. 'If it were yet in the place we took it from, it would be still a danger to the Frontier—a danger to other Legions. Also it was my father's Eagle and none of theirs. Let them keep it if they can. Only it is in my heart that I wish we need not have made Dergdian and his sword-brethren ashamed.'

They saw to their gear, tightened the ponies' belly-straps, and rode on.

Presently the loch began to narrow, and the mountains to crowd in on it, rising almost sheer from the water's edge; and at last they caught sight of the village; the distant huddle of turf bothies at the head of the loch, cattle grazing up the steep

glen behind, and the straight blue smoke of cooking-fires rising
pale against the sombre browns and purples of the mountains
that towered above them.

'It is time that I sickened of the fever,' said Esca, and
without more ado he began to sway from side to side, his eyes
half closed. 'My head!' he croaked. 'My head is on fire.'

Marcus reached out and took the reins from him. 'Slump
a little more and roll a little less; it is fever, not metheglin,
that lit the fire, remember,' he directed, beginning to lead the
other horse with his own.

The usual crowd of men and women, children and boys
gathered to meet them as they entered the village, and here and
there, people called out a greeting to them, glad in their remote
way to see them back again. With Esca slumped over Minna's
neck beside him, Marcus singled out the ancient headman,
greeted him with due courtesy, and explained that his servant
was sick and must rest a few days; two days, three at the most.
It was an old sickness that returned from time to time, and
would last no longer, given proper treatment.

The headman replied that they were welcome to share his
fireside, as they had done when they passed that way before.
But to that, Marcus shook his head. 'Give us some place to
ourselves; it matters not how rough, so long as it will keep out
the weather. But let it be as far from your living-huts as may
be. This sickness of my servant is caused by devils in his
belly, and to drive them out it is needful that I use strong magic.'
He paused, and looked round at the questioning faces. 'It
will do no harm to this village, but it cannot be looked upon
safely by any who have not the signs for protection. That is
why we must have lodging apart from the living-huts.'

They looked at each other. 'It is always dangerous to look
upon forbidden things,' said a woman, accepting the story
without surprise. There could be no question of refusing them
shelter; Marcus knew the laws of the tribes. They talked the
matter over quickly among themselves, and finally decided
that Conn's cow-byre, which was not now in use, would be the
best place.

Conn's cow-byre proved to be the usual turf bothy, exactly like the living-huts, save that it was not set so far below ground-level, and there was no hearth in the centre of the trampled earthen floor. It was well away from the main rath, with its doorway at an angle that would make it possible to slip out and in without showing up too clearly to any watchers among the living-huts. So far, so good.

The villagers, feeling perhaps that a man who could conjure out devils was best treated kindly, did their best for the two returned strangers; and by dusk the mares had been taken in charge, fresh fern stacked inside the hut for bedding, an old skin rug skewered up over the doorway; and the women had brought broiled boar's flesh for Marcus, and warm ewe's milk for Esca, who lay on the piled bracken, moaning and babbling most realistically.

Later, with the deerskin rug drawn close across the door, and the villagers crowded about their own hearths with faces and thoughts carefully turned from the outlying bothy and the magic that would be a-making there, Marcus and Esca looked at each other by the faint light of a floating reed-wick in a shell of rancid seal oil. Esca had eaten the lion's share of the meat, for he would need it most; and now, with a few strips of smoked deer meat thrust into the middle of a rolled-up cloak, he stood ready to go.

At the last moment, Marcus said savagely, ' Oh, curse this leg of mine! It should be me going back, not you.'

The other shook his head. ' That leg of yours makes no difference. If it were as sound as mine, still it would be better, quicker, and safer that I should go. You could not leave this place and return to it in the dark, without rousing the dogs; but I can. You could not find your way through the passes that we have traversed only once before. It is work for a hunter—a hunter born and bred, not a soldier who has learned a little forest-craft.' And he reached up to the little stinking lamp hanging from the roof tree, and pinched it out.

Marcus drew back a fold of the rug and peered out into the soft darkness of the mountains. Away to the right, a solitary glint of gold shone from the chink in a deerskin apron over a distant doorway. The moon was behind the mountains, and the waters of the loch were only a lesser darkness, without spark or lustre.

' All is clear,' he said.   ' You are sure you can find the way? '

' Yes.'

' Good hunting, then, Esca.'

A dark shadow slipped past him, and was gone into the night.   And he was alone.

He stood for a while in the bothy doorway, ears stretched for any sound to break the silence of the mountains, but heard only the wet whisper of falling water where the swift stream came tumbling into the loch, and a long while later, the belling of a stag.   When he was sure that Esca had got clear away, he dropped the rug.   He did not re-light the lamp, but sat for a long time on the piled bracken in the pitchy darkness, with his arms across his knees, thinking.   His one comfort was the sure knowledge that if Esca ran into trouble, he himself would very soon share it.

For three nights and two days Marcus kept guard over an empty hut.   Twice a day one of the women, with face averted, would bring broiled meat and fresh ewe milk, sometimes herrings, once a golden lump of wild honeycomb, and set them on a flat stone a little way off, and Marcus would collect them and later take back the empty bowls.   After the first day there were only women and children in the village; evidently the men had gone to answer some call from the dun.   He wondered whether he ought to provide noises for the benefit of the village, but decided that silence would probably be more effective; so save for a little muttering and moaning when he thought some-one was near enough to hear, just enough to keep it in their mind that there were two people in the bothy, he remained silent. He slept when he could, but he did not dare to sleep much, for fear that trouble should blow up suddenly when he was not on the alert for it.   Most of his time, day or night, was spent sitting just within the doorway watching, through a back-drawn chink in the rug, the grey waters of the loch and the sheer, boulder-strewn upward thrust of the mountains towering so high above him that he had to tip his head far back to see their jagged crests where the mist-rags trailed among the peaks and the high corries.

Autumn had come to the mountains almost overnight, he thought. A few days ago, summer had still lingered, though the heather was past its flowering and the flaming rowan berries long since gone. But now it was the Fall of the Leaf; one could smell it in the wind, and the trees of the glen grew bare and the brawling stream ran gold with yellow birch leaves.

Some while after moonset on the third night, without any warning, a hand brushed across the skin rug at the entrance, and as Marcus tensed in the close darkness, he heard the faintest ghost of a whistle: the broken, two-note whistle that he had always used to summon Cub. A sudden wave of relief broke over him, and he echoed the whistle. The rug was drawn aside and a black shape slipped through.

'Is it well?' Esca whispered.

'It is well,' Marcus returned, striking flint and steel to kindle the lamp. 'And with you? How went the hunting?'

'The hunting was good,' Esca said, as the tiny flame sprang up and steadied, and he stooped and set down something closely bundled in the cloak.

Marcus looked at it. 'Was there any trouble?'

'None, save that I pulled the bank down a little in landing with the Eagle. It must have been rotten, I suppose—but there is nothing in a bank slip to set anyone thinking.' He sat down wearily. 'Is there anything to eat?'

Marcus had made a habit of saving each meal that he was given, and eating it only when the next one came, so that he always had a meal in hand, packed into the old cooking-pot. He produced it now, and sat with his hand resting on the bundle that meant so much to him, while he watched the other eat, and listened to the story of the last three days, told in low snatches between mouthfuls.

Esca had cut back across the mountains without much difficulty, but by the time he reached the Loch of Many Islets

it had been near to dawn, and he had had to lie up in the dense
hazel-woods through the day. Twice during the day parties
of warriors had passed close to his hiding-place, carrying
coracles, and evidently bound, like himself, for the dun by the
short way across the loch. Also they had been carrying war-
spears, he said. As soon as it was dark, he had set out once
again to swim the loch. It was little more than a mile across
at the place he chose, and that, too, had not been difficult.
He had worked his way down the far shore until he came to the
spit of land that marked the place where they had hidden the
Eagle; found it, and landed again, pulling down the bank
a little in doing so, and bundled it in the wet cloak that he had
carried bound to his shoulder. Then he had returned the way
he came as fast as might be, for the dun was thrumming like a
disturbed bees' nest. Of a certainty the tribe was hosting. It
had all been very easy—almost too easy.

Esca's voice was growing blurred towards the close of the
story. He was blind weary, and the instant he had finished
eating, he stretched out on the piled bracken and sleep took him
like a tired hound after a day's hunting.

But before the sun was above the mountains next day they
were on their way once more, for though they were now clear
of suspicion, it was no time for lingering. The village had
shown no signs of surprise at Esca's sudden recovery; presumably when the devils were no longer in his belly the man
was whole again. They had given the travellers more of the
eternal smoked meat, and a boy—a wild, dark-faced lad too
young for the hosting and sulking in consequence—to guide
them on the next stage of their journey, and bidden them good
hunting and let them go.

That day they had gruelling travelling; no level loch-side
to follow, but a steep thrust northward into the heart of the
mountains, and then east—so far as they could hold to any
course—by narrow passes between sheer heather-washed crags
of black rock, skirting wide mountain shoulders, traversing
bare ridges, across what seemed to be the roof of the world;
until at last the lie of the country turned them south again into

the long downward sweep that ended afar off in the marshes of the Cluta. Here the boy parted from them, refusing to share their camp for the night, and set off back the way he had come, tireless as a mountain buck among his native glens.

They watched him go, easily, not hurrying, at the long, springing mountaineer's stride. He would walk like that through the night and arrive home before dawn, not much tired. Marcus and Esca were both hillmen, but they could never have equalled that, not among these crags and passes. They turned their back on the last glimpse of Cruachan, and set off southward, making for more sheltered country, for once again there was storm in the air, not thunder this time, but wind—wind and rain. Well, that would not matter much; mist was the one thing that would matter, and at least an autumn gale would keep the autumn mists away. Only once before had weather meant as much to Marcus as it did now: on the morning of the attack at Isca Dumnoniorum when mizzle rain had kept the signal smoke from rising.

In the last flush of the evening they came upon the ruins of a broch, one of those strange, chambered towers built by a forgotten people, perched like a falcon's eyrie on the very edge of the world. They made camp there, in company with the skeleton of a wolf picked bare by ravens.

Thinking it best not to light a fire, they simply knee-hobbled the mares, gathered fern for bedding, and after filling the cooking-pot at the mountain stream, which came leaping down through its own narrow gorge nearby, sat down with their backs to the crumbling stones of the entrance, to eat leathery shavings of dried meat.

Marcus stretched out thankfully. It had been a gruelling march; most of the day they had had to trudge and scramble, leading Vipsania and Minna, and his lame leg was aching horribly, despite the ready help that he had had from Esca. It was good to rest.

From their feet the land swept away southward over ridge after ridge into the blue distance, where, a thousand feet below and maybe two days' march away, the old frontier cut Valentia from the wilderness. Far below them, among dark ranks of pine-trees, the northern arm of a great loch reflected back the flame of the sunset; and Marcus greeted it as a familiar friend, for he and Esca had followed its shores on their way north, almost two moons ago. A straight journey now, no more sniping to and fro among sea-lochs and mist-wrapped mountains, he thought; and yet there was a queer superstitious feeling in him that it had all been too easy—a queer foreboding of trouble to come. And the sunset seemed to echo his mood. A most wonderful sunset; the whole western sky on fire, and high overhead, torn off, hurrying wind clouds caught the light and became great wings of gold that changed, even while Marcus watched them, to fiery scarlet. Stronger and stronger grew the light, until the west was a furnace banked with purple cloud, and the whole world seemed to glow, and the upreared shoulder of the mountain far across the loch burned crimson as spilled wine. The whole sunset was one great threat of coming tempest; wind and rain, and maybe something more. Suddenly it seemed to Marcus that the crimson of that distant mountain shoulder was not wine, but blood.

He shook his shoulders impatiently, calling himself a fool. He was tired, so was Esca and the horses for that matter, and there was a storm on the way. That was all. A good thing that they had found shelter for the night; with any luck it would have blown itself out by morning. It struck him that he had not so much as looked at the Eagle. It had seemed better not to, in the village they had left that morning; but now . . . It lay beside him, and on a swift impulse he picked up the bundle and began to unroll it. The dark folds of the cloak as he turned them back caught a more brilliant colour from the sunset, warming from violet to Imperial purple. The last fold fell away, and he was holding the Eagle in his hands; cold, heavy, battered, burning red-gold in the sunset. 'Euge!' he said softly, using the word he would have used to praise a victory in the arena, and looked up at Esca. 'It was a good hunting, brother.'

But Esca's suddenly widened eyes were fixed on one corner of

the cloak, outflung towards him, and he did not answer; and
Marcus, following the direction of his gaze, saw the cloth at that
corner torn and ragged.

'The ring-brooch!' Esca said. 'The ring-brooch!'

Still holding the Eagle in the curve of his arm, Marcus was
hastily flinging the folds this way and that, but he knew that it
was useless. The brooch had been in that corner. With
sudden sharp-edged vividness, now that it was too late, he
remembered that scene by the loch-side, the threatening faces
of the tribesmen gathered round, the gear tumbled on the
coarse grass, the cloak with its dangling brooch all but torn out
of the cloth by their furious handling. Fool that he was, it
had gone completely out of his mind; out of Esca's, too, it
seemed.

'It may have fallen at any time—even while you were in the
water,' he said.

'No,' Esca said slowly. 'It rang on the pebbles when I
dropped the cloak before I dived for the Eagle.' He rubbed
the back of one hand across his forehead, thinking back.
'When I picked up the cloak, it caught for an instant on an
alder root; you know how the alders grow right down to the
water's edge. I remember now, but at the time I scarcely
noticed.'

He dropped his hand and they sat quite still, staring at each
other. The ring-brooch was a cheap bronze one, but its
design was rather unusual, and the tribesmen must often have
seen Demetrius of Alexandria wearing it. Also, to judge by
the state of that jagged corner, there was probably a wisp of
violet cloth caught in it, to help their memories.

Marcus was first to break the silence. 'If they find it, they
will know that one of us has been back since they searched our
gear, and there could be but one reason for that.' As he spoke,
he began methodically to wrap up the Eagle once more.

'When they speak with the warriors from the village we left
this morning, they will know that it was I who went back,'
Esca said hurriedly, and checked. 'No, that will not serve,
for they will know that I went with your knowledge. . . .

Listen, Marcus. You must push on alone. If you take Vipsania and go now, you may stand a chance. I will put myself in their way. I will tell them that we quarrelled for possession of the Eagle; we fought for it down yonder, and you went into the loch, and the Eagle with you.'

' And Vipsania?' Marcus said, his hands still busy with the folds of the cloak. ' And what will they do to you when you have told them this story?'

Esca said very simply, ' They will kill me.'

' I am sorry, but I do not think much of that plan,' Marcus said.

' There is the Eagle to be taken into account,' Esca urged.

Marcus made a quick, impatient gesture. ' The Eagle will serve no useful purpose when we get it home. I know that well enough. So long as it does not fall again into the tribes-men's hands to be a weapon against Rome, it will lie as worthily in a Caledonian bog as on a Roman scrap-heap. If the worst comes to the worst, we will find means to dispose of the Eagle before they take us.'

' It seems strange that you have not cast a thing of so little worth into the loch before this. Why trouble to carry it south at all?'

Marcus was already drawing his legs under him; but he checked an instant, his gaze holding Esca's. ' For an idea,' he said. He got up stiffly. ' We are in this together, and we will win clear together, or not at all. It may be days before that accursed brooch is found, none the less the sooner we get down to Valentia the better.'

Esca got up also, saying nothing. There was no more to be said, and he knew it.

Marcus glanced up at the wild clouds; hurrying clouds like wind-driven birds. ' How long have we before the storm breaks?'

The other seemed to be smelling the weather. ' Long enough to get down to the loch-side, anyway; there will be some shelter from the wind down there among the pine-woods. We might make a few more miles tonight.'

XVII

THE WILD HUNT

Two mornings later, Marcus lay full length in a hollow of the lowland hills and looked down through the parted bracken fronds. Grey and tawny marshes lay below him, rising to the blue heights of Valentia to the south, and through the flatness of them wound the silver Cluta, spreading westward into its firth: with Are-Cluta, once a frontier town, still a meeting-place and market for all the neighbouring tribes, squatting within turf ramparts on its northern bank. There were coracles on the river, looking, from this distance, like tiny water-beetles; one or two larger vessels with blue sails furled, riding at anchor below the dun, from which the smoke of many cooking-fires rose towards a high grey sky; a sky that was gentle with exhaustion after the autumn gale, Marcus thought while he lay looking back over the past two days as it might be over a wild dream.

The storm had broken over them towards midnight, the wild westerly gale swooping at them down the shoulder of the mountains like a wild thing that wanted to destroy them;

whipping the waters of the loch into racing white-caps, bringing with it the bitter, hissing rain to drench them through and through. They had passed the greater part of the night crouching with the two frightened mares under a steep over-hang of rock, wrapped about with a shrieking turmoil of wind and rain and darkness. Towards dawn the storm had abated a little, and they had pushed on again until long past noon, when they had found a sheltered hollow under the bole of an uprooted pine, knee-hobbled the mares, and crawled under the upreared mass of torn roots, and slept. When they awoke it was well into the night, and the rain was falling softly before a dying wind that sobbed and roared through the pines but no longer beat against them like a live thing. They had eaten what was left of the smoked meat, and pushed on again through the dying storm, until, in the spent calm of the day-spring, with the wet oak-woods waking to the song of chaffinch and robin and wren, they had halted at last, here in the low hills above the Cluta.

As soon as it grew light, Esca had gone on down to Are-Cluta, to sell the mares. The parting was hard for all of them, for they had grown fond of each other, Marcus and Vipsania, Esca and Minna, in the months that they had been together; and the mares had known perfectly well that it was good-bye. A pity they could not have kept the mares, but with the old cavalry brand on their shoulders they were much too easily recognizable, and there was nothing for it but to trade them for others. But at least they would be sure of a good master, for the tribesmen loved their horses and hounds, using them hard but only as they used themselves hard, treating them as members of the family.

All would be well with Vipsania and Minna, Marcus told himself firmly. He stretched. It was good to lie here on the soft turf of the woodshore, to feel his tunic drying on him, and rest his aching leg, knowing that however fast the hunt came on their trail, they were past the last point where they could be cut off by men pouring down any side glen that linked loch with loch in the misty maze that was behind them. But how was it

going with Esca, down there in the dun? Always it was
Esca who had the extra task to do, the extra risk to run. It was
bound to be so, for Esca, who was British, could pass unnoticed
where Marcus, with his olive skin, his darkness that was of
quite a different kind from that of the tribesmen, would be
suspect at once. He knew that, but it infuriated him, none the
less; all his relief began to ebb away, and as the morning
dragged on he grew restless and yet more restless. He began
to feel sickeningly anxious. What was happening down there?
Why was Esca so long? Had word of the Eagle reached Are-
Cluta ahead of them?

It was near to noon when Esca suddenly appeared in the glen
below him, riding a shaggy mouse-coloured pony and leading
another. Relief flooded over Marcus, and as the other glanced
up towards his hiding-place he parted the bracken fronds more
widely and flung up a hand. Esca returned the signal, and a
few moments later, having joined Marcus in the little hollow,
he dropped from the back of the shaggy creature he rode, with
an air of duty well and truly done.

'Do you call these mossy-faced objects ponies?' Marcus
inquired with interest, rolling over and sitting up.

Esca was busy with the bundle he had taken from one of
them. For an instant his slow, grave smile lifted the corners
of his mouth. 'The man who sold them to me swore they were
sired out of the stables of the High King of Eriu.'

'Did you by any chance believe him?'

'Oh no,' said Esca. He had looped the reins of both ponies
over a low branch and sat down beside Marcus with the bundle.
'I told the man I sold ours to, that they were sired out of the
stables of Queen Cartimandua. He did not believe me, either.'

'They were game little brutes, whoever sired them. You
found them a good master?'

'Yes, and the same master for both; a little fox of a man,
but he had the right hands. I told him my brother and I were
taking ship for Eriu. It was a good enough reason for
selling the mares, and if anyone should ever ask him, it may
serve to start a false trail. We haggled for a long time, because

the mares were near foundering. I had to tell him a long story about wolves, to account for that, and so of course he swore their wind was broken, which was obviously a lie. But I sold them to him at last, for a fine sealskin rug and two enamelled war-spears, and a bronze cooking-pot and a sucking pig. Oh, and three fine amber bracelets.'

Marcus flung up his head with a croak of laughter. ' What did you do with the sucking pig? '

' It was a little black pig, very shrill,' said Esca reflectively. ' I sold it to a woman, for this.' He had been busy with the bundle while he spoke, and now shook out a hooded cloak of shaggy cloth that seemed to have once been chequered blue and red, but was now grease-stained and weather-faded to a uni-versal mud-colour. ' Even a small thing will help to change the look of a whole company—at least from a distance. . . . Also for dried meat. Here it is. Then I went back to the horse market and bought these two, with their head-gear on them, for the war-spears and all the other things. The other man had the best of the bargain; ill luck go with him! But there was no help for that.'

' We are in no case to drive a hard bargain,' Marcus agreed with his mouth full. They were both eating by that time. ' I should have liked to have seen you with that piglet,' he added thoughtfully.

Neither of them wasted more time on words. They ate quickly, and not over much, since there was no knowing how long the food would have to last them; and by noon they had loaded their few belongings into the yellow pack-cloth, flung the sheepskin saddle-pads across the backs of their shaggy little mounts, tightened the belly-straps, and were on their way once more.

Marcus wore the cloak for which Esca had traded the black piglet, the hood pulled well over his forehead, for he had laid aside the hand-shaped talisman which was too distinctive to serve him any longer; and under the greasy, evil-smelling folds, he carried the lost Eagle. He had contrived a kind of sling for it, with strips torn from the cloak in which it was closely

bundled, so as to have both hands free, but as he rode he
cradled it in the crook of his bridle arm.

.   .   .   .   .

They fetched a wide half-circle round Are-Cluta, and reached
the river again where it swung south-eastward into the heart of
Valentia.   Their return journey was very different from the
outward one.   Then, they had wandered openly from village
to village, with a meal and a place by somebody's fire at the
day's end.   Now they were fugitives, lying up in some remote
glen through the day, making southward through the night,
and somewhere behind them, the hunt was up.   For three days
they had no sign that it was so, but they knew it in their hearts,
and they pushed on grimly, listening always for sounds behind
them.   They made good speed, for the ponies, though not
beautiful, were game little brutes, bred in the mountains, tough
as whipcord and sure-footed as goats, and they were able to
ride much of the time.   Presently, they knew, they might have
to let the ponies go, and take to the heather on foot.   Meanwhile they pushed on in desperate haste, that they might be as
far south as possible before that time came.

The fourth evening found them on their way again, after a
day spent lying-up in a thicket of thorn-trees.   A murky
evening, closing in under a low grey sky.   In the low country
at their backs it was dusk already, but up here on the high
moors the daylight still lingered, reflected back by many little
silver tarns among the brown heather.

'Three more days,' Marcus said suddenly.   'Three more
days by my reckoning, and we should reach the Wall!'

Esca looked round to answer, and then suddenly his head
went up with a jerk, as though he heard something.   An instant
later, Marcus heard it too, very faint and far behind: a hound
giving tongue.

They had reached the crest of a long ridge of moorland, and
looking back, they saw a cluster of dark specks cresting a lesser
ridge behind them; a long way behind, but not too far to
be recognized for what they were: men on horseback and

o

many hounds.   And in that instant another hound took up the
cry.

'I spoke too soon,' Marcus said, and his voice jumped oddly
in his own ears.

'They have sighted us.'   Esca laughed sharply in his throat.
'The hunt is up with a vengeance.   Ride, brother quarry!'
And even as he spoke, his little mount leapt forward, snorting,
from the jab of his heel.

Marcus urged his own pony into a tearing gallop at the same
instant.   The ponies were fairly fresh, but both fugitives knew
that in the open it was only a matter of time before they were
ridden down by the better-mounted tribesmen—pulled down
by the yelling hounds as by a pack of wolves.   And with one
accord they swung a little in their course, heading for the higher
ground ahead; broken country by the look of it, in which they
might be able to shake off their pursuers.

'If we can keep the lead till dark,' Esca shouted above the
drumming hooves and the wind of their going, 'we've a chance
among the glens yonder.'

Marcus did not answer, but settled down to ride as he had
never ridden before.   The dark heather streaked backward
under his pony's thudding hooves, the long harsh hairs of its
mane sprayed back over his wrists, and the wind sung past his
ears.   For one flashing instant there rose in him the exultancy
of speed, the surge and splendour that he had once thought
never to know again.   The instant passed, swift as the darting
flight of a kingfisher.   He was riding for his life with the dark
hunt in full cry behind him, putting out all his skill to keep clear
of hidden pitfalls, the hummocks and snags and snarls among
the heather that might bring disaster, grimly aware that he
could not grip strongly with his right knee, and if the pony
stumbled at this flying gallop, he would go clean over its head.
On and on they hurtled, now skirting a reed-fringed upland
pool, now swerving from a patch of bog luminously green in
the fading light; uphill and down, through bronze tides of
dying heather, startling here a flock of plover, there a stray
curlew from the bents, and always, behind them, the hunt

drawing nearer. Marcus could hear the hounds giving tongue above the soft thunder of the ponies' hooves, nearer, steadily nearer; but there was no time for looking back.

On and on. Now the ponies were tiring. Marcus could feel the panting of his little mount's flanks, and foam flew back from its muzzle, spattering against him. He leaned far forward over its neck to ease it; he talked to it, sang and shouted, fondled its sweating neck and dug in his heels, urging it on by every means in his power, though indeed the poor brute was already winged by terror to its utmost speed, knowing as well as its rider the meaning of those sounds behind.

The land was rising under them, and the light fading moment by moment; the little glens and the hazel woods were very near; but so was the hunt. Snatching one glance over his shoulder, Marcus glimpsed a flying blur of horsemen and low-running hounds, smudged out of all clear shape by the twilight, streaking across the open turf, the leading hound scarce a bowshot away.

Near to their last gasp, and with the clamour of the hunt swelling in their ears, they struggled desperately over the crest of another ridge, and saw below them through the dusk the pale streak of running water. Very faintly, an unexpected scent drifted up to them, a sweet, heavy scent like musk, and Esca let out a sound that was half-way between a laugh and a sob. ' Down to the stream before they top the ridge, and we've a chance yet.'

Only half understanding, but content to trust to the other's better knowledge of the wild, Marcus drove his heel again and again into his pony's sobbing flank, urging it to one last effort. Shivering and sweating, the foam that flew from its muzzle blood-flecked now, it plunged forward in one last frantic burst of speed. Neck and neck they hurtled down through the tall bracken, the scent of musk growing every instant stronger; down and down toward the trampled hollow beside the stream, from which two battling, antlered shapes broke at their approach and went crashing away down the glen. Esca was already half off his pony, and in the musk-reeking hollow where only the instant before two great stags had been fighting for lordship of the herd, Marcus half fell, half flung himself from his own mount.   His friend's arm was round him almost before he touched the ground.   'Into the water, quick!'   Esca gasped, as, snorting with terror, the two ponies plunged on riderless into the dusk.

They dived through the alder scrub and scrambled headlong down the bank, Esca still with his arm round Marcus to help him, and slipped into the ice-cold, swift-running water, just as the first wave of the hunt topped the rise behind them. Crouching under the steep overhang, they heard the ponies crashing away downstream in terrified stampede, heard the hunt sweep down towards them, the check, the baying and the trampling and the sudden splurge of voices; and crouched lower yet, the water flowing almost to their nostrils.

It seemed an eternity that they crouched so, listening to the turmoil just above their heads, and praying that the dusk would hide the traces of their swift descent through the alder scrub, and that the hounds, having been set on to follow horses, would not concern themselves to pick up and follow the scent of men.   But in reality it could have been only a few moments before a triumphant yell told them that the movement of the stampeding ponies had been picked up.   The hounds were already away yelling on the hot scent of stags or ponies, or both. There was a fresh burst of shouts and trampling, the shrill, angry squeal of a horse, and with the confused speed of a dissolving nightmare, men, hounds, and horses were off in full cry after the flying shadows.

A little farther down, the glen curved, bringing them for an instant into full view of the two who crouched under the bank and stared after them with straining eyes, a shadow chase, sweeping down the dusk-sodden glen, the wild clamour of their passing growing fainter with every beat of flying hooves; swiftly come, and passed, and gone, as though they had been the Wild Hunt, the hunters of souls.

The dusk swallowed them; the last, long-drawn cry of a hound drifted back on the night wind, and that was all.   No sound now, but a curlew crying somewhere, and the racing of their own hearts.

Esca rose quickly to his feet. ' They will go like the wind for a while,' he said. ' Lightened of our weight, and terrified as they are; but they will be run down before long, and then the hunt will be back looking for us, so the sooner we are away from here, the better.'

Marcus was making sure he still had the Eagle safe in its sling. ' I feel sick about those ponies,' he said.

' There will be no harm come to them, unless their wind is broken. Those were hunting-dogs, trained to run down and bring to bay, and not to kill until the word is given. With us, I think the word would have been given, but the wanton waste of a horse is not in these hunters unless their tribe be different from all the other tribes of Britain.' Esca had been feeling about under the bank as he spoke, and now brought up his spear with a satisfied grunt. ' Better keep to the stream for a while, and break the trail,' he said, and put out a steadying hand to Marcus.

For what seemed an interminable time they struggled upstream, now wading knee deep through the shifting shallows, now plunged to the waist in the deep, swift flow where the stream narrowed. It was a fight every yard of the way, against the thrust of the water and the shifting footholds, against time, with every nerve on the stretch for the long-drawn cry of a hound that might rise at any moment above the soft rush of the stream.

It was quite dark now, for the moon was hidden by low cloud; and the hills closed round them, rising blackly on every hand. The stream began to lead them too far eastward, and anyway, they dared not stick to it too long; and at last, where a narrow side glen opened to the south, they scrambled out, chilled to the bone, and thankful to be done with icy water. They shook themselves like dogs, wrung as much water as they could from their clothes, and set off again.

Presently, coming over a steep rise, they dropped down into another glen, wooded with hazel and rowan, through which another burn fell in steep slides and cascades of white water. Indeed, one never seemed out of the sound of running water in these hills. And stumbling at last on a jagged hollow left by a landslip that the rain had torn away, they more or less fell into it, and sat there, huddled close together for warmth, to get their breath and take stock of the situation.

The little food that they had left had gone with the ponies, and from now on they would have to march empty, since they certainly could not stop to trap for food as they went. They were still at least two full marches from the nearest station on the Wall, and must cover the distance on foot, through unfamiliar country with the wild hunt on their trail. All in all, their prospects did not look very bright.

Marcus sat rubbing his leg, which was aching intolerably, and staring at the white water through the dark blur of the hazels. The sense of being hunted was heavy on him, and he knew that it was on Esca, too. The very countryside seemed to have grown hostile and menacing, as though not only men were on their trail, but the whole land up and hunting, the dark hills themselves closing in to the kill. And yet the Wild had stood their friend once tonight, he told himself, setting a pair of battling stags in their way, just in the moment of their direst need.

They sat silent a short while longer, snatching a breathing space before pushing on again; but they dared not rest long, for they must be much farther from the place where they had taken to the water, and in a much surer hiding, before dawn. Marcus sighed, and was actually drawing his legs under him to rise, when he became aware of Esca grown suddenly tense beside him, and then, above the soft wet rush of the stream, of someone, or something, moving far down the glen. Marcus crouched where he was, frozen, his head turned to listen, and gradually the sounds drew nearer: a queer confusion of sounds that might be one man or several, a great brushing and rustling through the hazel scrub. It came slowly up the glen towards them, while they crouched motionless in their hiding-place, nearer and louder until it seemed almost on top of them; and

Marcus, peering up through the overhanging screen of rowan and hazel, made out a pale blur and a dark one. Of all homely and unexpected things, a man leading a cow.

Furthermore, the man was whistling softly between his teeth as he came up the burnside; so softly that it was not until he was within a few feet, that the tune broke through. A catchy tune.

> ' Oh when I joined the Eagles,
> (As it might be yesterday)
> I kissed a girl at Clusium
> Before I marched away.'

Marcus reached up and parted the drooping rowan branches. ' Well met, Guern the Hunter,' he said in his own tongue.

XVIII

THE WATERS OF LETHE

THERE was a sudden pause; the white cow, startled by the unexpected voice, fidgeting and blowing, with lowered horns; the man, who had checked with a grunt, peering down through the rowan branches. Then the soft growling of the old dog, which Marcus had not at first noticed, rose suddenly to a sing-song snarl, and was checked by a backward thrust of the hunter's heel.

'Well met, Demetrius of Alexandria.'

There was no time to waste in surprise and explanation. Marcus said quickly, 'Guern, we need your help.'

'Aye, I know that well enough. You have brought away the Eagle, and the Epidaii are up after you,' Guern said. 'The word went by at sunset, and the Dumnonii and my own tribe at least will join spears with them.' He came a step nearer. 'What would you have me do?'

'We want food—and a false trail, if you can provide one.'

'Food is easily managed, but it is more than a false trail that you will need to get you in one piece to the Wall. Every pass to the south will be guarded by now, and there is but one way known to me that is likely to be left open.'

'Tell us how to find it.'

'Telling is not enough. It is a way that is death without a guide. That is why the tribesmen will not trouble to guard it.'

'And you know this way?' Esca spoke for the first time.

'Yes, I know the way. I—will take you by it.'

'How if you are caught with us?' Marcus said. 'How if you are missed from your own place, and any think to wonder where you are?'

'I shall not be missed from my own place, for there will be many out hunting these next few days. If any come upon us

together I can always knife one of you, and claim the honour
of being First Spear among the hunters.'

' It is a pleasant thought,' said Marcus. ' Do we come with
you now? '

' Yes. It is best that you come the first part of the way
now,' Guern decided. ' We shall have to take the cow; ill
luck to her. She is for ever straying.'

Marcus laughed, and got up, catching his breath as his overtaxed leg twinged under him. ' At least her straying has stood
us in good stead tonight. Give me your shoulder, Esca, this
place is—somewhat—steep.'

Many steep glens and moorland ridges lay between them and
the place of the fighting stags, and it was near dawn when
Guern at last led them down into an old sandstone quarry
that had not been worked since the Eagles flew from Valentia.
He thrust them into the crumbling cave or gallery of some sort
that seemed to have been the occasional lair of wild pig, and
bidding them be quiet until he came again, departed with the
cow, who seemed very weary. ' It may be that this will teach
you not to wander again, oh daughter of Ahriman! ' they heard
him say as he hauled her by the horns up the rough slope.

Left to themselves, Marcus and Esca drew the hanging
curtain of bramble and dog-rose across the mouth of their hole,
and lay down as comfortably as they could. ' If the roof
doesn't cave in and the pigs do not come back to challenge
our presence, we look like having a quiet day,' Marcus said,
pillowing his head on his arms.

Neither of these things happened, and the day dragged
slowly by, while Marcus and Esca slept fitfully, trying to forget
the emptiness of their stomachs. Beyond the bushes at the
entrance the light grew golden and then faded. It was after
dusk when Guern the Hunter returned, bringing with him,
beside the inevitable strips of leathery smoked meat, a lump of
fresh broiled venison. ' Eat the fresh meat now,' he said,
' and quickly.'

They did as he bade them, while he stood leaning on a spear
in the cave mouth, with the great dog lying at his feet, and

before it was full dark outside they were on their way again. They made slow marching at first, for Marcus's leg was stiff after the day's rest, but the way was easier than it had been last night, running mostly downhill, and little by little the stiffness wore off, and he was able to make better going. Silent as shadows, they followed Guern, by ways that only the hunter and the deer knew, with never a spoken word between them. But Marcus was puzzled as the hours went by, for so far there had been no real difference between this and any other march that they had made among the hills; no sign of this unguarded way which it was death to travel without a guide.

And then, as they came down a gentle slope, the air seemed to change, and with it, the feel of the ground under their feet; and suddenly he understood. Bog! Bog with presumably some hidden path across it for those who knew the secret. They came to the edge of it almost as abruptly as to the edge of a pool, and the queer rooty smell of it was all around them. Guern was casting about like a hound cutting across a scent. Suddenly he halted, and his dog with him.

'Here. It is here,' he said, speaking under his breath for the first time since their setting out. 'From now on we must go behind one another. Follow me exactly, and do not halt for so long as a heart-beat; even on the secret way the ground is soft. Do as I bid you and you will cross safely; disobey me, and you will sink.' It was as simple as that.

'Understood,' Marcus murmured back. It was no time or place for needless talk: Mithra alone knew how near the scouting tribesmen might be.

With the dog pressed against him, Guern turned outward to the bog. Marcus moved into place behind him, and Esca brought up the rear. The ground felt spongy under their feet, sucking at them gently at every step that seemed taken only just in time to keep from sinking; and they had gone only a short way when Marcus noticed that a faint mist had begun to rise. At first he took it for no more than the breath of the bog, but soon he realized that it was more than that. Higher and higher it rose, wreathing upward in faint gauzy swathes that closed together overhead. Looking up, he could still see the moon shining, but faintly, through mist-wreathes in a glimmering sky. Mist; the weather of all others that they had cause to dread! And that it should come now! There could be no turning back; yet how was it possible for any man to find such a way as they were following, in this murk? And if they lost it? But that was not good to think about.

The mist was thickening steadily. Soon they were walking almost blind, their world made up of a few feet of sodden turf and tufted bog-cotton, and the occasional glint of water, dissolving into a nothingness of glimmering mist; and there was no sign of any path. But Guern seemed never at a loss, walking lightly and steadily forward, changing his course from time to time, and the other two followed. The dank, rooty smell grew always stronger, colder; the moon was sinking low and the mist losing itself in darkness, and still Guern the Hunter walked on. On and on. It was very silent, only a bittern boomed somewhere to their right, and there came small, evil, sucking noises from the bog.

Marcus had long since got over his first unpleasant doubts of Guern's ability to find the secret way in the mist, but now he was beginning to wonder how much longer he could keep on at this light, unvarying stride; and then suddenly it seemed to him that the ground was growing firmer underfoot. A few more steps, and he was sure of it. They were drawing up out of the quag. The mist smelled different, chill as ever, but lighter and sweeter. Soon the secret way was behind them, like an evil dream.

By that time dawn was near, and the mist was growing out of the darkness again, no longer glimmering, but dully grey as the ash of a long-dead fire. In the growing light, clear of the last pocket of bog, they halted thankfully in the lea of a clump of ancient thorn-trees and turned to face each other, while the dog lay down at their feet.

'I have brought you as far as I can,' Guern said. 'Every man to his own hunting grounds, and from now on the land is strange to me.'

'You have brought us clear through the guard of our enemies, and we can fend for ourselves now,' Marcus said quickly.

Guern shook his ragged head doubtfully. 'They may be
drawing these hills also, for all I know. Therefore travel by
night and lie up by day; and if you do not go astray in the
mist, nor fall into the hands of the tribesmen, you should reach
the wall some time in the second night from now.' He
hesitated, tried to speak, and hesitated again. At last he said
with a kind of half-angry humility : 'Before our trails divide,
it is in my heart that I would see the Eagle once again. It was
my Eagle once.'

For answer, Marcus slipped the closely wrapped bundle from
its sling, and turning back the folds, laid bare the lost Eagle.
It was dark and lustreless in the grey dawn murk; a mere
bird-shaped lump of battered metal. 'It has lost its wings,'
he said.

Guern reached out eagerly as though to take it, then checked,
and dropped his hands back to his sides. The betraying
gesture tore harshly at something deep in Marcus's chest, and
suddenly he could have howled like a dog. For a long
moment he held the Eagle, while the other stood with rigidly
bent head, looking down at it, unspeaking. Then as Guern
stepped back, he folded the dark cloth once more over it, and
returned it to its place under his cloak.

Guern said, ' So. I have seen the Eagle once more. Maybe
after today I shall not look on a Roman face nor hear my own
tongue spoken again. . . . It is time that you were on your
way.'

' Come with us,' Marcus said on a sudden impulse.

Guern's ragged head went up, and he stared at Marcus under
his brows. For an instant he actually seemed to be considering
the idea. Then he shook his head. ' My welcome might be
an over-warm one. I have no yearning after death by stoning.'

' Tonight's work would alter that. We owe our lives to you,
and if we get the Eagle back to its own place, that will be your
doing.'

Guern shook his head again. ' I am of the Selgovae. I have

a woman of the tribe to wife, and she is a good wife to me.
I have sons, born into the tribe, and my life is here. If ever I
was—something else, and my life was elsewhere, all that lies
in another world and the men I knew in it have forgotten me.
There is no way back through the Waters of Lethe.'

'Then—good hunting to you on your own trails,' Marcus
said after a silence. 'Wish us well, between here and the Wall.'

'I will wish you well; and it is in my heart that I will wish
myself with you. If you win through, I shall hear of it, and be
glad.'

'You will have played no small part in it, if we do,' Marcus
said, 'and neither of us will forget. The Light of the Sun be
with you, Centurion.'

They looked back when they had gone a few paces, and saw
him standing as they had left him, already dimmed with mist,
and outlined against the drifting mist beyond. A half-naked,
wild-haired tribesman, with a savage dog against his knee;
but the wide, well-drilled movement of his arm as he raised it
in greeting and farewell was all Rome. It was the parade-
ground and the clipped voice of trumpets, the iron discipline
and the pride. In that instant Marcus seemed to see, not the
barbarian hunter, but the young centurion, proud in his first
command, before ever the shadow of the doomed legion fell
on him. It was to that centurion that he saluted in reply.

Then the drifting mist came between them.

As they turned away, Marcus found himself hoping that
Guern would get back safely to the new life that he had made
for himself, that he would not have to pay for the faith that he
had kept with them. Well, the mist would give him cover on
his homeward way.

Almost as though he had heard his friend's unspoken
thoughts and was answering them, Esca said: 'He will hear
if we come with our lives out of this, but we shall never hear
whether he does.'

'I wish that he had chosen to come with us,' Marcus said.
But even as he spoke, he knew that Guern the Hunter was right.
There was no way back through the Waters of Lethe.

Two dawns later, Marcus and Esca were still a long way from the Wall. The mist that had met them on the secret way had haunted them ever since; a patchy and treacherous mist that was sometimes no more than a faint blurring of the more distant hills, and at others swooped down on them, blotting out all landmarks in a swirling greyness in which the very ground seemed dissolving away. They would have become lost over and over again but for the hunter's sense of direction that made Esca able to smell the south as a townsman might smell garlic. And even with that to help them, they could only struggle on with maddening slowness, covering what distance they could when the mist thinned, and lying up wherever they happened to be when it grew too thick to push on any farther. Once or twice they came very near to disaster; many times they had to cast back for a way round some pitfall that the mist had hidden from them, and Marcus, who was leaving the route to Esca as usual, was having anxieties of his own. His lame leg, which had carried him well enough through the forced marches and weary scrambles of their way south, was beginning to let him down, and let him down badly. He held on doggedly, but he was growing clumsy, and when he stumbled the jar of it made him set his teeth.

That dawn brought them their first warning that the enemy were indeed, as Guern had said, drawing these hills also, when the fitful mist rolled back to show them the figure of a mounted man, evidently on watch, high on a hill-shoulder not more than a bowshot away. Luckily he was not looking their way, and they fell flat among the heather, and spent a bad few moments watching him ride slowly along the ridge, until the mist closed down again.

They spent part of that day lying up in the lee of a great boulder, but started out again while there were still several hours of daylight left. While the mist hung about them, they had had to abandon their plan of travelling only by night, and push on when and how they could.

' How far have we still to go, by your reckoning?' Marcus asked, as he stood trying to rub the stiffness out of his leg.

Esca tightened his rawhide belt, which had become too loose for him, collected his spear and brushed up, as well as he could, the flattened grass where they had been lying.

'It is hard to judge,' he said. 'It has been slow travelling in this murk, but I think that I have not brought us greatly out of our way. By the fall of the land, I should say twelve or fourteen of your Roman miles. There; if any hunter comes close to this place, he will see that we have lain there, but from a few paces distant, it will not show.'

They set out once more on the long march south.

Towards evening a faint wind began to stir; and before it, the mist, which had been thick all day, grew ragged as a beggar's cloak.

'If the wind rises, we may lose this witches' brew at last,' said Marcus, as they halted at the curve of a narrow glen to make sure of their direction.

Esca lifted his head and sniffed, like an animal grown suddenly wary. 'Meanwhile it is in my heart that we should do well to find ourselves a fox-hole until dusk.'

But they had left the finding of their fox-hole too late. The words were scarcely out of his mouth when the mist seemed to curl back on itself. It spread sideways like blown smoke; the brown heather and golden bracken across the burn warmed suddenly through the drifting swathes, and next instant a cry, high and carrying and oddly triumphant, pierced upward from the far side of the glen, and a saffron-kilted figure started from cover and ran, crouching low, for the hill-crest. Esca's spear followed him, but it was too far for a throw. In six racing heart-beats he had reached the sky-line and dropped out of sight, crying his summons as he ran.

'Downhill,' Esca said harshly. 'Into the woods.'

They swung in their tracks, towards the nearest tongue of the birch woods that were spreading like a stain through the ragged mist, but even as they did so, the signal cry rose from among the golden trees in answer. There was no escape that way; and as they turned again, from far up the glen behind them the same cry went up, thin as a bird's call. Only one way lay open for them, and they took it; straight uphill to their right, and what lay over the hill-crest only the Lord of the Legions knew.

They gained the crest somehow, Marcus was never sure how, and as they hesitated an instant on the bare ridge, the cry—it was changing its quality now, becoming a hunting cry—rose again behind them, and was answered and flung up out of the mist below, closing in. They must have blundered into a large band of the hunters. Southward along the ridge, a dark mass of furze seemed to offer a certain amount of cover, and they dived into it like hunted animals going to ground, and began to work their way forward into its heart.

After that all was a blurred confusion of mist and jagged furze branches, and a chaos of dark islands swirled through by tawny tides of bracken and bilberry; of lying rigid among the dagger-sharp furze-roots with a suffocating reek of fox in their throats and the horror of the hunted in their racing hearts, while death with many heron-tufted war-spears stalked them through the dark maze. There were men all round them, on horseback, on foot, thrusting heedless of torn skin through the spiney branches, leaping high on stiff legs like hunting dogs who seek their quarry in long grass, giving tongue like hunting dogs too, now on this side, now on that. Once a probing spear struck like a snake within a span of Marcus's shoulder. And then quite suddenly they realized that against all seeming possibility, the hunt had missed them. It had swept over them and was no longer all around them, but behind!

They began to work forward on their stomachs again, with slow, agonizing caution. They could not tell where they were going, save that it was away from the enemy behind them. A dark and evidently much-used tunnel in the furze opened to them, and they slid into it, Esca leading. The reek of fox grew stronger than ever. The tunnel curved, leading them slightly downhill, and there was nothing to do but follow it, no breaking out through the dense furze that walled and roofed it in. It ended suddenly on the edge of the cover, and before them a spur of rocky, bush-grown turf ran out at an angle from the main ridge. Swathes of mist, drawn up out of the deep glen, were still drifting across it before the rising wind, but at the farthest point, upward of a bowshot away, something that might be a broch loomed through the greyness. It did not look promising, but they could not stay where they were, for it seemed to them that the sounds of the hunt were drawing nearer again, and there could be no turning back.

So they struck out into the open, getting what cover they could from the rocks and scrub, in search of some way down. But it seemed that there was no way down. The north-western slope would have been easy enough, but as they crouched among the bushes at the edge of it, the jink of a pony's bridle-bit came up to them, and the movement of men waiting. That way was securely stopped up. The south-eastern scarp dropped practically sheer into drifting mist-wreaths, out of which rose the indefinable sense and smell of deep water. There might be a way out for the Eagle, there, but there was certainly none for Marcus. Driven on by the sound of the hunt questing through the furze behind them like hounds after a lost scent, they struggled on a few steps, then checked, panting and desperate, looking this way and that, with eyes that strained to find some way of escape. But Marcus was almost done, and Esca had his arm round him. They could go no farther even if the way were clear; they were trapped, and they knew it. The building that they had glimpsed through the mist was quite clear now; not a broch at all, but an old Roman signal-tower. They gathered themselves together and made for it.

It was a very obvious hiding-place, so obvious that it offered a bare chance of safety, or at all events respite, because the hunters might well have searched it already. At the worst it would give them a chance to put up some sort of fight; and there was always the dark coming.

The narrow archway, doorless now, gaped blackly in the wall, and they stumbled through into a small courtyard where grass had long since covered the cobbles. Another empty doorway faced them, and Marcus made for it. They were in

P

the guard-room now. Dead leaves rustled to and fro on the floor, and the milky light filtering from a high window embrasure showed them the foot of a stairway in the wall. 'Up here,' he gasped.

The steps were of stone and still in good condition, though slippery with damp, and they stumbled upward, the sound of their feet seeming very loud in the silence of the stone shell where a little Roman garrison had lived and worked, keeping watch over the border hills, in the short years when the province of Valentia was more than a name.

They ducked out through a low door under the signal platform, on to the flat roof of the tower, into daylight as translucent as a moonstone after the dark below. As they did so, Marcus was almost blinded by a thrashing of great black wings past his face, and a startled raven burst upward uttering its harsh, grating alarm cry, and flew off northward with slow, indignant wing-beats, caaking as it went.

'Curse! That will announce our whereabouts clearly to all who may be interested,' Marcus thought, but was suddenly too tired to care very much. Utterly spent, he lurched across to the far side of the roof, and looked down through a crumbling embrasure. Below him the ground dropped sheer from the tower foot, and through the last filmy rags of the mist he caught the darkness of deep water, far below, a still and sombre tarn brooding on its own secrets, between the spur and the main ridge. Yes, there would be a way out for the Eagle.

On the landward side, Esca was crouching beside a broken place in the parapet, where several large stones had fallen, leaving a gap. 'They are still beating the furze,' he muttered as Marcus joined him. 'It is well for us that there are no dogs with this band. If they do not come before dusk, we may escape them yet.'

'They will come before dusk,' Marcus murmured back. 'The raven has made sure of that. Listen. . . .' A sound came up to them from below the northern side of the spur, a confused, formless splurge of excitement, faint with mist and distance, that told them all too clearly that the waiting man had understood the raven's message. Marcus lowered himself stiffly on to his sound knee beside the other, slipped into an easier position, and stretched out sideways, leaning on one arm, his head hanging low. After a few moments he looked up. ' I suppose I should feel guilty about you, Esca. For me, there has been the Eagle; but what had you to win in all this? '

Esca smiled at him, a slow grave smile. There was a jagged tear in his forehead where a furze root had caught him, Marcus noticed, but under it his eyes looked very quiet. ' I have been once again a free man amongst free men. I have shared the hunting with my brother, and it has been a good hunting.'

Marcus smiled back. ' It has been a good hunting,' he agreed. The soft beat of unshod hooves on turf came drumming up from the mist below; the unseen hunters of the furze cover were casting back towards the open spur, beating as they came, making sure that their quarry did not again slip through them. They would be here soon, but the riders from below would be first. ' A good hunting; and now I think that is ended.' He wondered if any word of that ending would one day drift south across the Wall, would reach the Legate Claudius, and through him, Uncle Aquila; would reach Cottia in the garden under the sheltering ramparts of Calleva. He should like them to know. . . . it had been a good hunting, that he and Esca had had together. Suddenly he knew that, despite all outward seeming, it had been worth while.

There was a great quietness in him. The last of the mist was blowing clear away as the wind freshened; something that was almost sunshine brushed fleetingly across the old signal-tower, and he noticed for the first time that a clump of harebell had taken root in a cranny of the fallen parapet close to him, and, late in flowering because of the place in which it grew, still carried one fragile bell aloft on an arching thread-slender stem. It swayed as the wind blew over, and regained its place with a tiny, defiant toss. It seemed to Marcus that it was the bluest thing he had ever seen.

Up over the edge of the spur, three wild horsemen appeared heading for the gateway.

XIX

TRADUI'S GIFT

As they dropped from their ponies in the courtyard below, Marcus and Esca drew back from the parapet. 'Only three, so far,' Marcus whispered. 'Don't use your knife unless you have to. They may be of more use to us living than dead.'

Esca nodded, and returned his hunting-knife to his belt. Life and the urgency of doing had taken hold of them again. Flattened against the wall on either side of the stairhead they waited, listening to their pursuers questing through storehouse and guard-room. 'Fools!' Marcus breathed, as a shout told them that the stairway had been spotted; and then came a rush of feet that checked at the floor below and then came on, storming upward.

Marcus was a good boxer, and much practice with the cestus last winter had made Esca something of a boxer also; together, weary though they were, they made a dangerous team. The first two tribesmen to come ducking out through the low doorway went down without a sound, like poled oxen: the third, not so completely caught unawares, put up more of a fight. Esca flung himself upon him, and they crashed down several steps together, in a flailing mass of arms and legs. There was a short, desperate struggle before Esca came uppermost, and staggering clear, heaved an unconscious man over the doorsill.

'Young fools,' he said, stooping for a fallen spear. 'A hound puppy would have known better than that.'

Two of the tribesmen—they were all very young—lay completely stunned where they had fallen; but one was already stirring; and Marcus bent over him. 'It is Liathan,' he said. 'I'll see to him. Do you tie up and gag the other two.'

The young warrior groaned, and opened his eyes to find

P 2

Marcus kneeling over him with his own dagger to his throat, while close by, Esca was hastily trussing and gagging the two unconscious men with strips torn from the cloak of one of them. 'That was a mistake,' Marcus said. 'You should have kept with the rest of the hunt, not come thrusting in here on your own.'

Liathan lay looking up at him. His black eyes were hard with hate; blood trickled from the corner of his mouth. 'Maybe we saw the raven and we sought to be First Spear, lest a lowland tribe claim the Eagle-god for its own,' he said between shut teeth.

'I see. It was a brave thing to do, but extremely stupid.'

'Maybe; but though we fail, there will be others here soon.' There was a gleam of savage triumph in the black eyes.

'So,' Marcus nodded. 'When they come, these others, you will tell them that we are not here; that we must after all have slipped by in the mist; and you will send them back the way they came, over the main ridge yonder, towards the sunrise.'

Liathan smiled. 'Why will I do these things?' He glanced for a contemptuous instant at the dagger in Marcus's hand. 'Because of that?'

'No,' said Marcus. 'Because when the first of your friends sets foot on the stair, I shall send the Eagle—here it is—into the tarn which lies below this place. We are still a long way from the Wall, and you will have other chances—you or others of the hunt—before we reach it; but if we die here, you will lose whatever chance you have of retaking the Red Crests' god.'

For a long moment Liathan lay staring up into Marcus's face; and in that silent moment there grew a light smother of hoof-beats and a distant burst of shouting. Esca rose quickly and crossed, half crouching, to the broken parapet. 'The hunt is up,' he said softly. 'They have done with the furze cover. Aiee! Like a wolf-pack, they close in.'

Marcus withdrew the dagger, but his eyes never left the young tribesman's face. 'Choose,' he said, very quietly. He got up and moved backward to the far parapet, unwrapping the Eagle as he did so. Liathan had risen also, and stood swaying a little on his feet, looking from Marcus to Esca and back again. Marcus saw him swallow, saw him lick the cut on his lip. He heard the sounds of the in-closing hunt, very near now, the men giving tongue like excited hounds; and from the emptiness at his back, only the plaintive cry of a marsh bird in the wind-haunted silence. He let the last violet fold fall from the Eagle, and held it up. The evening light, spreading as the mist thinned, struck on the savage, gilded head.

Liathan made a queer gesture of defeat. He turned and strode rather shakily to the broken parapet, and leaned over. The first of the hunt was almost at the gateway, and a shout from under the walls greeted his appearance. Liathan called down to them: 'They are not here, after all. They must have slipped through the other way in this accursed mist.' He pointed wildly, and his voice broke like the crying of a storm bird. 'Try the woods yonder; they will likely have bolted that way.'

A confusion of fierce voices answered him and a pony whinnied shrilly; he drew back from the parapet as though coming hot-foot to follow his words, and as the hunt flung back on itself, turned once more to Marcus.

'It was well done, was it not?'

Marcus nodded without speaking. Through one of the em-brasures he was watching the hunt streaming back along the spur and into the furze cover of the main ridge, men on ponies and men on foot, calling to each other, gathering others as they went; dissolving into the last shreds of the mist. He brought his gaze back to the young tribesman. 'Truly it was well done,' he said, 'but keep your head down, lest any straggler should look back and think it strange to see you still here.'

Liathan lowered his head obediently—and sprang. Sprang like a wild cat. But Marcus, warned by some flicker of his eyes an instant before, flung himself sideways, half falling, with the Eagle under him, and as he did so, Esca was upon the high-lander and brought him crashing down.

'You fool,' Marcus said a moment later, staggering to his feet and looking down at Liathan, who lay squirming under

Esca's knees. 'You young fool; there are two of us and only one of you.'

He crossed to the two bound men, and after satisfying himself that all was well with them, tore off some more strips from the cloak that lay beside one of them, and returned to Esca. Between them they bound the hands and feet of the young warrior, who had ceased to struggle and lay rigid with his face turned from them.

'We can leave the gag for the moment,' Marcus said when it was done. He picked up the Eagle and began to fold it close once more. 'Esca, do you go and make sure the ponies are safe. We shall need them.'

When Esca was gone, he got up stiffly and turned to the southern parapet. The upland tarn lay clear and dark now beneath the steep fall of the spur. The hills were blown almost clear of the mist, though it still scarfed the glen with white; and the evening was coming swiftly, swiftly. And somewhere southward beyond those hills, not far now, surely, was the Wall.

'Why did you come among us, calling yourself a healer of sore eyes, to steal from us the winged god?'

Marcus swung round in answer to the furious voice behind him. 'In the first place, am I so lacking as a healer of sore eyes? At least your brother's son will not be blind.' He leaned one shoulder wearily against the parapet, and stood gazing down reflectively at his captive. 'In the second, I came to take back—not to steal, for it was never yours—*take back* the winged god, because it was the Eagle of my father's Legion.' Instinctively he knew that with Liathan, as with Cottia, that was the part that would make sense; knew also that it was better for the peace of the frontier that the thing be kept a private feud between himself and the tribes.

There was a queer little flicker in Liathan's dark eyes. 'So my grandfather was right,' he said.

'Was he? Tell me about this rightness of his.'

'When the priest-kind found the winged god was gone,' Liathan said, with a kind of defiant willingness to talk, 'my grandfather swore it was you who had taken it. He said you had the face of that Chieftain of the Red Crests he had seen killed under the wings of the god, and that he had been blind and doting not to know you for his son. But when we had followed you and searched your gear and found nothing, we said among ourselves that the grandfather grew old and fanciful. Then Gault the fisherman found your ring-brooch by the shore of the loch, and the bank pulled down and a hollow place under the water-line. And later, we heard a strange tale from the rath where your sword-brother was taken sick; and we knew. And my grandfather said, " I was right, after all, who am never wrong," and he sent for me, for my brother had been savaged by a seal and was too sick of the wound to go to the Hosting. He sent for me, and said: " It may be that it is you who will hunt him down, for there is a link of fate between his line and ours. If it be so, kill him if you can, for he has put shame on the gods of the tribe; but also give him his father's ring, for he is his father's son in more than blood." '

There was an instant's complete silence; and then Marcus said: ' You have it now? '

' On a thong round my neck,' Liathan said sullenly. ' You must take it for yourself, since my hands are bound.'

Marcus lowered himself on to his sound knee, and slipped a hand warily under the shoulder-folds of the other's cloak. But it was no trick; he found the ring, which had worked round to the back, and drawing it out, cut the thong, and slipped it on to his bare signet finger. The light was beginning to fade, and the great stone that had been full of green fire when he saw it last, was coolly dark as ilex leaves, lit only by a faint surface reflection of the sky. ' If the fortunes of war had gone otherwise, and Esca and I had fallen to your spears, you would have had small chance to give me my father's ring. How, then, would you have carried out your grand-father's bidding? ' he asked curiously.

' You should have had the ring to take with you, as a man takes his weapons and his favourite hound.'

' I see,' said Marcus. From the ring he looked back to

Liathan, suddenly half smiling. 'When you go back to your own place, say to Tradui that I thank him for the gift of my father's ring.'

Esca's step sounded on the stairs and a moment later he ducked out into the evening light. 'All is well with the ponies,' he said. 'Also I have looked round a little, and seen that our way lies down the glen westward. That way there is birch cover almost from the first, and moreover the hunt went toward the sunrise.'

Marcus glanced up at the sky. 'The light will be gone in the half of an hour, but much can happen in that time, and it is in my heart that we will go now.'

Esca nodded, reaching him a steadying hand as he rose; and in so doing, saw the flawed emerald, and gave him a quick, questioning glance.

'Yes,' said Marcus. 'Liathan has brought me my father's ring as a gift from his grandfather.' He turned to look down at the tribesman. 'We shall take two of your ponies, Liathan, to carry us to the Wall, but we will turn them loose when we have done with them, and with good fortune you will find them again—later. I hope you do, because you brought me my father's ring . . . See to the gag, Esca.'

Esca saw to it.

Meeting the furious eyes above the gag, Marcus said, 'I am sorry, but we can ill afford to have you shouting the moment we are gone, lest there be someone within hearing. It will assuredly not be long before your sword-brethren return and find you, but to make all safe I will see that word of your whereabouts reaches the tribesmen, when *we* have reached the Wall. That is the best that I can do.'

They crossed to the stairhead. Esca paused to collect the tribesmen's weapons from the place where he had stacked them, and sent them—all save one spear, which he kept to replace his own—over the parapet into the tarn below. Marcus heard them take the water in a stutter of faint splashes, while he bent over the other two captives, both conscious and hating hard by this time, to make sure that they had not yet contrived to

slacken their bonds. Then they ducked through the doorway
into the descending darkness.

The strain of their escape had taxed Marcus to the uttermost,
and the respite in the signal-tower, short as it had been, had
been long enough to let the old wound begin to stiffen. He had
to nerve himself to every step, and there seemed a great many
more steps on the way down than there had been on the way
up. But they reached the bottom at last, and came out into
the little courtyard, where three ponies stood with their reins
over their heads.

They chose the two of them, a black and a dun, who seemed
the freshest and, hitching the reins of the third one over a fallen
timber to prevent him following, led them out through the
narrow gateway. 'The last lap,' Marcus said, drawing a hand
caressingly down the neck of the black pony. 'We will break
fast in one of the Wall stations tomorrow morning.'

Esca helped him to mount, before he himself swung on to the
back of the dun. For a few moments Marcus had all he could
do to master his mount, for the fiery little brute objected
strongly to an unfamiliar rider, snorting and plunging like an
unbroken colt, until, seeming suddenly to tire of the fight, it
answered to his hand and set off at a canter, shaking its head
and spilling foam over its chest and knees.

Esca ranged alongside on the dun, and they swung over the
steep scarp of the spur, and headed downhill for the woods
below them. 'Praise be to Lugh, they are yet fairly fresh;
for we've a hard ride before us.'

'Yes,' said Marcus, rather grimly; and shut his teeth on
the word. That plunging tussle with his mount had taken
most of the endurance that was left in him.

The light was going fast, as they swung into the long southward curve of the glen. The wind was surging through the
birch and hazel of the woods, and overhead the sky between
the hurrying clouds was kindling yellow as a lantern.

.   .   .   .   .

A long while later, a sentry on the northern ramparts of
Borcovicus thought that in a lull of the tearing wind he heard

the beat of horses' hooves somewhere far below him. He checked his pacing to look down, far down where the burn cut through its wild glen a hundred feet below the fortress walls, but a racing, silver-fringed cloud had come across the moon, and the glen was a black nothingness below him, and the wind swooped back, blowing away all sound. Curse the wind! There was always a wind—save where there was mist —up here on the highest lift of the Wall; nothing to hear all day and all night but the wind and the peewits calling. It was enough to make a man hear worse than horses' hooves inside his head. The sentry spat disgustedly down into the dark abyss, and continued his measured pacing.

Some while later still, the guard on duty at the North Gate was surprised by a most imperious beating on the timbers and shout of ' Open in Caesar's name! ' So might a bearer of dispatches announce his arrival, if it were at any other gate; but the few who came from the north—horse-dealers, hunters, and the like—did not hammer on the gate as though they were the Legate himself demanding entrance in the name of the Emperor. It might be a trick of some kind. Leaving his gate-guard turned out and standing ready, the Optio clanked up to the look-out above the gateway.

The moon rode clear of the clouds now, and faintly, by its reflected light, the Optio could pick out two figures directly below him in the shadow of the arch. The sheer drop of the hillside was in shadow, but there was enough light to show it empty of men, clear down to the white streak of the burn. Not a trick, then.

' Who demands entrance in Caesar's name? '

One of the figures looked up, his face a pale blur in the darkness. ' Two who have urgent business with the Commander and would fain keep whole skins if possible. Open up, friend.'

The Optio hesitated an instant, then turned and clattered down the few steps. ' Open up,' he ordered.

Men sprang to obey him, the heavy oaken valve swung smoothly outward on its stone socket, and in the opening,

clearly lit now by the yellow light from the guard-room doorway, appeared two wild, bearded figures, who might have been
born of the autumn gale. One of them was leaning heavily
on the shoulder of the other, who seemed to be supporting him
by an arm round his waist; and as they stumbled forward,
the Optio, who had begun curtly, ' Now what——' went kindly
enough to steady him on the other side, saying, ' Run into
trouble, eh? '

But the other laughed suddenly, his teeth showing white in
the dark tangle of his beard; and staggering clear of his
friend's supporting arm, propped himself against the guard-
room wall, and drooped there, breathing hard and fast through
widened nostrils. Clad in filthy rags, gaunt as famine and
well-nigh as dirty, scratched and blood-smeared as though from
contact with many furze bushes, he was as villainous an object
as the Optio had seen for a long time.

As the gate clanged shut behind him, this apparition said in
the cool, clipped accents of a cohort centurion, ' Optio, I wish
to see the Commanding Officer immediately.'

' Ugh? ' said the Optio, and blinked.

Presently, after a queer confusion of changing faces, of
brusque soldiers' voices and clanging footsteps, and long
wavering alleyways between buildings whose corners never
seemed to be quite where he expected them, Marcus found
himself standing on the threshold of a lamp-lit room. It
flowered suddenly golden on his sight, out of the windy dark;
a small room, white-walled, and almost filled by a battered
writing-table and records chest. He blinked at it with a queer,
dreamlike sense of unreality. A square-built man in half uniform rose from the camp-chair, and turned inquiringly to the
door. ' Yes, what——' he began, much as the Optio had done.

As the door closed behind him, Marcus looked at the stocky
familiar figure, the square face with the dark hairs growing
out of the nose, and felt no surprise. He had come back to a
familiar world, and it seemed only natural that he should find
old friends in it. ' Good evening to you, Drusillus,' he said.
' My congratulations on—your promotion.'

The centurion's face was puzzled, and his head went up a little stiffly.

'Do you not know me, Drusillus?' Marcus said almost pleadingly. 'I am——'

But light had already dawned on his old centurion, and the bewilderment in his square brown face became blank astonishment and then lit into incredulous delight. 'Centurion Aquila!' he said. 'Yes, sir, I know you. I would know you in Tartarus itself, now that I come to look at you!' He came tramping round the table. 'But what in the name of Thunder brings you here?'

Marcus set his bundle carefully on the table. 'We have brought back the Hispana's lost Eagle,' he said, rather muzzily, and very quietly crumpled forward on top of it.

XX

VALEDICTORY

TOWARDS evening of a day in late October, Marcus and Esca came riding up the last lift of the Calleva road. Having learned at Eburacum that the Legate Claudius was not yet returned, they had pushed on south, knowing that they could not miss him by the way, to wait for him at Calleva.

They were rid of their beards and reasonably clean once more, and Marcus had had his hair clipped short again in the Roman manner; but still clad in the tatterdemalion clothes of their adventuring, still gaunt and hollow-eyed and disreputable, they had more than once needed the permit provided by Drusillus to save them from the awkward charge of having stolen the army post-horses on which they rode.

They were tired, bone tired, and without any glow of triumph to warm the leaden chill of their tiredness; and they rode with the reins loose on their horses' necks, in silence save for the strike of shod hooves on the metalled road and the squeak of wet leather. But after many months in the wild aloofness of the north, this gentler and more friendly countryside seemed to Marcus to hold out its arms to him, and it was with a sense of homecoming that he lifted his face to the soft grey mizzle, and saw afar off, beyond the rolling miles of dappled forest, the familiar and suddenly beloved outline of the South Downs.

They rode into Calleva by the North Gate, left the horses at the Golden Vine for return to the transit camp next day, and set out on foot for the house of Aquila. In the narrow street, when they turned into it, the poplar trees were already bare, and the way slippery with shrivelled wet leaves. The daylight was fading fast, and the windows of Uncle Aquila's watchtower were full of lemon-pale lamp-light that seemed somehow like a welcome.

The door was on the latch, and they pushed it open and went in. There was an air of most unwonted bustle in the house, as though someone had lately arrived or was expected to arrive at any moment. As they emerged from the narrow entrance closet, old Stephanos was crossing the atrium towards the dining recess. He cast one glance at them, uttered a startled bleat, and all but dropped the lamp he was carrying.

' It is all right, Stephanos,' Marcus told him, slipping off his wet cloak and tossing it over a convenient bench. ' It is only the Golden Vine that we are sprung from, not the realms of Hades. Is my uncle in his study? '

The old slave's mouth was open to reply, but nobody ever heard what he said, for his voice was drowned by a frenzied baying that rose on the instant. There was a wild scurry of paws along the colonnade, and a great brindled shape sprang over the threshold and came streaking across the floor, skidding on the smooth surface, ears pricked and bush tail flying. Cub, lying dejectedly in the colonnade, had heard Marcus's v oice and come to find him.

' Cub! ' Marcus called, and sat down hurriedly on top of his cloak, just in time to save himself from being bowled over like a stoned hare as Cub landed with a flying leap on his chest.

They slid together off the bench with a resounding thump. Marcus had his arms round the young wolf's neck, and Cub thrust against him, whining and yelping, licking his face from ear to ear with frantic joy. But by now news of their return had burst through the house, and Marcipor came scuttling with dignified haste to one door while Sassticca ran in through another, still clutching a large iron spoon; and somehow, between Cub's joyful onslaughts, Marcus was turning from one to the other, greeting and being greeted. ' You have not got rid of us, you see, Marcipor ! Sassticca, it is like the flowers in spring to see you! The nights that I have dreamed of your honey cakes—— '

' Ah, I thought I heard your voice, Marcus—among others.'

There was a sudden hush; and Uncle Aquila was standing

at the foot of the watch-tower stairs, with old grey-muzzled
Procyon at his side, and behind him, the dark, austere figure of
Claudius Hieronimianus.

Marcus got up slowly, one hand still on the great savage head
that was pressed against his thigh. 'It seems that we have
timed our arrival well,' he said. He started forward at the
same instant as his uncle strode to meet him, and next moment
they had come together in the middle of the atrium, and
Marcus was gripping both the older man's hands in his.

'Uncle Aquila! Oh, it's good to see you again. How goes
it with you, sir?'

'Strangely enough, it goes the better for seeing you safely
home once more, even in the guise of a Tiber rat,' said Uncle
Aquila. His glance went to Esca and back again. 'In the
guise of two Tiber rats.' And then after an instant's pause,
very quietly, 'What news?'

'I have brought it back,' Marcus said, equally quietly. And
that was all for the moment on the subject of the lost Eagle.
The four of them were alone in the atrium, the slaves having
slipped out to their own duties when the master of the house
appeared, and Uncle Aquila gathered both young men after
him with an imperious gesture to where the Legate, who had
drawn aside from their meeting, was quietly warming himself
at the brazier. In the general shifting Cub circled for an
instant to thrust his muzzle into Esca's hand in greeting, then
returned to Marcus again. Procyon greeted nobody, he was a
one-man-dog to the point of seldom appearing conscious that
other men existed.

'He has done it!' Uncle Aquila was announcing in a kind of
triumphant grumble. 'He has done it, by Jupiter! You
never thought he would, did you, my Claudius?'

'I am—not sure,' said the Legate, his strange black eyes
resting on Marcus consideringly. 'No, I am not—at all sure,
my Aquila.'

Marcus saluted him, then drew Esca forward from the
outskirts of the group. 'Sir, may I bring to your remembrance
my friend Esca Mac Cunoval?'

'I already remember him very well,' said Claudius with a quick smile to the Briton.

Esca bent his head to him. 'You witnessed my manumission papers, I believe, sir,' he said in a dead-level tone that made Marcus glance at him anxiously, realizing suddenly that there had been no real homecoming for Esca in this return to a house in which he had been a slave.

'I did. But I generally remember men by other things than the papers I may have witnessed for them,' the Legate said gently.

An exclamation from Uncle Aquila cut across the little exchange, and looking round, Marcus found the other staring at his left hand, which he had unconsciously curved about the precious bundle which he still carried in its sling. 'That ring,' said Uncle Aquila. 'Show it to me.'

Marcus slipped off the heavy signet-ring and passed it to him. 'Of course you recognize it?'

His uncle stood for a few moments examining it, his face unreadable. Then he gave it back. 'Yes,' he said. 'Yes, by Jupiter, I do recognize it. How came you by your father's ring?'

But with Sassticca's voice rising near at hand, and one or other of the slaves likely at any moment to come through the atrium about their preparations for dinner, Marcus could not bring himself to start on that story. Slipping the ring back on to his finger, he said, 'Uncle Aquila, could we leave that—with all the rest, for a fitter place and season? It is a long story, and there are many doors to this room.'

Their eyes met, and after a pause, Uncle Aquila said, 'Aye, well. Both matters have waited long enough for an hour to make little difference. You agree, Claudius?'

The Egyptian nodded. 'Most assuredly I agree. In your watch-tower, after we have eaten, we shall be safe from interruption. Then Marcus shall make his full report.' Suddenly his face crinkled into a thousand-creased smile, and with a swift change of manner that seemed to draw a silken curtain over the whole affair of the lost Eagle, shutting it decently from view until the time came to take it out again and deal with it, he turned to Marcus. ' It seems always that I visit this house at a happy hour. The last time, it was Cub who came back, and this time it is you, but the reunion remains the same.'

Marcus looked down at Cub, who was leaning against him, head up and eyes half closed in ecstasy. 'We are glad to be together, Cub and I,' he said.

' So it seems. It is almost past believing that a wolf should be so much a friend. Was he greatly more difficult than a hound, in the making? '

' I think he was more stubborn; certainly fiercer to handle. But it was Esca rather than I who had the making of him. He is the expert.'

' Ah, of course.' The Legate turned to Esca. ' You come of the Brigantes, do you not? More than once I have seen Cub's brethren running among the dog-packs of your tribe, and wondered how——'

But Marcus heard no more. He had stooped quickly, and was running an exploring hand over the young wolf, suddenly aware of something that he had not really taken in, in the first flush of home-coming. ' Uncle Aquila, what have you done to Cub? He is nothing but skin and bone.'

' *We* have done nothing to Cub,' said Uncle Aquila in accents of acute disgust. ' Cub has been breaking his own wilful heart for his own amusement. Since you left, he has refused food from any but that chit Cottia, and since her going, he has pre- ferred to starve. That brute has been deliberately dying in our midst with the entire household buzzing round him like blow- flies round a stranded fish.'

Marcus's caressing hand had checked on Cub's neck, and something seemed to twist and turn cold inside him. ' Cottia,' he said. ' Where has Cottia gone? ' He had scarcely thought of her, save twice, in all the months that he had been away; but it seemed a long, long time before his uncle answered.

' Only to Aquae Sulis for the winter. Her Aunt Valaria discovered a need to take the waters, and shifted the whole household, a few days ago.'

Marcus let go the breath that he had been holding. He
began to play with Cub's ears, drawing them again and again
through his fingers. ' Did she leave any word for me? '

' She came to me in a fine flaming passion, the day before
she was swept away, to bring back your bracelet.'

' Did you tell her—about keeping it? '

' I did not. Some things are best unsaid until the need
comes for saying them. I told her that since you had left it in
her charge, it seemed to me best that she keep it until she came
back in the spring and could give it into your hands. I also
promised to tell you that she would guard it well through the
winter.' He held one great blue-veined hand to the warmth
of the brazier, and smiled at it. ' She is a vixen, the little one,
but a faithful vixen.'

' Yes,' Marcus. ' Yes . . . sir, with your leave I will take
the Cub and feed him now.'

Esca, who had been answering the Legate's questions about
the taming of wolf-cubs, said quickly. ' I will take him.'

' Maybe if we both take him, we can wash off some of the
journey while we are about it. We have time for that, Uncle
Aquila?'

' Time and to spare,' said his uncle. ' Dinner will doubtless
be put back to Jupiter knows what hour, while Sassticca
ransacks her store shelves for your benefit.'

Uncle Aquila was perfectly right. For Marcus's benefit,
Sassticca ransacked her store shelves with joyful abandon; and
the sad thing was that it was all as good as wasted. To
Marcus at all events, that dinner was completely unreal. He
was so tired that the soft light of the palm-oil lamps seemed a
golden fog, and he tasted nothing of what he ate and scarcely
even noticed the handful of rain-wet autumn crocuses which
Sassticca, proud of her knowledge of Roman ways, had
scattered on the table. It seemed odd, after so many meals
eaten in the open or squatting beside peat fires, to eat at a
civilized table again, to see the clean-shaven faces of the other
men, and the tunics of soft white wool that they wore—Esca's
a borrowed one of his own—to hear the quiet, clipped voices of

his uncle and the Legate when they spoke to each other.   Very
odd, like something out of another world; a familiar world,
grown suddenly unfamiliar.   He had almost forgotten what
to do with a napkin.   Only Esca, clearly finding it strange and
uncomfortable to eat while reclining on his left elbow, seemed
real in the queer brittle unreality.

It was an uneasy meal, eaten without lingering and almost
in silence, for the minds of all four were on one subject, carefully
shut away behind its silken curtain, but making it hopeless to
try to talk of something else.   A strange home-coming meal,
with the shadow of the lost Eagle brooding over it; and Marcus
was thankful when at last Uncle Aquila set down the cup after
pouring the final oblation, and said, ' Shall we go up to my
study now? '

Following the two older men, and once again carrying the
Eagle, Marcus had mounted four or five of the watch-tower
steps before he realized that Esca was not coming up behind,
and looking back, he saw him still standing at the foot of the
stairs.

' I think that I will not come,' Esca said.

' Not come?   But you must come.'

Esca shook his head.   ' It is between you and your uncle and
the Legate.'

Followed as ever, by Cub, Marcus came down the few steps
again.   ' It is between the four of us.   What maggot has got
into your head, Esca? '

' I think that I should not go to your uncle's private sanc-
tum.'   Esca said stubbornly.   ' I have been a slave in his
house.'

' You are not a slave now.'

' No, I am your freed-man now.   It is strange.   I never
thought of that until this evening.'

Marcus had never thought of it either, but he knew that it was
true.   You could give a slave his freedom, but nothing could
undo the fact that he had been a slave; and between him, a
freed-man, and any free man who had never been unfree, there
would still be a difference.   Wherever the Roman way of life

held good, that difference would be there. That was why it
had not mattered, all these months that they had been away;
that was why it mattered now. Suddenly he felt baffled and
helpless. 'You did not feel like this before we went north.
How is it altered now?'

'That was at the beginning. I had not had time to—
understand. I knew only that I was free—a hound slipped
from the leash; and we were going away from it all in the
morning. Now we have come back.'

Yes, they had come back, and the thing had got to be faced,
and faced at once. On a sudden impulse Marcus reached out
his free hand and caught his friend's shoulder, not at all gently.
'Listen to me,' he said. 'Are you going to live all the rest of
your life as though you had taken a whipping and could not
forget it? Because if you are, I am sorry for you. You don't
like being a freed-man, do you? Well, I don't like being lame.
That makes two of us, and the only thing we can do about it,
you and I, is to learn to carry the scars lightly.' He gave the
shoulder a friendly shake, and dropped his hand. 'Come up
with me now, Esca.'

Esca did not answer for a moment. And then slowly his head
went up, and his eyes wore the dancing look they always wore
in action. 'I will come,' he said.

When they emerged into Uncle Aquila's watch-tower, the
two older men were standing over the wrought-iron brazier
that glowed red in its alcove at the far side of the room. They
looked round as Marcus and Esca entered, but nobody spoke;
only the rain whispered softly, delicately, against the narrow
windows. The small lamplit room seemed very remote from
the world, very tall above it. Marcus had a sense of immense
depths dropping away beneath him in the darkness, as though,
if he went to the window, he might look down and see Orion
swimming like a fish below him.

'Well?' said Uncle Aquila at last; and the word fell
sharply into the silence, like a pebble dropping into a pool.

Marcus crossed to the writing-table and set his bundle down
upon it. How pathetic and shapeless it seemed; a bundle that

might contain boots or washing. 'It has lost its wings,' he said. 'That is why it bulks so small.'

The silken curtain had been drawn back now, and with it was gone the brittle surface of ordinariness that they had kept all evening. 'So the rumour was a true one,' the Legate said.

Marcus nodded, and began to undo the shapeless mass. He turned back the last fold, and there, amid the tumble of tattered violet cloth, the lost Eagle stood, squat and undignified, but oddly powerful, on its splayed legs. The empty wing sockets were very black in the lamplight which kindled its gilded feathers to the strong yellow of gorse flowers. There was a furious pride about the upreared head. Wingless it might be, fallen from its old estate, but it was an Eagle still; and out of its twelve-year captivity, it had returned to its own people.

For a long moment nobody spoke, and then Uncle Aquila said, 'Shall we sit down to this?'

Marcus folded up thankfully on one end of the bench which Esca had drawn to the table, for his unsound leg had begun to shake under him. He was warmly aware of Cub's chin settling contentedly on his foot, and Esca sitting beside him, as he began to make his report. He made it clearly and carefully, abating nothing of the stories told him by Guern the Hunter and by old Tradui, though parts of them were hard in the telling. At the appropriate places he handed over to Esca, to speak for himself. And all the time, his eyes never left the Legate's intent face.

The Legate sat leaning forward a little in Uncle Aquila's great chair, his arms crossed on the table before him, his face, with the red weal of his helmet rim still faintly showing on his forehead, like an intent golden mask against the shadows behind.

No one moved or spoke at once when the report was finished. Marcus himself sat very still, searching into the long black eyes for their verdict. The rain sharpened to a little impatient spatter against the window. Then Claudius Hieronimianus shifted, and the spell of stillness was broken. 'You have done well, both of you,' he said; and his gaze moved from Marcus to Esca and back again, drawing them both in. ' Thanks to you, a weapon which might one day have been used against the Empire, will never be so used. I salute two very courageous lunatics.'

' And—the Legion? '

' No,' said the Legate. ' I am sorry.'

So Marcus had his verdict. It was ' thumbs down ' for the Ninth Legion. He had thought that he had accepted that from the night when he had heard Guern's story. Now he knew that he had never quite accepted it. In his heart of hearts he had clung, against all reason, to the hope that his own judgement was wrong, after all. He made one desperate appeal for his father's Legion, knowing as he did so, that it was hopeless.

' Sir, there were upward of three cohorts who were not with the Legion when it marched North. Many Legions have been re-formed from fewer survivors than that—if the Eagle was still in Roman hands.'

' Those cohorts were broken up twelve years ago, and distributed among other Legions of the Empire,' the Legate said very kindly. ' By now more than half the men will have finished their military service, and those that have not, will have changed their allegiance to their new Eagles, long ago. On your own showing, the name and number of the Ninth Hispana is no heritage for a new Legion to carry. It is better that it be forgotten.'

' There is no way back through the Waters of Lethe.' Behind the Legate's words, Marcus seemed to hear Guern the Hunter. ' No way back through the Waters of Lethe—no way back——'

Uncle Aquila crashed up from the table. ' And what of their last stand, that Marcus has just told us of? Is not *that* a heritage fit for any Legion? '

The Legate turned a little in his chair, to look up at him. ' The conduct of a few score men cannot counterbalance the conduct of a whole Legion,' he said. ' You must see that, Aquila, even though one of them was your brother.'

Uncle Aquila grunted savagely, and the Legate turned back

to Marcus. 'How many people know that the Eagle has been brought back?'

'South of the Wall, we four, your own Camp Commandant, who I gather knew of the matter from yourself, and the Commander of the garrison at Borcovicus. He was my old Second at Isca Dumnoniorum, and gained his cohort for his defence of the fort after I was wounded. We took pains that no one else in Borcovicus should know what it was all about; and he will say nothing unless I give him leave. Rumour may come down from the North, of course, but if so, I imagine that it will die out as the earlier rumour did.'

'Well enough,' said the Legate. "Naturally I shall lay the whole matter before the Senate. But I have no doubt of their verdict.'

Uncle Aquila made a small, expressive gesture, as though screwing something up and tossing it into the brazier. "What do you suggest becomes of this?' he nodded to the defiant, squatting Eagle.

'Give it honourable burial,' said the Legate.

'Where?' Marcus demanded huskily, after a moment.

'Why not here in Calleva? Five roads meet here, and the Legions are for ever passing by, while the place itself is the territory of no particular Legion.'

He leaned forward to brush the gilded feathers lightly with one finger, his face thoughtful in the lamplight. 'So long as Rome lasts, the Eagles will pass and re-pass under the walls of Calleva. What better place for it to lie?'

Uncle Aquila said, 'When I had this house built, there had lately been a flare-up of unrest hereabout, and I had a small hiding-place made under the floor of the shrine, to take my papers in case of further trouble. Let it lie there and be forgotten.'

.   .   .   .   .

Very much later that night, the four of them stood together in the small alcove shrine at the end of the atrium. The slaves had long since gone to their own quarters, and they had the house and the silence of the house to themselves. A bronze

Q

lamp on the altar sent up a long tongue of flame the shape of a
perfect laurel leaf; and by its light the household gods in their
niches in the lime-washed walls seemed to look down, as the
four men were looking down, into the small square hole in the
tesselated floor, just before the altar.

Marcus had brought the Eagle down from the watch-tower,
carrying it as he had carried it so many miles and slept with it
so many nights, in the crook of his arm.   And while the others
watched in silence, he had knelt down and laid it in the small
square cist that reached down through the hypercaust into the
dark earth beneath.   He had laid it—no longer bundled in
tattered violet cloth—on his old military cloak, and drawn the
scarlet folds closely over it with a gentle hand.   He had been
very proud to wear that cloak; it was fitting that his father's
Eagle should have it now.

The four men stood with bent heads; three who had served
with the Eagles in their different times, one who had suffered
slavery for taking up arms against them; but in that moment
there was no gulf between them.   The Legate stepped forward
to the edge of the square hole, looking down to where the
scarlet of Marcus's cloak was all but lost in the depths beyond
the reach of the lamplight.   He raised one hand, and began,
very simply, to speak the Valedictory, the Farewell, as he might
have spoken it for a dead comrade.

Suddenly, to Marcus's tired mind, it seemed that there were
others beside themselves in the little lamplit shrine; notably
two: a slight, dark man, with an eager face beneath the tall
crest of a First Cohort Commander; and a shock-headed tribesman in a saffron kilt.   Yet when he looked at the tribesman,
he was gone, and in his place the young centurion he had once
been.

'Here lies the Eagle of the Ninth Legion, the Hispana,' the
Legate was saying.   'Many times it found honour in the wars,
against foes abroad and rebellion at home.   Shame came to it;
but at the end it was honourably held until the last of those who
held it died beneath its wings.   It has led brave men.   Let it lie
forgotten.'

He stepped back.

Esca looked questioningly to Uncle Aquila, then at a sign from him, stooped to the segment of solid-moulded tessera which stood upreared against the wall, and fitted it carefully back into place over the hole. It had been well contrived, this hiding-place that Uncle Aquila had had made for his papers; with the segment replaced and the pattern completed, no trace of it remained, save for one all but invisible chink just wide enough to take a knife-blade.

'Tomorrow we will seal it up,' said Uncle Aquila, heavily.

Faintly into the silence, down the soft wet wind, stole the long-drawn, haunting notes of the trumpets from the transit camp, sounding for the third watch of the night. To Marcus, still gazing down blindly at the place where the square hole had been, it seemed that they were sounding with unbearable sadness for the lost Eagle, and for the lost Legion that had marched into the mist and never come marching back. Then, as the distant trumpets quickened into the shining spray of notes that ended the call, suddenly his sense of failure dropped from him like a tattered cloak, and he knew again, as he had known in the ruined signal-tower while the hunt closed in below, that it had all been worth while.

He had failed to redeem his father's Legion, since it was past redeeming, but the lost Eagle was home again, and would never now be used as a weapon against its own people.

He raised his head at the same time as Esca, and their eyes met. 'A good hunting?' Esca seemed to be asking.

'It was a good hunting,' Marcus said.

XXI

THE OLIVE-WOOD BIRD

THAT winter was not an easy one for Marcus. For months he had mercilessly overtaxed his lame leg, and when the strain was over, it quite suddenly took its revenge. He did not much mind the pain it gave him, save when it kept him awake at night, but he did most bitterly mind finding himself shackled by the old wound again, when he had thought that all that was over. He felt ill, and he was wildly impatient; and he missed Cottia through the dark winter days as he had never missed her before.

Also there was the old nagging question of the future still to be settled. For Esca, the future was simpler—simpler as to the outward things at all events. 'I am your armour-bearer, though I am no longer your slave,' he said when they discussed the question. 'I will serve you, and you shall feed me, and between whiles maybe I will turn hunter, and that will bring in a sesterce from time to time.' Even before the year turned Marcus had spoken to his uncle about his old idea of becoming somebody's secretary; but Uncle Aquila had disposed of his capabilities to be anybody's secretary in a few well-chosen and blistering words, and when he proved stubborn in the plan, finished up by making him promise to wait at least until he was strong again.

The year drew on to spring, and slowly Marcus's leg began to strengthen under him once more. March came, and the forest below the ramparts was flushed with rising sap, and the many thorn-trees which gave it its name began to feather the wooded hills with white. And quite suddenly the House of Kaeso woke up. For a few days slaves came and went, scurrying about it; hangings were shaken out of doors, and the fumes of the freshly lit hypercaust fire blew into the slaves' quarters of Uncle Aquila's house and created unpleasantness between the two households. Then one evening, returning from the baths, Marcus and Esca met a hired mule-carriage being driven away empty from the house of Kaeso, and glimpsed a mass of luggage being carried indoors. The family had returned.

Next morning Marcus went down to the foot of the garden, and whistled for Cottia, as he had been used to do. It was a wild day of blustering wind and thin, shining rain, and the little native daffodils in the rampart curve tossed and streamed before the gusts like points of wind-blown flame, with the shrill sunshine slanting through their petals. Cottia came with the wind behind her, up round the end of the swaying hedge, to join him under the bare fruit-trees.

' I heard you whistle,' she said, ' and so I came. I have brought your bracelet back to you.'

' Cottia! ' Marcus said. ' Why, Cottia! ' and stood looking at her, making no move to take the bracelet that she held out to him. It was almost a year since their last meeting, but he had expected her to wait as she had been then. And Cottia had not waited. She stood before him much taller than she had been, with her head up, and returned his look, suddenly a little uncertain. Her soft golden-green mantle was swathed closely round her over the straight white folds of her tunic; one end of it, which had been drawn over her head, had fallen back, and her flaming hair that had been used to blow wild, was braided into a shining coronal so that she seemed more than ever to carry her head like a queen. Her lips were touched with red, and her eyebrows darkened, and there were tiny gold drops in her ears.

' Why, Cottia,' he said again, ' you have grown up,' and felt suddenly a little ache of loss.

' Yes,' said Cottia. ' Do you like me grown up? '

' Yes—yes, of course,' Marcus said. ' Thank you for looking after my bracelet for me. Uncle Aquila told me how you came to see him about it before you went away.' He took the heavy gold bracelet from her and sprang it on to his wrist, still looking at her as he did so. He found that he did not know how to talk to her, and as the silence lengthened, he asked with desperate politeness, ' Did you like Aquae Sulis? '

' *No*! ' Cottia spat the word between little pointed teeth, and her face was suddenly bright with fury. ' I hated every moment of Aquae Sulis! I never wanted to go there; I wanted to wait for you because you told me you might be home before the winter closed in. And all winter I have had no word of you save one little—*little* message in some silly letter your uncle sent mine about the new town water supply; and I have waited, and waited, and now you are not at all glad to see me! Well, neither am I at all glad to see *you*! '

' You little vixen! ' Marcus caught her wrists as she turned to run, and swung her round to face him. Suddenly and softly he laughed. ' But I am glad to see you. You do not know how glad I am to see you, Cottia.'

She was dragging away from him, wrenching at her wrists to free them, but at his words she checked, looking up into his face. ' Yes, you are now,' she said wonderingly. ' Why were you not, before? '

' I did not recognize you, just at first.'

' Oh,' said Cottia, a little blankly. She was silent a moment, and then asked with sudden anxiety: ' Where is Cub? '

' Making love to Sassticca for a bone. He is growing greedy.'

She drew a deep breath of relief. ' All was well with him, then, when you came home? '

' He was very thin; he would not eat after you left. But all is well with him now.'

' I was afraid of that; that he would fret, I mean. It was one of the things that made me not want to go to Aquae Sulis; but I could not take him with me, truly I could not, Marcus. Aunt Valaria would never have allowed it.'

' I am very sure she would not,' Marcus said, his mouth quirking as he thought of the Lady Valaria confronted with the suggestion that she should take a young wolf to a fashionable watering-place.

By this time they were sitting side by side on Marcus's cloak

spread on the damp marble bench, and after a few moments
Cottia asked: ' Did you find the Eagle? '

He looked round at her, his arms resting across his knees.
' Yes,' he said at last.

' Oh, Marcus, I *am* so glad! So very glad! And now? '

' Nothing now.'

' But the Legion? ' She searched his face, and the sparkle
died in her own. ' Will there not be a new Ninth Legion,
after all? '

' No, there will never be a Ninth Legion again.'

' But Marcus——' she began, and then checked. ' No, I will
not ask questions.'

He smiled. ' One day, maybe, I will tell you the whole
story.'

' I will wait,' said Cottia.

For a while they sat there, talking by fits and starts, but silent
for the most part, glancing at each other from time to time
with a quick smile, and then away again, for they were unexpectedly shy of each other. Presently Marcus told her about
Esca, that he was no longer a slave. He had expected her to
be surprised, but she only said, ' Yes, Nissa told me, just after
you went away, and I was glad—for you both.' And then they
were silent again.

Behind them, in the bare swaying branches of the wild pear-
tree, a blackbird with a crocus-coloured bill burst into song,
and the wind caught and tossed the shining notes down to
them in a shower. They turned together to look up at the
singer, swaying against the cold blown blue of the sky. Marcus
narrowed his eyes into the thin dazzle of sunlight and whistled
back, and the blackbird, bowing and swaying on the wind-
blown branch, its throat swelling with an ecstasy of song,
seemed to be answering him. Then a cloud came sailing across
the sun, and the bright world was quenched in shadow.

At the same moment they heard a horse coming down the
street, its hoof-beats ringing on the wet roadway. It stopped
before the house, or before the next one; Marcus could not be
sure which.

The blackbird was still singing, but when he turned to look at Cottia, a shadow that was not merely the passing cloud seemed to have touched her. ' Marcus, what is it that you will do now? ' she asked suddenly.

' Now? '

' Now that you are strong again. You are strong again, aren't you? ' Then swiftly: ' No, I do not believe you are, you were limping more, just now, than you were when I saw you last.'

Marcus laughed. ' I have been lying up like a sick badger all winter, but I am mending fast now.'

' That is the truth? '

' That is the truth.'

' Then—what will you do? Will you go back to the Legions? '

' No. I should do well enough in a skirmish, maybe, but I could not march my cohort down from Portus Itius to Rome at twenty miles a day, and I should certainly be no use on the parade ground.'

' The parade ground! ' Cottia said indignantly. ' I have seen them on the parade ground through the gates of the transit camp. They march about in straight lines with all their legs working together, and make silly patterns of themselves while a man with a voice like a bull shouts at them. What has *that* to do with the fighting of wars? '

Marcus hastily gathered his wits together to make Cottia understand what it had to do with the fighting of wars, but he did not have to struggle with the explanations, for she hurried on without waiting for an answer. ' Then if you cannot go back to the Legions, what *will* you do? '

' I am not—quite sure.'

' Perhaps you will go home,' she said; and then seemed suddenly to realize her own words, and her eyes grew frightened. ' You will go back to Rome, and take Cub and Esca with you! '

' I do not know, Cottia, truly I do not know. But I do not suppose for a moment that I shall ever go home.'

But Cottia did not seem to hear him. ' Take me too.'

Suddenly her voice broke almost into a wail. ' They will build
the city wall round here soon, and you could not leave me in a
cage! You could not! Oh, Marcus, take me too! '
' Even if it were to Rome? ' Marcus said, remembering her
old wild hatred of all things Roman.

Cottia slipped from the bench, and turned to him as he got
up also. ' Yes,' she said. ' Anywhere at all, if only it was
with you.'

Two distinct waves of feeling swept over Marcus, so close
upon each other that they were almost one. The first was the
joyful surprise of finding, and the second the desolation of
losing again . . . How was he to explain to Cottia that
possessing nothing in the world, without even a trade to his
hands, he could not take her with him?

' Cottia,' he began wretchedly. ' Cottia, my heart—it is
no use——'

But before he could get any farther, he heard Esca calling,
with a note of excitement in his voice. ' Marcus! Where are
you, Marcus? '

' Down here. I am coming,' he shouted back, and caught
Cottia's hand. ' Come with me now, anyway.'

Rain had begun to spatter round them, but the sun was out
again and the rain shone as it fell. Cub met them at the courtyard steps, circling about them and barking joyously, his
straight bush of a tail streaming out behind. And hard behind
Cub, was Esca. ' This has just come for you,' he said, holding
out a slim, sealed papyrus roll.

Marcus took the roll from him, raising his brows at sight of
the Sixth Legion's signum on the seal; while Cottia and Esca
and Cub all greeted each other after their fashion. In the act
of breaking the thread he glanced up to see Uncle Aquila
stalking towards them.

' Curiosity is one of the privileges of extreme old age,' said
Uncle Aquila, towering over the group in the entrance to the
colonnade.

Marcus unrolled the crackling papyrus sheet. He was half
blind with the dazzle of the day outside and the written words

seemed to float in the midst of red and green clouds. 'To Centurion Marcus Flavius Aquila, from Claudius Hieroni-mianus, Legate of the Sixth Victrix, Greeting,' the letter began. He skimmed the few close lines to the end, then glanced up and met Cottia's wide golden eyes fixed on him. 'Are you a witch out of Thessaly, to draw down the moon in a net of your hair? Or is it only the Other Sight that you have?' he said; and returned to the letter in his hand.

He began to read it a second time, more carefully, taking it in, as he had scarcely been able to do at first, and giving them the gist of it as he went along. 'The Legate has laid that matter before the Senate, and their ruling is as we knew it must be. But he says that " in just recognition of service to the State, which is none the less real that it must remain unpub-lished ..."' He looked up quickly. 'Esca, you are a Roman citizen.'

Esca was puzzled, almost a little wary. 'I am not sure that I understand. What does it mean?'

It meant so much; rights, and duties. It could even, in a way, mean the cancelling of a clipped ear, for if a man were a Roman citizen, that fact was stronger than the fact that he had been a slave. Esca would find that out, later. Also, in Esca's case, it was his honourable quittance, the wooden foil of a gladiator who had won freedom with honour in the arena; the settlement of all debts. 'It is as though they gave you your wooden foil,' he said; and saw Esca, who had been a gladiator, begin to understand, before he returned again to his letter.

'The Legate says that for the same service, I am to be awarded the gratuity of a time-expired cohort centurion—paid in the old style, part sesterces, part land.' A long pause, and then he began to read word for word. 'Following the estab-lished custom, the land-grant will be made over to you here in Britain, as the province of your last military service; but a good friend of mine on the Senate benches writes me that if you so wish, there should be no difficulty in working an exchange for land in Etruria, which I believe is your own country. The official documents will be reaching both of you in due course, but since the wheels of officialdom are notoriously slow, I hope that I may be the first to give you the news. . . .'

He stopped reading. Slowly the hand which held the Legate's letter dropped to his side. He looked round at the faces that crowded him in: Uncle Aquila's wearing the look of someone watching with detached interest the result of an experiment; Esca's face with an alert and waiting look in it; Cottia's, grown all at once very pointed and white; Cub's great head upraised and watchful. Faces. And suddenly he wanted to escape from them all; even from Cottia, even from Esca. They were part of all his plans and calculations, they belonged to him and he to them, but for this one moment, he wanted to be alone, to realize what had happened without any-one else entering in to complicate it. He turned away from them and stood leaning against the half wall beside the court-yard steps, staring away down the rain-wet garden where the little native daffodils were a myriad points of dancing flame under the wild fruit-trees.

He could go home.

Standing there with the last cold spattering of the shower blowing in his face, he thought ' I can go home,' and saw be-hind his eyes, the long road leading South, the Legion's road, white in the Etruscan sunlight; the farmsteads among their terraced olive-trees, and the wine-darkness of the Apennines beyond. He seemed to catch the resiny, aromatic smell of the pine forests dropping to the shore, and the warm mingling of thyme and rosemary and wild cyclamen that was the sum-mer scent of his own hills. He could go back to all that now, to the hills and the people among whom he had been bred, and for whom he had been so bitterly home-sick, here in the North. But if he did, would there not be another hunger on him all his life? For other scents and sights and sounds; pale and changeful northern skies and the green plover calling?

Suddenly he knew why Uncle Aquila had come back to this country when his years of service were done. All his life he would remember his own hills, sometimes he would remember them with longing; but Britain was his home. That came to

him, not as a new thing, but as something so familiar that he
wondered why he had not known it before.

Cub thrust a cold muzzle under his hand, and he drew a
long breath and turned once again to the others. Uncle
Aquila stood still with arms folded and huge head a little bent,
looking on with that air of detached interest.

'My congratulations, Marcus,' he said. 'It is by no means
everyone for whom my friend Claudius will sweat as he must
have sweated to drag justice out of the Senate.'

'I could lay my head on his feet,' Marcus said softly. 'It is
a new beginning—a new beginning, Esca.'

'Of course, it will take a little time to work the exchange,'
said Uncle Aquila, thoughtfully. 'But I imagine that you
should be back in Etruria by autumn.'

'I shall not be going back to Etruria,' Marcus said. 'I shall
take up my land here in Britain.' He looked at Cottia. She
was standing just as she had stood ever since he began to read
the Legate's letter, still and waiting as a winter-bound withy.

'Not Rome, after all; but you did say, " Anywhere ", did
you not, Cottia sweet,' he said, holding out a hand to her.

She looked at him for an instant, questioningly. Then she
smiled, and making a little gesture to gather her mantle as
though she were quite prepared to come now, anywhere, anywhere at all, put her hand into his.

'And now I suppose that I shall have to arrange matters
with Kaeso,' said Uncle Aquila. 'Jupiter! Why did I
never realize how peaceful life was before you came!'

.   .   .   .   .

That evening, having written to the Legate for both of them,
Marcus had wandered up to join his uncle in the watch-tower,
while Esca went to arrange about getting the letter sent. He
was leaning at the high window, his elbows propped on the
sill, his chin in his hands, while behind him Uncle Aquila sat
squarely at the writing-table, surrounded by his History of
Siege Warfare. The high room held the fading daylight as in
a cup, but below in the courtyard the shadows were gathering,

and the rolling miles of forest had the softness of smoke, as Marcus looked out over them to the familiar wave-lift of the Downs.

Down country: yes, that was the country for farming. Thyme for bees, and good grazing; maybe even a southern slope that could be terraced for vines. He and Esca, and what little labour they could afford, little enough that would be at first; but they would manage. Farming with free or freed labour would be an experiment, but it had been done before, though not often. Esca had given him a distaste for owning human beings.

'We have been talking it over, Esca and I; and if I have any choice in the matter, I am going to try for land in the Down Country,' he said suddenly, still with his chin in his hands.

'I imagine that you should not have much difficulty in arranging that with the powers that be,' said Uncle Aquila, searching for a mislaid tablet among the orderly litter on his table.

'Uncle Aquila, did you know about this—beforehand, I mean?'

'I knew that Claudius intended bringing your names before the Senate, but whether any result would come of it was quite another matter." He snorted. " Trust the Senate to pay its debts in the old style! Land and sesterces; as much land and as few sesterces as may be; it comes cheaper that way.'

'Also one Roman citizenship,' said Marcus, quickly.

'Which is a thing apart from price, though not costly in the giving,' agreed Uncle Aquila. 'I think they need not have economized on your gratuity.'

Marcus laughed. 'We shall do well enough, Esca and I.'

'I have no doubt of it—always supposing that you do not first starve. You will have to build and stock, remember.'

'Most of the building we can do ourselves; wattle and daub will serve until we grow rich.'

'And what will Cottia think of that?'

'Cottia will be content,' Marcus said.

'Well, you know where to come when you need help.'

'Yes, I know.' Marcus turned from the window. 'If we should need help—really need it, after three bad harvests—I will come.'

'Not until then?'

'Not until then. No.'

Uncle Aquila glared. 'You are impossible! You grow more and more like your father every day!'

'Do I?' Marcus said, with a glint of laughter and hesitated; there were some things that it was never easy to say to the older man. 'Uncle Aquila, you have done so much for Esca and me already. If I had not had you to turn to——'

'Bah!' said Uncle Aquila, still searching for his missing tablet. 'No one else to turn to me. No son of my own to plague me.' He found the tablet at last, and began with delicate precision to smooth the used wax with his quill pen, evidently under the impression that it was the flat end of his stylus. Suddenly he looked up under his brows. 'If you had applied for that exchange, I believe I should have been rather lonely.'

'Did you think I would be away back to Clusium on the first tide?'

'I did not think so, no,' said Uncle Aquila slowly, looking with surprised disgust at the wreck of his quill, and laying it down. 'You have now made me ruin a perfectly good pen and destroy several extremely important notes. I hope you are satisfied . . . No, I did not think so, but until the time came, and the choice was between your hands, I could not be sure.'

'Nor could I,' Marcus said. 'But I am sure now.'

All at once, and seemingly for no particular reason, he was remembering his olive-wood bird. It had seemed to him as the little flames licked through the pyre of birch-bark and dead heather on which he had laid it, that with the childhood treasure, all his old life was burning away. But a new life, a new beginning, had warmed out of the grey ash, for himself, and Esca, and Cottia; perhaps for other people too; even for an unknown downland valley that would one day be a farm.

Somewhere a door slammed, and Esca's step sounded below in the colonnade, accompanied by a clear and merry whistling.

> ' Oh when I joined the Eagles,
> (As it might be yesterday)
> I kissed a girl at Clusium
> Before I marched away.'

And it came to Marcus suddenly that slaves very seldom whistled. They might sing, if they felt like it or if the rhythm helped their work, but whistling was in some way different; it took a free man to make the sort of noise Esca was making.

Uncle Aquila looked up again from mending the broken pen. ' Oh, by the way. I have a piece of news that may interest you, if you have not heard it already. They are rebuilding Isca Dumnoniorum.'

List of Place-Names

ROMAN BRITAIN

Aquae Sulis	Bath
Are-Cluta	Dumbarton (Cluta is Celtic for the Clyde)
Anderida	Pevensey
Borcovicus	The next station on the Wall to the modern Housesteads
Calleva Atrebatum	Silchester
Chilurnium	On the Wall just north of Corbridge
Deva	Chester
Dubris	Dover
Durinum	Dorchester
Eburacum	York
Glevum	Gloucester
Isca Dumnoniorum	Exeter
Isca Silurium	Caerleon
Luguvallium	Carlisle
Regnum	Chichester
Segedunum	Wallsend
Spinaii, Forest of	Forest which covered a large part of Southern England, of which all that now remains is the New Forest
Caledonia	Highland Scotland; the Celtic name is Albu
Hibernia	Ireland; the Celtic name is Eriu
Valentia	The Roman province between the Northern and Southern Walls—broadly speaking Lowland Scotland

SCOTTISH TRIBAL TERRITORIES

The Selgovae	Dumfries and Ayrshire
The Novantae	Kirkcudbrightshire and Wigtown
The Dumnonii (the same tribe as in Devon)	Ayr, Lanark, Renfrew, Dumbarton and Stirling
The Epidaii	Kintyre and Lorn, and the country round Loch Awe